A LAUGH A DAY KEEPS THE DOCTOR AWAY

IRVIN S. COBB

BY THE AUTHOR OF
"SPEAKING OF OPERATIONS," ETC.

A LAUGH A DAY KEEPS THE DOCTOR AWAY

*His Favorite Stories as Told by
Irvin S. Cobb*

GARDEN CITY, NEW YORK
GARDEN CITY PUBLISHING CO., INC.

CL
Copyright, 1923,
By George H. Doran Company

Copyright, *1921,*
By the Central Press Association

Copyright, *1922, 1923,*
By the McNaught Syndicate, Inc.

A Laugh a Day Keeps the Doctor Away.
Printed in the United States of America

To
Three of the Best Story-Tellers I Know:
ROBERT H. DAVIS   SAMUEL G. BLYTHE
HAL S. CORBETT

FOREWORD

The anecdotal form of humor is largely, I think, a native institution. Americans did not invent or discover the short humorous story, it is true. Indeed, some short stories still are making their rounds which were old when the Pyramids were young. Probably the piper who piped before Moses rounded out his act with one of the standard jokes of the period—a joke which, dressed in new clothes, is doing duty somewhere today. The mother-in-law joke could not have originated with Adam, because Adam had no mother-in-law, but I have not the slightest doubt that Cain began using it shortly after his marriage. And beyond peradventure Father Noah wiled away many a dragging half hour in the Ark by telling Shem, Ham and Japhet one of the ones which begin: "It seems there were two Irishmen named Pat and Mike. And Pat said to Mike, 'Faith, an' be jabers!—'"

So it would not do for us to lay claim to sole responsibility for the short humorous story. But I am quite certain that we, more than any other people, have made it a part of our daily life, using it to point morals, to express situations, to help us solve puzzles. To these extents, at least, it is a national institution with us.

Americans like to tell short stories and like to laugh at them. We are by inheritance a race of story-tellers. There are short stories which sum up the characteristics of white Americans or black Americans, Jews or Gentiles, city folk or country folk more completely than could ponderous essays or scholarly expositions. It is of record that Abraham Lincoln, in the darkest days of the Union, cured more than one crisis with some homely anecdote, some aptly barbed retort.

After-dinner speakers and professional jokesmiths of the stage or the printed page are not responsible for the spread of good stories to the extent with which they generally are credited. That honor properly belongs to telegraph operators and notably to telegraph operators serving on "leased" wires in newspaper offices. Late at night when the flood tides of news matter have slackened off, the operator, say, in New York, tells his friend in Buffalo a good one he heard that afternoon. The Buffalo man passes it along to Kansas City. The Kansas City man conveys it by dot-and-dash to a pal in Denver and next morning folks are grinning over it in the streets of San Francisco.

FOREWORD

I always have loved short funny stories. I prefer them to be new, but an old one, properly told, is often better than a new one badly presented. For the contents of this book I have sought to choose those short stories which made the greatest appeal to me. Some of them I heard years ago; others no longer ago than yesterday.

For the book I claim two distinctions, namely, as follows:

There is only one mother-in-law story in it.

There is not a single story in it in which a colored character is referred to as "Rastus."

I. S. C.

CONTENTS

[*Topically Arranged*]

A

ACTORS	64, 178, 179
AERONAUTIC	153, 187
AFTER-DINNER SPEAKERS	16, 130, 342, 355
AGRICULTURAL	66, 84, 348, 360
ALCOHOLIC	1, 11, 18, 33, 36, 64, 65, 68, 89, 150, 157, 203, 212, 232, 242, 263, 319
AMERICANS ABROAD	10, 24, 94, 215, 219
ANIMAL FRIENDS	5, 15, 25, 71, 117, 167, 216, 232, 233, 248, 291, 293, 344
ARCTIC	120, 221
ART	8, 168
ARMY (A. E. F. mostly)	21, 30, 34, 39, 62, 69, 71, 73, 97, 156, 161, 162, 163, 354, 359
AUTOMOBILING	105, 303

B

BANKING	44, 52, 113, 218
BASEBALL	32, 184, 228, 278, 357
BATHING	66, 127
BRIDAL COUPLES	92, 200, 205, 320
BUNCO STEERERS	110, 273
BUSINESS	8, 35, 44, 136, 165, 277, 341

C

CANADIAN	180
CARRIER-PIGEONS	71
CENSUS	40
CHILDREN	95, 128, 129, 223, 231, 240, 290, 293, 324, 347, 352
CHINESE	40, 99
CIRCUSES	19, 123, 171, 209, 336
CLERGYMEN	33, 45, 49, 56, 94, 103, 116, 158, 187
COCKNEY	199, 201
COWBOY	22, 51, 349
CRICKET	164
CRITICISM	362

* These figures refer to the numbers of the stories and not to the pages in the book.

CONTENTS

D

DANCING 9
DENTISTS 301, 303, 312
DINING 53, 65, 77, 128, 160, 192, 261, 304, 313
DOCTORS 98, 146, 226, 285, 314, 361
DOGS 190
DWARFS 262, 325

E

EDUCATIONAL 57, 268, 276, 346
ENGLISH ... 16, 24, 46, 130, 142, 184, 235, 249, 321, 337, 345

F

FEMININE 9
FEUDS 3, 101, 138, 143
FINANCE 70, 241, 250, 296
FISHING 111, 175
FOOTBALL 78
FORTUNE TELLING 158
FRENCH 30, 196, 225, 280
FRUGALITY 35, 42, 108, 147, 265, 300, 309

G

GHOSTS 86, 351
GOLF 182, 237, 270, 317

H

HANGINGS 14, 17, 54, 56, 295, 316
HEALTH 131
HEBREW 8, 12, 44, 52, 113, 132, 197, 213, 237, 244, 245, 255, 276, 304, 305, 308-310, 335, 365
HORSE-RACING 141, 327
HOTELS 11, 227, 330
HUNTING 5, 337, 345

I

INDIAN 122
IRISH ... 2, 49, 107, 118, 188, 247, 251, 258, 267, 294, 297, 339

CONTENTS

J

JAILS 63, 170, 278, 328
JAPANESE 149, 239
JOURNALISTIC 41, 195, 281
JUDICIAL 38, 90, 91, 115

K

KU KLUX 305, 353

L

LAWYERS 7, 28, 31, 58, 63
LAZINESS 350
LEGACIES 2, 274
LIARS 6, 60
LITERATURE 280, 284
LUNACY 268

M

MATHEMATICAL 323
MATRIMONIAL ... 29, 81, 92, 106, 124, 135, 205, 229, 238, 302
MENTAL HEALING 256, 285
MINING 333
MISCELLANEOUS 75, 82, 109, 131, 172, 185, 186, 189, 191, 193, 202, 208, 211, 214, 227, 230, 234, 236, 243, 248, 257, 259, 260, 277, 284, 286, 296, 298, 307, 315, 329, 331, 343, 346, 348, 356
MORTUARY 107-132, 254, 256, 266, 288, 308, 322
MOVIES 13
MULES 173, 287, 332
MUSIC 197, 282

N

NEGRO 5, 14, 17, 25, 34, 37, 38, 39, 42, 43, 53, 54, 55, 56, 57, 61, 67, 69, 72, 73, 74, 76, 77, 81, 83, 85, 86, 88, 90, 92, 93, 97, 100, 104, 111, 144, 146, 148, 192, 198, 205, 217, 278, 283, 289, 292, 299, 326, 363

O

ORATORY 28, 220, 364

CONTENTS

P

POLITICS 67, 169, 204, 217
PROPHECY 47, 49, 58, 80, 104, 145, 149, 158, 162, 172, 207, 222, 235
PUGILISTIC 41, 139, 253, 272, 338

R

RAILROADING 174, 210
REVIVALS 80, 206, 358
ROGUES 48, 110, 133, 273, 279, 334
ROYALTY 152, 311

S

SCIENCE 181
SCOTCH 27, 35, 103, 108, 112, 116, 147, 224, 265, 300
SECRET ORDERS 74, 318
SOUTHERN 3, 15, 20, 23, 26, 28, 29, 58, 60, 79, 84, 127, 137, 140, 154, 155, 159, 206, 252, 275
SPIRITUALISM 59
SPORTS 102, 166, 183
SUNDAY SCHOOLS 167, 240, 269
SWEDISH 134, 340

T

THEATRICAL 12, 114, 126, 151, 246, 271
TRAVELING 4, 47, 55, 93, 96, 157, 221, 222, 310

V

VAUDEVILLE 176, 177, 194

W

WEATHER 87, 121, 145, 199, 287
WESTERN 4, 22, 50, 51, 264, 279, 291, 349

Y

YANKEE 6, 19, 119, 125, 135, 145, 160, 207, 341, 360

A LAUGH A DAY KEEPS
THE DOCTOR AWAY

A LAUGH A DAY KEEPS THE DOCTOR AWAY

§ 1   The Untraveled Stranger

Back in those sinful days which ended in January, 1919—that is, officially they ended then—a group of congenial spirits were gathered one Saturday night in a local life-saving station on the principal corner of a small Kentucky town, engaged in the quaint old pastime of pickling themselves.

In the midst of these proceedings the swinging doors were thrust asunder and there entered one of those self-sufficient, self-important persons who crave to tell their private affairs to others, and who, in those times, preferably chose as a proper recipient for their confidences, a bar-keeper—as I believe the functionary was called.

The newcomer wedged his way into the congenial group of patrons, and apropos of nothing which up until then had been said or done, introduced himself to the notice of the company by stating in a loud clear voice:

"The doctor wants me to take a trip. I haven't been feelin' the best in the world and my wife got worried—you know how women are—and tonight she sent for the doctor. And he came over, a little while ago, and he asked me a lot of foolish questions and took my temperature and five dollars and then he says to me that I should rest up for a spell and travel 'round. He says I ought to go out to California and see the sights. Ain't I been to California? I have —more'n half a dozen times. Ain't I seen every sight there is in the whole state of California? I have. As a matter of fact, I don't mind tellin' you fellers that I've been everywhere and I've seen practically everything there is."

At this a gentleman who was far overtaken in stimulant, slid the entire length of the bar, using his left elbow for a rudder. Anchoring himself alongside the stranger he hooked a practiced and accomplished instep on the brass rail to hold him upright and he focused a watery, wavering, bloodshot eye upon the countenance of the other and to him in husky tones he said:

"Excus'h me, but could I ash you a ques'shun?"

"Sure, you could ask me a question," said the stranger. "Go ahead."

"The ques'shun," said the alcoholic one, "'s as follows: Have you ever had delirium tremens?"

"Certainly not," snorted the indignant stranger.

"Well, you big piker!" said the inebriate, "then you ain't never been nowheres—and you ain't never seen nothin'."

§ 2   The Prudent Mr. Finnerty

The lawyer picked his way to the edge of the excavation and called down for Michael Finnerty.

"Who's wantin' me?" inquired a deep voice.

"I am," said the lawyer. "Mr. Finnerty, did you come from Castlebar, County Mayo?"

"I did."

"And was your mother named Mary and your father named Owen?"

"They was."

"Then Mr. Finnerty," said the lawyer, "it is my duty to inform you that your Aunt Kate has died in the old country, leaving you an estate of twenty thousand dollars in cash. Please come up."

There was a pause and a commotion down below.

"Mr. Finnerty," called the lawyer, craning his neck over the trench, "I'm waiting for you!"

"In wan minute," said Mr. Finnerty. "I just stopped to lick the foreman!"

For six months Mr. Finnerty, in a high hat and with patent leather shoes on his feet, lived a life of elegant ease, trying to cure himself of a great thirst. Then he went back to his old job. It was there that the lawyer found him the second time.

"Mr. Finnerty," he said, "I've more news for you. It is your Uncle Terence who's dead now in the old country; and he has left you his entire property."

"I don't think I can take it," said Mr. Finnerty, leaning wearily on his pick. "I'm not as strong as I wance was; and I'm doubtin' if I could go through all that again and live!"

§ 3   Enough for Wilkins

From the lowlands a special judge was sent up to the Kentucky mountains to try some murder cases growing out of a desperate and bloody feud. He took with him as his official stenographer a young man from Louisville, who dressed smartly and, in strong contrast to the silent mountaineers, did considerable talking. For convenience let us call him Wilkins.

On his first Sunday morning in the mountain hamlet Wilkins felt the need of a shave. He had no razor and there was no regular barber in the town; but he learned from the hotelkeeper that there was an old cobbler living a few doors away who sometimes shaved transients.

In a tiny shop Wilkins found an elderly native with straggly chin whiskers and a gentle blue eye. The old chap got out an ancient razor and was soon scraping away on the patron's jowls. Wilkins felt the desire for conversation stealing over him.

"This is a mighty lawless country up here, ain't it?" he began.

"I don't know," said the old chap mildly. "Things is purty quiet jist at present."

He paused to put a keener edge on his blade.

"Well," said Wilkins, "you won't deny, I suppose, that you have a lot of murders in this town?"

"We don't gin'rally speak of 'em as murders," said the old man in a tone of gentle reproof. "Up here we jest calls 'em killin's."

"I'd call 'em murders, all right," said Wilkins briskly. "If shooting a man down in cold blood from ambush isn't murder, then I don't know a murder when I see one, that's all. When was the last man killed, as you call it, here in this town?"

"Why, last week," said the patriarch.

"Whereabouts was he killed?" continued Wilkins.

"Right out yonder in the street in front of this here shop," stated the old man, with the air of one desiring to turn the conversation. "Razor hurt you much?"

"The razor's all right," said Wilkins snappily. "What I want to know are the facts about the killing of this last man. Who killed him?"

The cobbler let the edge of the razor linger right over the Adam's apple of the stranger for a moment.

"I done so," he said gently.

There was where the conversation seemed to begin to languish.

§ 4   Why the Major Didn't Suit

On a voyage of one of the Cunard liners from New York to Liverpool a Major H. Reynolds of London was registered on the passenger list. The purser, running over the names, assigned to the same stateroom as fellow travelers, this Major Reynolds and a husky stockman from the Panhandle of Texas.

A little later the cattleman, ignoring the purser, hunted up the skipper.

"Look here, cap," he demanded, "what kind of a joker is this here head clerk of yours? I can't travel in the same stateroom with that there Major Reynolds. I can't and I won't! So far as that goes, neither one of us likes the idea."

"What complaint have you?" asked the skipper. "Do you object to an army officer for a traveling companion?"

"Not generally," stated the Texan—"only this happens to be the Salvation Army. That there major's other name is Henrietta!"

§ 5   Grandfather Laughed at This One

On a Georgia plantation a group of darkies went coon hunting one night. Because of his love for the sport they took with them Uncle Sam, the patriarch of the colored quarters. Uncle Sam was over eighty years old and all kinked up with rheumatism. He hobbled along behind the hunters as they filed off through the woods.

The dogs "treed" in a sweet gum snag on the edge of Pipemaker Swamp, five miles from home; but when the tree fell there rolled out of the top of it, not a raccoon but a full-grown black bear, full of fight and temper.

The pack gave one choral ki-yi of shock and streaked away, yelping as they went; and the two-legged hunters followed, fleeing as fast as their legs would carry them.

When they came to a moonlit place in the woods they discovered that Uncle Sam was missing; but they did not go back to look for him—they did not even check up.

"Pore ole Unc' Sam!" bemoaned one of the fugitives, between pants. "His ole laigs must 'a' give out on him 'foh he went ten jumps. I reckin dat bear's feastin' on his bones right dis minute."

"Dat's so! Dat's so!" gasped one of the others. "Pore Unc' Sam!"

When they reached the safety of the cotton patches they limped to Uncle Sam's cottage to break the news to the widow. There was a light in the window; and when they rapped at the door, and it opened, the sight of him who faced them across the threshold made them gasp.

"Foh de Lawd!" exclaimed one. "How you git heah?"

"Me?" said Uncle Sam calmly, "oh, I come 'long home wid de dawgs."

§ 6   The Day Denver Was Surprised

Swifty, the High Diver, was imported to give his performance as a crowning feature on the last day of the annual fair and races in a certain small county-seat of interior Vermont.

Those who remember the late Swifty may recall that it was his custom, clad in silken tights, to ascend to the top of a slender ladder which reared nearly ninety feet aloft and after poising himself there for a moment to leap forth headlong into air, describing a graceful curve in his downward flight, then with a great splatter and splash to strike in a tank of water but little larger and wider and deeper than the average well-filled family bathtub, and immediately thereafter to emerge from it, in his glittering spangles, amid the plaudits of the admiring multitude. That is to say, he did this until the sad and tragic afternoon when, just as Swifty jumped, some quaint practical joker moved the tank.

But on this particular occasion no mishap marred the splendor of the feat. Naturally enough that night, when the community loafers assembled at their favorite general store, the achievement of the afternoon was the main topic of the evening.

The official liar held in as long as he could; and when he no longer could contain himself, he spoke up and said:

"Wall, I hain't denyin' but what that there Swifty is consid'able of a diver—but I had a cousin onc't that could a-beat him."

The official skeptic gave a scornful grunt.

"Ah, hah!" he exclaimed, "I rather thought you'd be sayin' somethin' of that general nature before the evenin' was over. Who, for instance, was this yere cousin of yourn?"

"Wall, for instance," said the liar, modestly, "he wan't no one in especial and perticular, exceptin' the champeen diver of the world— that's all."

"And what did he ever do to justify his right to that there title?" demanded the skeptic.

"Wall," said the liar, "he done consid'able many things in the divin' line, which was his speciality. I remember onc't he made a bet of a hundred dollars, cash, that he could dive from Liverpool, England, to Noo York City."

The skeptic gave a groan of resignation.

"I suppose," he said, "that you're goin' to ask us to believe he won that there bet."

"No I hain't," stated the liar. "I hain't a-goin' to lie to you. That wuz the one bet in his hull life my cousin ever lost. He miscalculated and come up in Denver, Colorado!"

§ 7   And Worth the Money, Too!

A noted lawyer down in Texas, who labored under the defects of having a high temper and of being deaf, was trying a case in a courtroom presided over by a younger man, for whom the older practitioner had a poor opinion.

Presently in an argument over a motion there was a clash between the lawyer and the judge. The judge ordered the lawyer to sit down, and as the lawyer, being deaf, didn't hear him and went on talking, the judge fined him $10.

The lawyer leaned toward the clerk and cupped his hand behind his ear.

"What did he say?" he inquired.

"He fined you $10," explained the clerk.

"For what?"

"For contempt of this court," said the clerk.

The lawyer shot a poisonous look toward the bench and reached a hand into his pocket.

"I'll pay it now," he said. "It's a just debt!"

§ 8   The Spirit of Seventy-six, with Improvements

A New York East Sider met a friend on Third Avenue and told him he had quit the buttonhole-making trade.

"I'm in the art business now," he said, proudly—"such a fine business, too! Lots of money in it!"

"What do you mean—art business?" demanded his friend.

"Well," explained the East Sider, "I go by auction sales, and I buy pictures cheap; then I sell 'em high. Yesterday I bought a picture for twenty-five dollars and to-day I sold it for fifty."

"What was the subject?"

"It wasn't no subject at all," said the art collector—"it was a picture."

"Sure, I know," said the other. "But every picture has got to be a subject or it ain't a regular picture, you understand. Was this here picture a marine, or a landscape, or a still life, or a portrait—or what?"

"How should I know?" said the puzzled ex-buttonholer. "To me a picture is a picture! This here picture now didn't have no name. It was a picture of three fellers. One feller had a fife and one feller had a drum and one feller had a headache!"

§ 9 Protecting the Gentler Sex

A certain young lady who gives interpretative dances in rather scanty costume was engaged to go to a staid community in New England and dance before the local dramatic and literary society.

The day after her appearance the entertainment committee—all women—held a meeting to discuss the affair of the night before. Several had been heard, when one member raised her voice.

"Personally," she said, "I enjoyed it ever so much. To me it was most artistic and symbolic and everything. But if you ask me, I must say this: It certainly was no place to take a nervous man!"

§ 10 Not at All Singular

An American journalist in poor health spent the summer of 1910 at a resort in Southern France. The proprietor was an English woman, and all of the other guests were English too. They were friendly and kind to the invalid—all excepting one very austere and haughty lady.

On his first day as a guest at the house he heard this lady say to the landlady:

"I distinctly understood that you did not admit Americans as lodgers here, and I wish to know why you have broken the rule."

The other woman explained that the stranger had come with good references and that he seemed a quiet, well-mannered person who hadn't offered to scalp anybody and who knew how to eat with a knife and fork. Nevertheless the complaining matron was not at all pleased.

She took frequent opportunity of saying unkind things about the States and those who lived in the States. The sick American maintained a polite silence. Finally one day at the dinner table she addressed him with direct reference to a certain ghastly murder case which even after the lapse of all these years will be remembered by most readers today.

"What do you Yankees think of your fellow-American, Doctor Crippen?" she inquired.

"We think he's crazy," said the American.

"How singular!" said the lady, arching her eyebrows.

"Not at all," said the American. "He must have been crazy to kill an American woman in order to marry an English one."

§ 11   Strictly in Confidence

The time was in the early hours of a new day; the place was the lobby of a hotel; the principal character was a well-dressed gentleman in an alcoholic fog, who had come in and registered for the night a few minutes earlier. Now, half dressed, he descended the stairway from the second floor and stood swaying slightly in front of the desk.

"Mish' Night Clerk," he said politely but thickly, "I'll 'ave requesh you gimme 'nozzer room."

"Well, sir," stated the clerk, "we're a little bit crowded. I don't know whether I could shift you immediately. It's pretty late, you know."

"Mish' Night Clerk," said the guest in a courteous but firm voice, "I repeat—mush gimme 'nozzer room."

"Isn't the room I gave you comfortable?" parleyed the functionary.

"Sheems be perf'ly so," admitted the transient. "Nev'less, mush ash be moved 'mediately."

"Well, what's the matter with your room?" demanded the pestered clerk.

The stranger bent forward, and with the air of one imparting a secret addressed the clerk in a husky half whisper:

"If you mush know, my room's on fire!"

§ 12 He Didn't Believe in Signs

A fireman on duty behind the scenes of one of the big New York theatres and charged with the responsibility of seeing to it that the regulations were strictly obeyed back-stage, suffered a profound shock as he came around from behind a stack of scenery, just before the evening performance. Standing in the opposite wings was a salesman for an East Side cloak and suit concern, who had procured entrance via the stage door for the purpose of soliciting orders for his wares among the young ladies of the chorus. This person was vehemently puffing on a large, long, black, malignant-looking cigar.

In three jumps the scandalized fireman had the violator by the arm.

"Say," he demanded, "what the hell do you mean, comin' in here with that torch in your face? Don't you see that sign right up over your head?"

The trespasser's eyes turned where the fireman's finger pointed.

"Sure, mister," he said, "I see it."

"Well, can't you read?" demanded the fireman.

"Sure I can read," admitted the other calmly.

"Then read what it says there. Don't you see what it says in big letters? It says—'No Smoking.'"

"Yes," agreed the East Sider with a winning smile, "but it don't say 'Positively.'"

§ 13 Advice to Charlie Chaplin

When General Neville, the hero of the defense of Verdun, made his tour of America he was the guest of honor at a big public reception in one of the Los Angeles hotels. Among those invited to greet the distinguished visitor were the more prominent members of the moving-picture colony.

At the doors of General Neville's suite Will Rogers met Charlie Chaplin. Chaplin, who in private life is a reserved and rather shy little man, was considerably fussed up over the prospect ahead of him.

"I suppose we're expected to say a few words to the General," he confided to Rogers. "But for the life of me I can't think of the best way to start the conversation."

Rogers gave to the problem a moment of earnest consideration.

"Well," he said, "you might ask him if he was in the war, and which side he was on."

§ 14 What Aunt Myra Desired

They brought a darky out of the jail in a North Carolina town with intent to hang him for murder. This was in the day when capital punishment was publicly inflicted. As a special mark of attention the widow of the murderer's victim was permitted to witness the event from a position of vantage directly facing the gallows. She had had a sort of small grandstand rigged up and she had decorated it with bunting, and when the march to the scaffold started, there she sat in a white mother-hubbard wrapper, gently agitating a palmleaf fan, flanked and surrounded by relatives, invited friends and sister members of her lodge.

When the condemned had been properly trussed up, with the noose dangling about his neck, the sheriff, holding the black cap in his hand, edged up to him and said:

"Well, Jim, we're about ready. If you've got anything to say, I reckon this would be a mighty good time to say it."

"Yas, suh," said the doomed, "I has got sump'n to say. I jest wants to say dat I is fully repented fur whut I done. I taken it to de Lawd in prayer an' I knows it's all right wid Him. I ast de jedge w'ich tried me an' de persecutin' attorney an' de foreman of de jury ef they bore me any gredge, w'ich, one an' all, they said they did not. An' now I kin go right straight to Hebben an' nestle in de bosom of Father Abraham ef only I kin git de fergiveness of dat nigger lady sittin' yonder—de wife of de man I kil't."

He lifted his voice, addressing the white-clad figure in front of him:

"Lady," he entreated, "does you fergive me fur shootin' yore husband six times wid a fo-ty-fo' caliver revolover?"

Excepting that her under lip jutted out a trifle farther there was no sign she had heard him. She calmly fanned on.

The darky on the scaffold tried again:

"Lady," he pleaded, "for de secont time I axes you, ain't you, please ma'am, gwine fergive me?"

Still from her there was no response. It was as though she had not heard him. The sympathetic sheriff felt moved to add his intercession:

"Aunt Myra," he called, "Jim, here, will be goin' away from us in a minute and we don't expect him back. Surely you don't enter-tain any hard feelin's against him now? Won't you speak to him and let him go in peace?"

This time the obdurate widow shook her head in an emphatic negative. Yet still she uttered no sound. The sheriff turned to the condemned.

"Jim," he said, "you see how it is; that old woman is set in her ways. What's the use of wastin' any more time on her? Besides, it's hot as the devil out here and I ought to be gettin' on home to dinner. Just hold still a second and we can have this all over."

"Mr. Lucas," sobbed Jim, "lemme see ef I still can't sof'en dat nigger woman's stony heart. Lady," he cried out, "wid mouty nigh my dyin' bre'f I begs you fur jest a word. I ain't hopin' no mo' dat you'll fergive me, but won't you please, ma'am, jest speak to me?"

And now she did speak. She motioned with her fan as though it had been a baton of authority, and in impatient tones she said:

"Go on, nigger, git hung—git hung!"

§ 15   When the Dawn of Understanding Came

The caller was undeniably large. When he walked he rippled and one had the feeling that should he sit down suddenly he'd splash.

He wallowed into the office of a lawyer in the foothills of the Tennessee mountains and stated that he desired to bring suit against a neighbor for ten thousand dollars' damages on account of libel.

"How did he libel you?" asked the lawyer.

"Well, suh," stated the aggrieved party, "he up an' called me a hippopotamus—that's wut he done, consarn his picture!"

"When did he call you this name?"

"It's a' goin' on two years ago."

"When did you first hear about it?"

"That very next day."

"Indeed," said the lawyer; "then why did you wait nearly two years to begin taking steps to bring suit against him?"

"Well, suh," stated the prospective plaintiff, "ontil that there Ringling Brothers' circus showed yistiddy in Knoxville an' I went down fur to see it I hadn't never seen no hippopotamus."

§ 16   As Translated into the English

One night at dinner in honor of a distinguished visiting Englishman I was reminded of a yarn. I told it, and it went very well. It had to do with a prospector in Oklahoma who, on a Saturday night, bought a quart of moonshine whiskey and took it to his lonely cabin, anticipating a pleasant Sunday. But as he crossed the threshold he stumbled and fell, dropping his precious burden and smashing the bottle, so that its contents were wasted upon the floor. Depressed by his misfortune, the unfortunate man went to bed. As he lay there, a mangy, furtive, half-grown rat with one ear and part of a tail, emerged timorously from a hole in the baseboard, sat up, sniffed the laden air and then, darting swiftly to where the liquor made a puddle in a depression of the planking, ran out its tiny pink tongue, took one quick sip of the stuff and fled in sudden panic to its retreat. But it didn't stay; shortly it again appeared, and now a student of rats would have discerned that a transition had taken place in the spirits of this particular rat. Suddenly it had grown cocky, debonair, almost reckless. It traveled deliberately back to the liquor and imbibed again. Seemingly satisfied it started for home but, changing its mind, it returned and partook a third time of the refreshment. Immediately then its fur stood on end, its eyes burned red, like pigeon-blood rubies, and straightening itself upon its hind legs it waved its forepaws in a gesture of defiance and shrilly cried out:

"Now, bring on that dad-blamed cat!"

No one seemed to enjoy my story more than did the guest of the evening. After the party broke up he made me tell it to him all over again. I could read from his expression that he was trying to memorize it. In fact, he confessed to me that he expected to use it when he got home as a typical example of American humor.

Six months later I was in London. I attended a dinner. My English friend was the toastmaster. Perhaps my presence recalled to him the anecdote he had so liked. At any rate, he undertook to repeat it.

His version ran for perhaps twenty minutes. He entered into a full exposition of the potency of the illicit distillation known among the Yankees, he said, as "shining moon." He went at length into the habits of rats, pointing out that inasmuch as rats customarily did not indulge in intoxicants a few drops of any liquor carrying high alcoholic content would be likely, for the time being at least, to alter the nature of almost any rat. At length he reached his point. It ran like this:

"And then, this little rodent, being now completely transformed by its repeated potations, reared bolt upright and, voicing the pot-valor of utter intoxication both in tone and manner, it cried out in a voice like thunder:

"'I say, I wonder if there isn't a cat about somewhere?'"

§ 17 Absolutely no Hurry about It

One chilly evening in the early part of March the sheriff entered the county jail and addressing the colored person who occupied the strongest cell, said:

"Gabe, you know that under the law my duty requires me to take you out of here to-morrow and hang you. So I've come to tell you that I want to make your final hours on earth as easy as possible. For your last breakfast you can have anything to eat that you want and as much of it as you want. What do you think you'd like to have?"

The condemned man studied for a minute.

"Mr. Lukins," he said, "I b'lieves I'd lak to have a nice wortermelon."

"But watermelons won't be ripe for four or five months yet," said the sheriff.

"Well, suh," said Gabe, "I kin wait."

§ 18 One Who Desired to Know

A suburbanite in New Jersey was moving from one street to another. Observing with dismay the care-free way in which the moving crew yanked his cherished antiques about, he was filled with a desire to save from possible damage a tall grandfather's clock which he prized highly.

Taking the clock up in his arms he started for the new house. But the clock was as tall as its owner, and heavy besides, and he had to put it down every few feet and rest his arms and mop his streaming brow. Then he would clutch his burden to his heaving bosom and stagger on again.

After half an hour of these strenuous exertions he was nearing his destination when an intoxicated person who had been watching his labors from the opposite side of the road took advantage of a halt to hail him.

"Mister," he said thickly, "could I ash you a quest'n?"

"What is it?" demanded the pestered suburbanite.
"Why in thunder don't you carry a watch?"

§ 19 The Poor Aim of Mr. Zeno

When the circus reached the small New Hampshire town the proprietor feared that his afternoon performance might lack its chief feature. The star of the aggregation was Zeno, the Mexican Knife Thrower, answering in private life to the name of Hennessy. Twice a day Zeno, dressed in gaudy trappings, would enter the arena accompanied by his wife, a plump young woman in pink tights, and followed by a roustabout bearing a basket full of long bowie-knives and shining battle-axes. While the band played an appropriate selection of shivery music the young woman would flatten herself against a background of blue planking which had been erected in the middle of the ring. There she would pose motionless, her arms outstretched. Then Zeno, stationing himself forty feet from her, would fling his knives and axes at her, missing her each time by the narrowest of margins. Presently her form would be completely outlined by the deadly steel, but such was Zeno's marvelous skill that she took no hurt from the sharp blades which pinned her fast.

But on this day Mrs. Zeno had fallen ill and although the circus owner offered a reward for someone who would take her place, he could find no volunteers among the members of his staff. In this emergency the invalid's mother, who traveled with the show in the capacity of wardrobe mistress, agreed to serve as an understudy in order that the performance might not be marred.

Forth came Zeno, wearing his professional scowl, slightly enhanced. His mother-in-law, skinny and homely, with her hair knotted in a knob on her head and her daughter's fleshings hanging in loose folds upon her figure, followed him closely. She plastered herself flat against the wooden background. Zeno gave her a look seemingly fraught with undying hate. He took up his longest, sharpest bowie-knife. He tested its needle-like point upon his thumb. He poised it, aimed it, flung it.

Like a javelin it hurtled and hissed in its flight through the air. Striking tip first a scant quarter of an inch from the lobe of the mother-in-law's left ear, it buried itself deep in the tough oaken planking and stood there, the hilt quivering.

The pause which ensued was broken by the astonished voice of a lank native sitting on the lowermost tier of blue seats industriously milking his whiskers:

"Wall, by Heck—he missed her!"

§ 20 Curing the Great Thirst

There was a philanthropic Tennessee distiller who believed in spreading sunshine wherever he could. One Christmas he sent a gift of prime whiskey to an improvident acquaintance who lived in a cabin up in the hills.

Along toward the end of January the beneficiary dropped in on him and intimated that if his friend was so inclined he could use a little more liquor.

"Aren't you rather overdoing things, Zach?" inquired the distiller. "If my memory serves me rightly, it has been less than five weeks since I gave you a whole keg."

"Well, Colonel," explained the mendicant, "you got to remember that a kag of licker don't last very long in a fambly that can't afford to keep a cow."

§ 21 The Ways of the Army

The officer of the day was inspecting the guard.

"What are your orders?" he inquired of a drafted man.

"Sir," said the sentry, in his newly-acquired military manner "my orders are to be vigilant."

"What does vigilant mean?" said the officer.

"I don't know," said the sentry.

"Call the corporal of the guard and we'll find out," said the officer.

The corporal of the guard came.

"Corporal," said the officer, "this man here doesn't know the meaning of the word vigilant. Suppose you tell him."

"It means, sir, to be alert," answered the corporal promptly.

"And what does alert mean?" said the commander, anxious that the lesson should be driven home to the pupil.

"I don't know," said the corporal.

§ 22 Remote from the Real Centers

A Wyoming ranch foreman was sent East by his employer in charge of a carload of polo ponies. He was gone four weeks.

When he arrived back at the ranch he wore an air of unmistakable pleasure and relief.

"Gee," he said, "it's good to git home again. So fur as I'm concerned I don't want never to travel no more."

"Didn't you like New York?" asked one of the hands.

"Oh, it's all right in its way," he said, "but I don't keer for it."

"What's chiefly the matter with it?"

"Oh," he said, "it's so dad blame far frum everywhere."

§ 23 The Way of the Neighborhood

It is not so very long ago that life in the Kentucky mountains was primitive. They used to tell a story to illustrate how primitive things actually were. It may not have been true. Probably it wasn't, but at any rate it was an illustration, even though an exaggerated one, of a prevalent condition.

There was a narrow-gauge, jerk-water road which skirted through the knobs. One day the train—there was only one train a day, each way—was laboring slowly upgrade when the engineer halted his locomotive to let a cavalcade cross the track ahead of him. First there streaked past a pack of hounds, all baying. Behind the dogs followed men, on horse-back and mule-back, galloping at top speed and cheering the hunt on with shrill whoops and blasts from a horn. The troupe had vanished into the deep timber bordering the right-of-way when a Northern man, riding in the shabby day-coach, addressed a fellow-passenger who was a native.

"Sheriff's posse, I suppose?" he said.

"Nope," said the mountaineer.

"Perhaps your people are seeking to lynch somebody?" suggested the Northerner.

"No, 'tain't that neither."

"Then may I ask what is the purpose—the intent—of this chase?"

"Well, mister," said the native, "it's like this: County Judge Sim Hightower's oldest boy, Simmy Junior, comes of age to-day and they're runnin' him down to put pants on him."

§ 24 A Radical Difference Noted

A friend of mine has a friend who went abroad while Victoria the beloved, was still on the throne of Great Britain.

In London one night the traveler saw Madame Bernhardt play in "Anthony and Cleopatra."

The scene came where Cleopatra receives news of Mark Antony's defeat at Actium. Bernhardt was at her best as Egypt's fiery queen that night. She stabbed the unfortunate slave who had borne the tidings to her, stormed, raved, frothed at the mouth, wrecked some of the scenery in her frenzy and finally, as the curtain fell, dropped in a shuddering, convulsive heap.

As the thunderous applause died down, the American heard a middle-aged British matron in the next seat remarking to her neighbor in tones of satisfaction:

"How different—how very different from the home life of our own dear queen!"

§ 25   Where the Partnership Dissolved

One of the oldest stories in the known world—and in my humble judgment one of the best ones—deals with three actors—an aged negro, an itinerant conjurer and a twelve pound snapping-turtle.

It is a hot day in a Mississippi countryside. The conjurer, who is making his way across country afoot, is sitting alongside the dusty road, resting. There passes him an ancient negro returning from a fishing expedition. The darky is not going home empty-handed. He has captured a huge snapping-turtle. He is holding it fast by its long tail, which is stretched tautly over his right shoulder so that the flat undershell of the captive rests against his back. He bids the stranger a polite good-morning and trudges on. He has gone perhaps twenty feet further when an impish inspiration leaps into the magician's brain. In addition to his other gifts he is by way of being a fair ventriloquist.

He throws his voice into the turtle's mouth and speaking in a muddy, guttural tone such as would be suitable to a turtle if a turtle ever indulged in conversation, he says sharply:

"Look here, nigger, where are you taking me?"

The old man freezes in his tracks. He rolls his eyes rearward. There is the look of a vast, growing, terrific bewilderment on his face.

"W-h-who—who dat speakin' to me?" he asks falteringly.

"It's me speakin' to you," the turtle seemingly says, "here on your back. I asked you where you were taking me."

"Huh, boss," cries the old man, "I ain't takin' yo' nowhars—I'se leavin' you right yere!"

§ 26 Absolutely Unfitted for the Rôle

A few months before his death Gen. Basil Duke of Kentucky, who commanded Morgan's Cavalry after the killing of his brother-in-law, Gen. John Morgan, told this tale at a Confederate reunion:

During one of the Tennessee campaigns Morgan's Men surprised and routed a regiment of Federal troopers. In the midst of the retreat one of the enemy, who was mounted upon a big bay horse, suddenly turned and charged the victorious Confederates full-tilt, waving his arm and shrieking like mad as he bore down upon them alone. Respecting such marvellous courage, the Confederates forebore shooting at the approaching foe, but when he was right upon them they saw there was a reason for his seeming foolhardiness.

He was a green recruit. His horse had run away with him—the bit had broken, and, white as a sheet and scared stiff, the luckless youth was being propelled straight at the whooping Kentuckians, begging for mercy as he came.

Jeff Sterritt, the wit of the command, stopped the horse and made a willing prisoner of the rider. Sterritt, who had not washed or shaved for days and was a ferocious looking person, pulled out a big pistol and wagged its muzzle in the terrified Federal's face.

"I don't know whether to kill you right now," he said, "or wait until the fight is over!"

"Mister," begged the quivering captive, "as a favor to me, please don't do it at all! I'm a dissipated character—and I ain't prepared to die!"

§ 27 The Careful MacTavish

Mr. MacTavish attended a christening where the hospitality of the host knew no bounds except the capacities of the guests.

In the midst of the celebration Mr. MacTavish rose up and made the rounds of the company, bidding each person present a ceremonious farewell.

"But, Sandy, mon," objected the host, "ye're no' goin' yet, with the evenin' just startin'?"

"Nay," said the prudent MacTavish, "I'm no' goin' yet. But I'm tellin' ye good night while I know ye."

§ 28 The Sway of Eloquence

Down in my part of the country in the old days we were a high strung and sentimental people, and oratory moved us as nothing else would. There was once a brawny blacksmith in our county who was elected justice of the peace on the strength of his Confederate record. The first case he sat to hear was one growing out of the death of a cow under a freight train. After the evidence was all in, the attorney for the plaintiff made a most effective argument. In vivid word pictures he sketched the abundant virtues of the late cow; he described her sweetness and her gentleness, her capacity as to milk; he told of the great bereavement to her immediate family, consisting of a young calf, and he dwelt upon the heartlessness of a railroad system which by its brutal carelessness had at one fell swoop, as it were, made stew meat of the parent and an orphan of the offspring. His peroration is still remembered.

"And, finally, squire," he said, "if the train had been run as she should have been ran, and if the bell had been rung as she should have been rang, and if the whistle had been blowed as she should have been blew—both of which they done neither—this here cow would not have been injured at the time she was killed."

As he sat down the new justice in a voice husky with feeling, said: "I've done heared enough! Plaintiff wins!" and proceeded to enter judgment for the full amount of damages. But the lawyer for the other side protested. He insisted he had a right to be heard, and, though the justice said he had already made up his mind, he admitted that it was no more than fair for the young gentleman to make a speech, too, if he wanted to.

The lawyer for the railroad cut his moorings and went straight up. He was a genuine silver tongue. He soared right into the clouds. Among other matters pertinent to the issue, he introduced the American Eagle, Magna Charta, First and Second Manassas, Paul Revere's Ride and the Bonny Blue Flag Which Bears but a Single Star, concluding the whole by giving the Rebel Yell.

As he sank into his seat the justice, with a touch of the true old Jeffersonian simplicity, wiped his streaming eyes upon his shirt sleeve, and in a voice quivering with sobs exclaimed:

"Well, don't that beat all! Defence wins!"

§ 29 The Unuttered Wish

A North Carolina mountain woman fell ill, and for the first time in his life her husband had to work. It devolved upon him to nurse the invalid, look after a large family of tow headed children, milk the cow, feed the pig, cook the meals and tend a straggly acre of corn.

After ten days of these frightful labors he staggered down to the general store at the forks of the road and fell at the doorway in an exhausted heap.

The storekeeper came out and said: "Hello, Anse, how's yore wife?"

"She ain't no better," moaned the husband. "I paid out a whole four bits fur a bottle of bitters fur her, but it seems like hit don't do her no good. I'm plumb wore out!"

He paused a moment and sighed deeply.

"Sometimes," he said, "I git to wishin' the old woman would git well—or somethin'!"

§ 30   The Gift of Tongues

Over in France the average doughboy had a gorgeous confidence in his ability to speak the language of the country. In a Norman village one day a perplexed looking private, who had not been abroad very long, approached a seasoned campaigner of the A. E. F. and asked the latter if he spoke French.

"Sure I speak French," said the veteran. "What's the matter?"

"Here's what's the matter," said the green soldier. "The Frog that keeps that shop yonder across the street sold me some post cards, and I gave him a ten franc note, and now he's holding out part of my money on me. I wish you'd come on over there with me and straighten the thing out and make that guy hand me back what's coming to me."

"Sure I will," said the other.

Moved by curiosity, a friend of mine trailed behind them, arriving just in time to hear the following dialogue between the linguist and the storekeeper:

"Parley voo Fransay?"

"Oui, oui, Monsieur."

"Then, why the hell don't you give this here boy his right change?"

§ 31   He Lacked Storage Space

Congressman John K. Hendrick of Kentucky, now deceased, was notoriously soft hearted. He was sitting in a courtroom one day when a young and struggling member of the local bar, who was not especially renowned for mental brilliancy, undertook to read a petition in a divorce suit and speedily got himself badly tangled up in a confused maze of legal phrases. The judge sought to set the young lawyer right, but the only result was to tangle him worse than ever. The judge was showing signs of losing his temper when Col. Hendrick arose.

"I hope, your Honor," he said, "that you will bear patiently with our young friend here. He is doing his best."

"I know that, Col. Hendrick," said the judge, somewhat testily, "and I intend to bear patiently with him. I am merely trying to give Mr. So-and-So an idea."

"Your Honor," said Col. Hendrick, "don't do it. He's got no place to put it."

§ 32   The Voice of the Purist

In the National League formerly was an umpire who was a stickler for correct deportment on the diamond. In a game in which he officiated at the Polo Grounds Chief Meyers, catcher for New York, came to bat. Certain of the Boston players sitting on their bench began to guy the brawny red man.

In an instant the umpire had left his place behind the catcher and was running toward the visitors' bombproof.

"Cut out them personalities!" he ordered. "Cut out them personalities!"

A high pitched voice filtered out from the grandstand:

"Cut out them grammar!"

§ 33   There Spoke Envy's Voice

The town drunkard of a small Scotch community went on an especially vehement tear. The village authorities locked him up.

On the second day of his captivity, as he sat in his cell, thirsty beyond words, the minister, who was of a full habit of life, came to give him consolation and good advice.

They sat down side by side and the dominie read the parable of the Prodigal Son. The prisoner seemed to hang on the words. He nudged up closer and closer, bending forward until his face almost was in the minister's face, and listened.

"Please read it over once more," he said when the dominie had finished the chapter and started to close the Good Book.

Touched by this further sign of penitence, the minister read it again.

"Tell me, poor man," he said when he was done, "what was it held you so close the while I was reading—was it the lesson of the Scripture or was it the words?"

"Nay, nay," said the tippler—" 'twas your grand breath!"

§ 34   The Treacherous Warehouse

When the Yanks prepared to make their advance through Belleau Wood there was brought up from the south of France, a negro labor battalion, not a man of which until that time had ever heard a big gun crack in anger, but who, before this, had been employed in building roads and mending bridges and unloading freight cars. This outfit was set to work constructing defences of fallen timbers in the lower fringe of the forest, on the contingency that our troops, after their first onslaught might be driven back and need shelter behind which to fight on the retreat.

On a morning when the enemy, for reasons best known to themselves, were feeling unusually peevish and fretful, one of the correspondents, picking his cautious way through the thickets, came upon a coal black woodchopper in a ragged khaki shirt, who was swinging his ax on a fallen tree and between strokes looking up to where German shells were whistling through the ragged foliage overhead and occasionally exploding in his vicinity with a large, harsh, grating, unpleasant sound.

At each fresh report the darky would say—and even a perfect stranger to him could tell that from the very bottom of his soul he meant it—

"Oh, Lawsy, how I does wish't I wuz home!"

"Well," asked the correspondent, "why did you enlist if you didn't care to face some danger?"

"Huh, man," he snorted, "I never onlisted!"

"Well, why did you come over here, then?"

"I didn't exac'ly come."

"Well, you weren't born over here, were you?"

"Naw suh, an' I trusts not to die yere."

"Well," said the newspaper man, "you're evidently past the draft age, and since you did not enlist and didn't come over here of your own free will and weren't born here, what I want to know is, how did you get here?"

"Mister," said the negro, "it meks a kind of a sad story. My reg'lar home is Waycross, Georgia, an' I suttinly does crave to be there right this minute! Here 'bout a yeah ago a w'ite man come down frum de Nawth, an' he corralled a whole passel of us together an' he say to us, he say: 'Boys, I want you all to go up Nawth wid me an' wuk fur de gove'mint. Plain niggers is gwine git eight dollars a day; fancy niggers 'at shows speed, is gwine git ten.' An' I sez to myse'f, I sez: 'W'ite man, you don't know it yit, but you's lookin' at one of the ten dollar ones right now!'

"So he loads a whole raft of us on board de steam cyars an' he totes us plum' to Noo Yawk city. An' w'en we gits thar we wuks jest one mawnin', down by de water. W'en de time come to knock off for dinner de w'ite man gets up on a box an' meks us a speech. 'Boys,' he says, 'I wuz wrong 'bout you—w'y, they ain't a eight dollar nigger in the lot. Come on wid me to de warehouse an' sign up for ten!'

"Natchelly I led de parade. Right behind me comes de w'ite man yellin': 'Dis way to de warehouse!' An' right behind him comes all de rest of dem Waycross niggers, jest runnin'.

"So he teks us th'ough a kind of a long shed. An' he 'scorts us 'crost a lil' narrow plank. An' he leads us th'ough a kind of a lil' round iron do'.

"An' w'en we wuz all inside, de w'ite man slammed de iron do'—AN' DE WAREHOUSE SAILED AWAY!"

§ 35 A Scotchman's Conscience

The purchasing agent of a big jobbing concern was a Scotchman. He gave an extensive order—to a salesman for a supply house. Although he had obtained the business in open competition, the salesman felt gratitude at being favored and sought a way to show it.

He knew he dare not offer the Scot a commission; likewise a gift of money, he figured, would be regarded as an insult. The Scot, he noticed, constantly smoked cigars. So the salesman slipped out to a cigar store and bought a box containing fifty of the finest Havanas the tobacconist carried in stock. The price for the fifty was fifteen dollars. He brought the box back and asked the purchasing agent to accept it with his compliments.

The latter explained that it was against the policy of his house for its buyers to accept presents of any sort from those with whom the concern did busines. He was sorry, he said, but he could not take the cigars as a present, even though he felt sure his young friend had tendered them with the best of intentions and in absolute good faith.

The salesman had another idea:

"Well," he said, "I hate to throw these cigars away. They are of no use to me—I smoke only cigarettes. I wonder if you would buy them from me?—there's no harm in that, I'm sure."

"What would you be asking for them, laddy?" inquired the prudent Scot.

"I'll sell the whole fifty to you for a nickel," stated the salesman.

The purchasing agent lifted one of the cigars from the top row, smelled it, rolled it in his fingers and eyed it closely.

"Very well," he said, "at that price I'll take four boxes."

§ 36   Establishing an Identity

It was plain the stranger was suffering from an excess of alcoholic stimulant. He wavered and lurched and wabbled as he ran to catch the trolley car; he slipped and almost fell as he swung aboard; he trampled on the toes of those who rode upon the rear platform and at length when he fell into a seat he struck with considerable violence a somewhat testy gentleman alongside him.

The latter resented being jostled. Probably he had scruples against the use of intoxicants in any form and at any time. He fixed a stern and condemning eye upon the new passenger and of him demanded to know why he did not exercise a little more care when entering a public vehicle.

The person thus reproved, focused his uncertain vision upon the face of the other.

"Dye shee me when I gotta board thish car?" he asked.

"I did."

"Dye ever shee me before in your who' life?"

"No."

"Ever hear an'body call my name?"

"No."

"Ever hear an'body speak 'bout me?"

"Certainly not."

"Then how the hell did you know it was me?"

§ 37   An Earnest Cry for Help

Our town—I mean the one where I was born—formerly abounded in characters. One of our local institutions twenty years ago was a black driver named Abe, but called Old Abe for short. Abe was popular with both races. He had one social shortcoming, though.

About once in so often he would slip out on a dark night and acquire something of value without the formality of speaking to the owner about it. For awhile he escaped a penitentiary sentence.

But eventually he was caught with what the Grand Jury and the prosecuting attorney regarded as the goods, the said goods consisting of a stray calf. He was lodged in jail to await trial. His cell was in the upper tier. On the Sunday afternoon following his incarceration his wife, accompanied by five or six pickaninnies, came to pay him a visit. It was the first time she had seen him since his arrest.

On her way out she was halted by the deputy jailer, whose name was Grady.

"Dora," he said, "have you hired a lawyer for Abe yet?"

"Naw, suh," she said, "effen Abe was guilty, right away I'd git him a lawyer. But he p'intedly tells me he ain't de leas' bit guilty. So, of co'se, dat bein' de case, he ain't needin' no lawyer to git him clear."

From the floor above, down the iron stairwell, came floating the voice of Abe:

"Mr. Grady, oh, Mr. Grady!—you tell 'at fool nigger 'oman down thar to git a lawyer—an' git a damn good one, too."

§ 38 The Pride of Creative Genius

A colored person of a formidable aspect was arraigned on a charge of mayhem. As Exhibit A, for the case of the prosecution, the mutilated victim of his wrath was presented before the jurors' eyes. The face of the victim was but little more than a recent site—a place where a face had been, but was no longer.

When the jury very promptly had returned a verdict of guilty, His Honor, pointing to the chief complaining witness and addressing the defendant, said:

"This is the most lamentable example of brutality I have ever seen in a long experience on the criminal bench. Surely no human being, unless he were inspired by infernal influences and suggestions, could deliberately work such wreckage as you have worked upon the countenance of a defenseless and helpless fellow creature. Demons from below surely must have prompted you in what you did. It must have been the devil himself who urged you on."

"Well, Jedge," said the prisoner, "come to think it over, I ain't shore but whut you're right. As I look back on it now it do seem lak to me 'at w'en I wuz cuttin' his nose loose frum his face wid a razor, the devil wuz right behind me sayin' 'Tha's right, separate him frum his nose.' An' I 'spects it must a been them demons you mention w'ich suggested to me stompin' out his front teeth.

"But, Jedge, bitin' off his ear wuz stric'ly my own idea!"

§ 39 The Prompt Response

Of all the stories relating to our colored troopers in their services overseas, I think the one I like best has to do with a brawny black infantryman, who, on his way up to the front for his first taste of actual combat, fortified himself on a full quart of French wine.

As a result, he reached the forward position in a somewhat elevated and groggy state. He had been warned in advance that he was going into an exceedingly dangerous sector, but it so happened at the moment of his arrival the immediate vicinity was strangely quiet. He glanced about him in a foggy but disappointed way, and then, addressing his fellow occupants of the trench, spoke as follows:

"Wha's de war?—tha's whut I wants to know! White folks suttinly is mouty deceivin'. Yere dey promises me a war. So dey rides me 'crost mo'n a million miles of ocean an' dey marches me th'ough mo'n a thousand miles of mud, an' all de w'ile dey keeps on tellin' me 'at w'en I gits up yere dey'll be a war waitin' fur me. An' yere I is all organized fur a war an' dey ain't no war! Dat ain't no way to act. Ef ary of you folks is got ary war jest fetch it on an' leave it to me."

A veteran of several months' experience told him that his desires should shortly be gratified, inasmuch as the hostile positions were only about two hundred yards away, and the enemy was both active and alert.

Hearing this, the green hand leaped upon the parapet and, standing there in the moonlight, like a great black statue of defiance, he shook a broad fist in the direction of the foes' lines, and in a voice which might have been heard half a mile away he cried out:

"Come on, you Heinie Germans, an' gimme war! Gimme all de war you's got! Gimme exploserives! Gimme gas shells! Gimme scrapernel! Gimme bung shells! Most in 'special I asts you fur bung shells!"

At this particular moment a German minnenwerfer, two feet long and nine inches in diameter and filled with potential ill-health, went whirring in its wabbly, uncertain flight just over his head, and with a crash like the crack of doom struck not fifty yards behind him, tearing a hole in the earth big enough for the foundations of a

A LAUGH A DAY KEEPS THE DOCTOR AWAY

smoke house. The belligerent warrior was slapped flat and instantly covered in a half inch coating of powdered grit and gravel and dust.

There he lay, stunned, until the last reverberation had died away and the tortured earth had ceased from its quiverings. Then, slowly and cautiously, he sat up. First he felt himself all over to make sure he was intact; then he stole a respectful glance rearward to where the huge, new formed crater behind him still was smoking and fuming and throwing off noxious smells, and then he cast a cautious look in the direction from which the devilish visitor had come, and, finally, in a small, curiously altered voice, he said:

"Well, suzz, dey's one thing you's got to say fur dem Germans—dey suttinly does give you service!"

§ 40 Once Every Ten Years

Every time the Government takes a census this story is revived, which means it enjoys a rejuvenated popularity at intervals of ten years. When I catch myself laughing at it, I know that another decade has slipped by.

The story has to do with the enumerator who called at a humble home, and there found the head of the family humped up over a large volume. It developed, in the course of the conversation, that the householder some months before had been induced by a traveling agent to invest in an encyclopedia. To get the worth of his money he had been reading the books of the set pretty constantly ever since.

In reply to the caller's questions he gave his name and age and his wife's name and age.

"How many infant children have you?" asked the census taker.

"I've got three," said the citizen. "And that's all there ever will be, too, you take it from me."

"What makes you so positive about that? asked the visitor.

"I'll tell you why there won't never be but three," said the man "It's wrote down in this here book that every fourth child born in the world is Chinese."

§ 41 One Detail Was Missing

On the historic afternoon when Jack Johnson fought Jim Jeffries in Nevada for the world's championship there was a baseball game at the old Polo Grounds. In the press stand, among others, sat Sid Mercer, the sporting writer, and Franklin P. Adams, the column conductor. For some reason or other, ringside bulletins were not being received at the ball park. Naturally, the crowd wanted to know how the fight was going.

Several hundred spectators, drawn by the fact that telegraph instruments were clicking in the press stand, packed themselves solidly behind the wire netting in the hope of hearing tidings from Reno over the wire. Mercer and Adams had a joint inspiration. They pretended to be taking a ringside description off one of the instruments. First one would chant off a purely imaginary account of a round, and then the other would.

Adams had a bet down on the negro to win, and accordingly favored the dark contender. In his turn to "read" a round, he would depict Johnson as hammering Jeffries to a pulp. But Mercer, who was a partisan of Jeffries, would each time retaliate with a spirited but, of course, purely fictitious account of how the white man, having rallied heroically, was now dealing mighty blows upon the head and body of the tottering, weakening black.

Naturally, the listening crowd was torn by conflicting emotions. Cheers and groans marked the utterances of the two gifted romancers. Eventually, when the multitude had grown in numbers until the pressure of its bulk threatened to break down the netting, the conspirators decided to bring their joke to a climax.

Mercer, cocking his head above an instrument as though the better to hear, began reciting, somewhat after this fashion:

"Round-seven! At-the-sound-of-the-bell-the-two-men-leap-to-the-center-of-the-ring! They-exchange-a-whirlwind-of-jabs-and-upper-cuts! The-fighting-is-the-fiercest-ever-seen-in-a-heavyweight-contest! Suddenly-the-knockout-blow-is-delivered-full-upon-the-point-of-the-jaw! The-defeated-man-drops-like-a-log! His-seconds-drag-his-unconscious-form-into-his-corner! The-maddened-throng-acclaims-the-winner-and-pandemonium-reigns-supreme!"

Here he paused with the air of one who has completed a hard job.

From a thousand throats behind him one question arose in a mighty chorus:

"Who wins?"

Dramatically Mercer raised his hand for silence. A deep hush befell.

The dispatches do not state," he said, simply, and sat down.

§ 42   In Permanent Storage

Once upon a time, in the middle part of Georgia, there lived a banker who was known far and wide as the Human Safety Clutch. In his day he was accused of many things, but nobody ever charged him with being a spendthrift. His home was on a plantation a mile from town. One Sunday he remembered that he had left some important papers on his desk, and he gave an aged negro servitor on the place his keys and sent him for the documents.

It was a hot day and the road was dusty, but in an hour the old darky had returned with the papers intact. The owner felt in all his pockets, one after the other.

"That's too bad, Uncle Jim," he said finally; "I thought I had a nickel here that I was going to give you."

"Cap'n Henry," said Uncle Jim, "you look ag'in. Ef ever you had a nickel you got it yit."

§ 43 What Might Be Called an Active Man

The wharf at New Orleans was crowded with foot travelers, vehicles and freight piles. A brawny Irishman, driving a truck, locked wheels with another truck operated by a negro.

As the trucks jammed the negro opened his mouth in profane and highly disrespectful protest. But before he had uttered six words unconsciousness shut off further speech from him.

For the Irishman, with one flying leap, had reached the earth. His left hand closed on the negro's ankle, and as the latter was jerked violently into space the enemy's right fist landed a wing shot squarely on the point of his jaw, and for the time being he knew no more.

Ten minutes later the victim half opened his eyes. A policeman was bending over him.

"What's the matter with you?" demanded the officer.

"A w'ite man hit me," said the darky, "an' I wants him arrested."

"What's his name?"

"I don't know whut his name is, boss—never seed him befo' in my life."

"Well, then, what does he look like?"

"I don't rightly know dat, neither. Hit all happen' so quick-lak I didn't got a good look at 'im."

"Then how do you expect me to find him if you can't describe him?" asked the puzzled policeman.

"Boss, dat ain't goin' be no trouble," stated the negro. "You jest go lookin' for the doin'est man they is in Newerleans!"

§ 44 Sauce for the Goose

An East Sider of foreign birth prospered to the extent where he graduated from the ranks of the sidewalk merchants and became a regular business man, with a store and showcases and everything. Also, for the first time in his life he was able to start a bank account.

One day he was engaged on the telephone by the assistant cashier of the bank where he kept his checking fund.

"Mr. Abrams," stated the cashier, "I called you up to tell you that on the first day of this month your account appears overdrawn $108."

"So?" droned Mr. Abrams. "Say, young man, would you do it for me a favor?"

"Sure."

"Then, please, you should look at your books und tell me how stood the account on the foist day of last month."

In a minute or two the bank functionary was back at the 'phone.

"Oh, Mr. Abrams," he said, "on the first day of last month you had a balance to your credit of $322.25."

"So!" shouted Mr. Abrams. "Und did I call you up?"

§ 45 Driven Beyond His Strength

There was a down-and-outer, who made a precarious living as a sandwich man. Encased front and back, like a turtle in its shell, between broad boards which bore advertisements for a dairy lunch, he marched the Bowery all day long for wages barely sufficient to keep body and soul together.

One day, as he plodded his weary route, he saw a shining coin lying upon the sidewalk. Instantly he set his foot upon it, and then, stooping with difficulty because of his wooden waistcoat, he clutched it in his eager fingers and raised it to his eyes. His heart inside of him gave a great throb. It was a twenty-dollar gold piece. He was wealthy beyond his wildest ambitions.

Across the street was an excavation for a new building. He hurried thither. Standing on the edge of the digging he unbuckled the straps which bound the squares of planking to him, and, kicking them to pieces with a glad, exultant cry, he flung the shattered emblems of his servitude down into the hole below. Then straightway he departed for the nearest saloon. Stalking in, a triumphant figure even in his tatters, he slapped his precious gold piece down upon the bar and called for a drink of whiskey. It was to have been the first of a long and gorgeous succession of drinks of whiskey.

Some one jostled him in the side. He turned his head, and when he looked back again his double eagle mysteriously had vanished, and the barkeeper was motioning him to depart.

He protested, naturally. Whereupon the barkeeper reached for the bung starter, swung it with a skill born of long practice, and struck him squarely between the eyes. A moment later the ex-sandwich man found himself sprawling on the sidewalk, his happy visions gone forever.

A prey to melancholy, filled with deep disappointments and a yet deeper sense of injustice, he got upon his feet and started to limp away.

Next door to the saloon was a basement barber shop. From it at this instant there emerged a Bowery mission worker, an elderly gentleman of a benevolent aspect, his pink jowls newly scraped and his face powdered. As he climbed up the steps to the level of the sidewalk this gentleman bent over to refasten a loosened shoelace.

Now, to the best of his knowledge and belief, the derelict never before had seen the missionary, but as the latter stooped, presenting before him an expanse of black coat tails, the misanthrope hauled off and dealt the gentle stranger a terrific kick.

With a yell of astonishment and pain the clergyman landed ten feet away.

"What did you mean by that?" he demanded, rubbing the seat of his trousers with both hands. "Why did you kick me?"

"Oh," said the ex-sandwich man, in tones of an uncontrollable annoyance, "you're *always* tying your shoestring!"

§ 46 The Custom of the Country

The English have the credit for being a conservative race—a breed in which respect for traditions is so strong that they hesitate to change anything which has behind it the merits of antiquity and established comfort. The story which follows would tend to indicate that this trait really does persist in our Anglo-Saxon cousins.

Through the fields between two villages in Sussex ran a footpath. It was not the quickest route for one going from one of the hamlets to the other, for it wandered about, but it had been traced originally by the horny, naked feet of Saxon serfs, and now was worn deep into the turf by the heels of countless generations, and everybody in the neighborhood used it, because everybody always had.

A country gentleman lived midway between the towns. One day he heard a vicious bull was straying about the countryside, chasing pedestrians, frightening children and generally misbehaving himself.

Seeking for variety from the monotony of his life, the gentleman went forth in the afternoon hoping to glimpse the bull. Once he heard him bellow, but he did not see him.

He lingered afield until nearly dusk. He had reached a stile where a hedge crossed the footpath when he heard in the distance, through the thickening gloom, the patter of flying feet, mingled with the thud of heavy hoofs, a convulsive panting and the snorts of some large animal.

Into sight came the local postman, an elderly person. He was legging along at top speed, his mail pouch bouncing on his hip, his whiskers neatly parted by the wind and blowing backward over his shoulders, and just behind him came the bull, lunging with his horns at the seat of the fugitive's trousers.

By half a length the fleeing man reached the hedge ahead of his pursuer. He flung himself headlong over the stile and in its protection lay breathless, while the bull, bellowing his disappointment, strolled off to seek an easier victim.

The spectator aided the quivering postman to his feet.

"He almost had you to-night, Fletcher," said the gentleman, sympathetically.

" 'E's almost 'ad me every night this week, sir," gasped Fletcher.

§ 47 Sight Unseen, As It Were

Once upon a time—this, as the sequel will show, was before prohibition came—the Palm Beach Flier, northbound, was compelled by reason of a wreck ahead to detour over a side line. When the passengers on the Pullmans awoke in the morning they found the train halted for an indefinite stop at a small settlement set among the scrub oaks, jack pines and dwarf palmettos of interior Florida. Next only to the tiny station the most important looking structure in sight was an unpainted frame shack facing the tracks. Over its doorway, in awkward capitals, was lettered this imposing promise:

NEW YORK BAR.

ALL KINDS OF FANCY DRINKS SERVED HERE.

Reading this sign, two Easterners on board one of the sleeping cars were seized with a waggish idea. They left their stateroom and, crossing the rails, entered the establishment.

Its interior decorations were exceedingly simple. At the front was a broad, unpainted board, supported on two barrels. Behind this barrier, against the wall, a small bleared mirror hung. On either side of the mirror, upon a narrow shelf, stood a black bottle, flanked by a meagre store of smeary toddy glasses. Beneath it was a beer keg, resting upon the floor on its side.

In the rear was a small rusty stove. The air being chilly, a fire of pine knots blazed in it. A lanky individual, plainly the proprietor, sat in a broken chair close up to the stove with his bare feet in the warm ashes, reading a tattered copy of a Jacksonville paper.

He did not raise his head as the strangers entered, nor did they hail him. They lined up side by side before the makeshift bar and one of them, addressing space, said:

"Seeing that they serve all sorts of fancy drinks here, I'll have a gin rickey. What are you going to take?" he added, addressing his fellow joker.

"Well," said the other, "I think I'll take a dry martini cocktail, made with French vermouth."

Without shifting his position or lifting his eyes from his paper the proprietor now spoke:

"I kin lick airy dam' Yankee in the house—an' I ain't even looked yit!"

§ 48   A Born Snob

In those bygone times when New York's Chinatown was in its heyday—whatever a heyday is—there were three cronies among its habitués who were popular with newspaper reporters and others in search of local color. One was Blinky Britt and one was Honest John Clary, so called because once upon a time when Blinky went to sleep and his glass eye fell out of its socket and rolled across the floor Honest John picked it up and gave it back to him; and the third was Dingo Katz. Honest John was a barkeeper in a Doyers street saloon. Blinky was a lobby-gow, or messenger, for Chinese residents, and Dingo was a pickpocket, making a specialty of robbing women passengers on crosstown trolley cars. They were the Three Musketeers of the Oriental quarter.

In an evil hour the law broke up the triumvirate. Dingo, while plying his profession, was arrested and lodged in the Tombs. At his trial he was found guilty, and the Judge sentenced him to three years at Sing Sing. Although the Underworld agreed that his friends had done all for him that it was humanly possible to do, it is said that an unreasonable rancor filled his soul on the morning when he was taken to prison.

Some months later a journalist prowling through Chinatown looking for material happened upon Blinky Britt sitting in Nigger Mike Callahan's bar.

"Hello, Blinky," he said; "when did you hear from your old side-kick, Dingo?"

"Aw, say," answered Blinky, "cheese on dat sidekick stuff. I'm off of dat Dingo for life."

"Why, I thought you two were pals," said the newspaper man.

"So did I t'ink we wuz pals," said Blinky, "so did I t'ink so. But, say, lissen, bo, and lemme slip you de lowdown on dis Dingo. Like you knows already, Dingo he gits sloughed up fur moll-buzzin' on a Canal street rattler. Well, it looks like de sneezers is got him nailed fur fair wid de goods. But all de same I'm de one dat goes to de bat wid de fall-money fur to hire him a swell mouthpiece to git him cleared. But it ain't no use. A jury of twelve delicates-seners and the likes of dat dey t'rows de hooks into him and de old pappy-guy in the silk nightshirt on the bench hands him a t'reetime jolt at Warble-Twice-on-the-Hudson.

"Well, w'en de poor nut is been up dere fur going on maybe two or t'ree weeks I says to myse'f dat it's no more'n de act of a friend dat I should go to see him. So I rolls a come-on fur five iron men and I takes t'ree of dem front wheels and I buys some makin's and some crullers and some sweet slum out of a candy shop and some soft scoffin' out of a pie shop and one t'ing and another dat I knows Dingo likes, and, come a Sunday I gits on de rattler and I rides up dere to dat town of Boid Center and I walks up de road to de big stone hoosgow on de hill. Dere's a bull in harness on de gate. See? So I says to dis here bull, I says, 'Is dis visitors' day?' And he says, 'It 'tis.' So I says, 'You pass de news to Dingo Katz dat his old pal, Blinky Britt, is come to see him.'

"And say, cull, do you know de woid dat Dingo sends back to me?

"HE SENDS ME WOID HE AIN'T IN."

§ 49 Maybe Not on the Second Day, Either

For his topic that Sabbath morning the reverend father chose the Judgment. He painted a shining picture of the scene which would be presented on the Last Day, when all the race of mankind, the quick and the dead, the old and the young, from Adam to the newest born babe, assembled before the throne of the Almighty to be judged according to their deeds done in the flesh.

When the service was over an elderly Irishman tarried after the rest of the congregation had departed. He halted the priest as the latter was leaving.

A LAUGH A DAY KEEPS THE DOCTOR AWAY 45

"Your Riverince," he said, "I want to ask you a question or two, if you please. I followed your sermon close this mornin', but still I don't know if I got your meanin' quite clear."

"I rather thought my language was sufficiently plain for any understanding," said the clergyman.

"Oh, it was plain, and most beautiful besides," said the parishioner. "But, Father, what I want to know is this: Do you mane to say thot on the Last Day whin Gabriel's Trumpet blows iverybody thot iver lived in this world will be gathered togither at the wan place and the wan time?"

"That is my conception of the meaning of the Scriptures and the Gospels," said the priest.

"Do you think now, f'rinstance, thot Cain and Abel 'll be there, side be side?"

"Beyond a doubt."

"And thot little fella David and thot big slob Goliath—thim also, you think?"

"Surely."

"And Brian Boru and Oliver Cromwell?"

"Of course, they will."

"And the *A. P. A.*'s and the *A. O. H.*'s?"

"Naturally."

"Father," said the parishioner, "there'll be dom little judgin' done the first day."

§ 50 Calling a Spade a Spade

A Christmas entertainment was being planned in a remote Nevada town. The affair was to take place at the church, and the local Sunday school superintendent, a mild and gentle man, with a temperamental Adam's apple and an aggravated habit of wearing white string ties on week days, had charge. Up until the eleventh hour it looked as though the manager of the show must depend exclusively upon home talent in making up the bill. But late in the afternoon of Christmas eve, as though directed by Providence, a shabby stranger dropped off a passing freight train carrying a slender instrument case under his arm. He sought out the superintendent, introduced himself—modestly—as a distinguished musician on tour and volunteered to take part in the night's program. Delighted at having enlisted a visiting star from out of the East, the superintendent assigned him the place of honor.

At the proper moment the pleased promoter in his rôle of master of ceremonies, came forth upon the improvised stage and announced that he had a delightful surprise and a wonderful treat for the audience. Prof. Bilbus, a famous clarinet player direct from New York city and at present sojourning temporarily in their midst, would now favor the assembled citizens with a solo. He stepped to one side and from the wings issued the visitor, who bowed low, and then, lifting his instrument to his lips, emitted one of the sourest and most dismal of notes.

In his shock and disappointment a big miner at the back of the house forgot the proprieties.

"Well, the blanketty blank!" he exclaimed in a voice which reached beyond the footlights.

Quivering with indignation the introducer sprang forward again to the centre.

"Wait!" he called out. "Who called the clarinet player a blanketty blank?"

From the audience a third voice was lifted:

"Who called the blanketty blank a clarinet player?"

§ 51   Poor Aim but Good Intent

After his retirement from the presidency Colonel Roosevelt was making one of his periodical trips through the Southwest, when word came to him in a town in New Mexico that one of his old Rough Riders, a cow hand, was in jail on a serious charge over in Arizona and craved that his beloved commander would come to see him and, if possible, aid him in his present troubles.

Promptly the Colonel crossed the line. In a small brick coop of a county prison he found the veteran. When greetings had been exchanged through the bars, Col. Roosevelt said:

"Jim, I'm certainly sorry to see you in this place."

"Kernel," stated the captive, "I'm sorry 'bout it myself. And I'm hopin' you kin use your influence to git me out pronto. They really ain't got no right to keep me locked up. My bein' here is all due to a mistake anyway."

"A mistake?" echoed the Colonel. "Why, I understood you were charged with some serious offence—shooting somebody, wasn't it?"

"Well," said the prisoner, "it's true I did shoot a lady in the eye. But it was an accident, Colonel."

"An accident?"

"Yes suh, a pure accident. I wasn't shootin' at that lady at all I was shootin' at my wife."

§ 52 There Spake True Friendship

To a prosperous cloak and suit merchant on the lower East Side came an acquaintance of many years' standing. The newcomer had made a failure of it as a pushcart huckster, and then as a dealer in castoff garments. But he was undismayed; his ambition still soared. It seemed that now he aspired to open a regular store—on borrowed capital.

"But I don't want I should ask my friends for the money," he explained. "So this morning I go by that bank over yonder on the other side of the street and I talk with the bank president, a feller named Howard, about it. But what should I know about banks? Nothing, that's what. He says to me I should make him a note with indorsements. I asks him what is a note, and what is this here indorsement? So he asks me who do I know in this neighborhood what has plenty money, and I says to him that I know you—that we came over together, greeners, on the same ship from Poland eighteen years ago. And then he fixes up this here piece of paper, and he says to me I should bring it over here and get you to sign your name on the back of it, and then I should bring it back to him and he would right away give me the two thousand dollars I need. So, here I am, Goldberg."

Mr. Goldberg's voice was husky with emotion as he answered:

"Moe," he said, "honestly for you I am positively ashamed that you should do this thing. Ain't always we been friends both in the old country and over here? Ain't always I loved you like a brother? And now when you need some money do you come to me and ask for it, man to man? No, you go to a goy like that Howard. Oy! Oy! for you I hang my head that you should do so!

"Listen: I am the one which is going to help you and not some feller in a bank. You get that Howard to sign his name on the back of this paper and then I give you the money!"

§ 53 The Tools Were Lacking

Two traveling men sat at breakfast in the hotel dining room of a South Carolina mill town. To them came a polite negro, soliciting their orders.

Said the first:

"Bring me grape fruit, coffee with hot milk, corn muffins, bacon and eggs."

"Yassuh," confirmed the waiter. He addressed the second patron:

"Whut's yourn goin' be, Cap'n?"

"I'll take the same as my friend here, except that the eggs should be eliminated."

At the sound of that last mysterious word the darky stiffened.

"Scuse me, suh—how'd you say you wanted 'em aigs?" he asked.

The white man caught the point. He was by way of being something of a practical joker anyhow. He raised his voice slightly for added emphasis:

"I said I wanted them eliminated."

The waiter blinked hard but recovered gallantly.

"Yas suh," he said, and departed for the kitchen. Almost immediately there floated in through the swinging doors which separated kitchen from dining room, a medley of sounds betokening a violent debate between two persons of African antecedents. And then on the heels of this the waiter reappeared, perspiring freely, and returned to where the two white men sat.

"Cap'n," he said, "wouldn't you des' ez soon have yore aigs fried? Or mebbe scrambled? We also meks a mouty tasty om'let yere. Folks w'ich tries our om'lets speaks mos' highly of 'em. Or mout——"

The joker broke in on him:

"Say," he demanded, "what's the matter with you? I gave you my order once—told you what I wanted. Now, I'm on a diet. Under the doctor's orders I must always have my eggs eliminated. And I'm going to have them that way here or else some nigger's going to be looking for a job."

"'Tain't my fault, suh," pleaded the waiter. "Hit's de cook. I tells him jes' ez plain. I sez, 'Liminate a couple of fresh aigs fur a Naw'the'n genelman,' I sez, an' 'en he starts argufyin'. An' he tell me to come on back yere an' suggest to you——"

"Never mind that," snapped the humorist, now seemingly in a highly indignant state. "You go tell that cook that I want him to fill my order according to instructions or there'll be trouble."

Once more the waiter sped away. Half a minute later he came through the swinging doors. With him was a large, coal black person in a greasy apron, and with a look of grave concern upon his face.

"Whar's de gen'elman?" asked the newcomer.

"Thar he set," said the waiter, pointing.

The cook presented himself at the table and bowed low.

"Boss," he said, "I'se de cook yere an' I strives to please. But you'll please, suh, haf' to 'scuse me reguardin' yore desires 'is mawnin' fur 'liminated aigs—an' tha's a fact."

"Don't you know how to eliminate an egg?" demanded the joker.

The cook favored him with a winning smile.

"Who, me?—w'y to be suttinly, I does. Any other time dem 'liminated aigs'd be settin' right dar in front of you now, smokin' hot. But to tell you de truth, boss, dey wuz a flighty nigger gal come foolin' round de kitchen yistiddy w'ich she rightly didn't have no business to be there neither; an' she drapped the 'liminator an' bruk de handle off of it."

§ 54   A Tribute to Moderation

It befell in the old days that a mob one night took a negro out of a county jail in southern Kentucky and carried him just across the line into Tennessee and there hanged him at the roadside. As he dangled they riddled him with bullets and then kindled a fire under him with intent to destroy the body.

By the light of the mounting flames somebody saw something stirring in a brush pile, close by the scene of execution. He kicked the brush away and dragged out an old colored man, who had been on his way home when he saw the lynchers coming. He had deemed it the part of prudence to take cover immediately. But as luck would have it, he had gone into retirement at the very spot where the mob halted to do its work.

Men poked big guns in his face and swore to take his life if ever he dared reveal what he had that night beheld. The old man protested that the whole thing was purely an affair of the white folks, in which he had no concern nor interest. He was quite sure that by daybreak of the following morning all memories of the night would be gone from his mind.

The leader of the mob felt it incumbent to press the lesson home to the consciousness of the witness. Still casually cocking and uncocking a long pistol, he flirted a thumb over his shoulder toward the gallows-tree and said:

"Well, you know that black scoundrel yonder got what he deserved, don't you?"

The old man craned his neck about and gazed for a moment upon the grisly spectacle.

"Boss," he said fervently, "it looks lak to me he got off mighty light."

§ 55   The Instantaneous Diagnosis

The traveling man had occasion to pass through the colored compartment of the train on his way to the baggage car, where he wished to open one of his trunks. He took note of a large black person who slept audibly, with his head lolled back against the seat, his mouth agape and his tongue hanging down on his chest like a pink plush necktie.

Now the traveling man was by way of being a practical joker. Also he had in his waistcoat pocket a number of five-grain quinine capsules.

When he returned from the baggage car he held in his hand one of those capsules, with its top removed. Along the furry surface of that pendant tongue he gently sifted the crystals of quinine. The sleeper stirred but did not waken.

The wag halted at the rear door of the Jim Crow section to await results. Presently a fly lit on the nose of the slumbering one, and he sucked his tongue back inside of his mouth. Instantly he was wide awake. He spat violently, then arose with a look of deep concern on his face and headed for the back platform.

At the door he encountered the traveling man. "Mister," he demanded, anxiously, "does you know ef dey's a doctor on dis yere train?"

"Who needs a doctor?" countered the white man.

"I does, tha's who."

"Are you sick?"

"I shore is. An' whut's more I knows whut ails me, an' I knows I needs to git to a doctor right away."

"Well, what does ail you?"

"Boss, my gall's busted!"

§ 56   In Fact, a Positive Fad

Not long ago a very wise literary critic suggested in my presence the attractiveness of the idea of compiling a funny book about hangings. He pointed out that there were scores of yarns, all dealing more or less humorously with the unhumorous subject of hangings, legal and otherwise. He thought that a suitable beginning for the volume might be found in the ancient anecdote of the shipwrecked mariner who, after drifting for days on an improvised raft, was carried by a friendly current within sight of a strange land. As he drew nearer he saw some men on the shore erecting a gallows, and, falling upon his knees, cried out: "Thank Heaven, I have reached a Christian country!"

I do not know whether my friend will carry out his threat of compiling such a work, but if he ever does I claim the collection will be incomplete unless in his pages he includes the narrative pertaining to that colored person who was condemned to death on the scaffold, and who was unable to readjust himself to the prospect. The nearer the date of execution came the greater became the reluctance on his part, until toward the end it amounted with him to what might be called a positive diffidence.

On the night before the fatal day a clergyman sat with the prisoner striving by counsel and admonition to prepare him for the ordeal.

"My brother, my poor brother," said the minister, soothingly, "try to face the fate which confronts you on the morrow with courage and resolution. Remember that thousands and thousands before you all through the ages, some justly condemned and some unjustly, have suffered this same punishment with fortitude. Even the early Christian martyrs died much as you must die."

"Yas, suh, I knows," quavered the condemned, "but—but it wuz a hobby wid them."

§ 57 Something Like a Wampus, Probably

They were holding an examination of aspirants for the position of principal of a colored grade school in Louisville. One of the most promising candidates for the vacancy was a small yellow man, who wore shiny, gold-rimmed spectacles, and bore himself with that air of assurance which learning sometimes imparts.

The superintendent of the public school system was sounding the qualifications of this person. The subject was syntax. The inquisitor would choose a word at random from the lexicon and the applicant would give his conception of its proper definition.

Out of a clear sky, so to speak, the superintendent sped this one: "Jeopardy."

The candidate froze stiff. His eyes rolled in his head as he recoiled from the shock.

"Which?" he inquired softly.

"Jeopardy."

"I believe you said 'jeopardy,' didn't you, suh?" said the little yellow man, still sparring for time.

"Certainly, 'jeopardy.' You know the word, don't you?"

"Oh, yas, suh, fluently."

"Well, then, since you are familiar with it, what is your understanding of its meaning?"

Like a man preparing to dive from a great height into vasty depths the candidate took a deep breath. Then gallantly he leaped headlong.

"Well, suh," he stated, "in reply to the question just propounded I should say that 'jeopardy' would properly refer to any act committed by a jeopard."

He got the job on the spot.

§ 58   An Education in Peril

The original of my fiction character of "Judge Priest" was a certain Judge William Bishop, now deceased. He was a wonderful old man—shrewd, simple, kindly, witty, gentle.

One time the old Judge was acting as chairman of a committee of three lawyers who sat to examine a gangling young man from the country who sought a license to practice at the local bar. The candidate had started out to be a blacksmith, but he had decided that wearing a frock coat and making speeches to juries would be easier than bending mule shoes and shrinking wagon tires.

Judge Bishop opened the inquiry.

"Henry, my son," he began in his usual benignant fashion, "I suppose you have done a course of reading with a view to acquiring the rudiments of this calling of ours and thereby fitting yourself for your new career?"

"Well, Jedge, I done some readin' but not so very much," confessed Henry. "I aims to do the most of my readin' after I opens an office."

"Well, let's see just what reading you have done," pursued Judge Bishop. "I assume naturally that you have read Blackstone?"

"Black which, Jedge?"

"Blackstone, author of great textbooks on the practice and principle of the law."

The candidate shook his head.

"I ain't never heared of him," he confessed.

"Well, how about Coke?"

"I don't know ez I ever heared tell of him, neither."

"Well, surely then you have studied the Constitution of the United States of America and the Constitution and the Bill of Rights of the State of Kentucky?"

"To tell you the truth, Jedge, I ain't got round to them yit," admitted the aspiring blacksmith.

"Henry," pressed Judge Bishop, "suppose you tell us just what books—what authorities—you have studied since you became seized with the desire to be a member of our bar?"

Henry pondered a moment. Then his face brightened.

"I tell you, Jedge," he said, "I read one big book called 'Revised Statutes of the State of Kintucky' mighty nigh through, an' I kin remember part of what it says."

"My son," stated Judge Bishop, "the trouble with you is that the next Legislature is liable to meet and repeal every damn thing you know."

§ 59   A Lover of Statistics

There was a seance on—a regular seance, with a trance medium and a black cheesecloth cabinet and a mysterious table rapper and a ghostly guitar picker and everything orthodox, like that. The medium was a stout lady whose controls took those liberties with the English language which seemingly is permitted in a realm where there is neither space nor time—nor grammar. The audience was of fairish size. Amid the throng sat a half-grown youth from about five miles out on R. F. D. No. 3. He was attending his first spiritualistic seance. As manifestation succeeded manifestation, his eyes popped and his ears twitched.

Presently the medium's husband, who acted, so to speak, as ringmaster, desired to know whether there was yet another present desirous of having speech with some dear departed one. If so, Madame would undertake to establish liaison.

This was the cue for the yokel. He mustered courage to stutter an embarrassed plea. He wished to hear from the shade of his late father.

After a proper wait there were sounds in the cabinet and through the darkness there spoke the tones of one of seeming hoary age.

"Is that you, my son?" asked the voice.

"Yes, paw, this here is me," answered the youth.

"Was there any questions you wished to ast me concernin' my present state?" continued the accommodating voice.

The boy thought a moment. Then:

"Where air you, Paw?" he inquired with simple directness.

"Heaven, my son."

"Air you an angel, Paw?"

"Oh, yes, my son."

"An angel with wings and a harp and everything?"

The answer was somewhat muffled but seemingly in the affirmative. The son considered a moment.

"Say, Paw," he demanded eagerly, "whut do you measure frum tip to tip?"

§ 60   History in the Un-Making

There used to be a character in George Creel's town in Missouri a transplanted Kentuckian and a veteran of Shelby's command, who was a born orator and an inspired romancer.

One sunny afternoon he was holding forth to an attentive audience upon the part he had played in the war between the States. It was rather to be inferred that he was one of the main reasons why the Confederacy endured, against odds, for four years. He progressed to where he was enriching history with an account of the first engagement in which he had participated.

"Gentlemen," he proclaimed, "envisage the scene. There we stand, a little group, armed for the most part with nondescript weapons, with flint lock muskets, with scythes, with axes, even with cudgels. We are underfed, half shod and ragged, yet inspired by the dauntless resolution and splendid valor which sustained the Southern heart. Over the slope and straight against our line come pouring the Northern hordes, those relentless invaders of our beloved Southland, lusty and strong and equipped with every appliance for conducting warfare that modern science can provide.

"We are outnumbered three to one; we are weak from hunger while they are lusty with bacon and beef. But none among us quails. A righteous belief in our sacred cause inspires us, every one. Each one feels himself a giant. And what is the result? Suddenly we leap forward in the charge. We grapple with them, we fight like demons. And, gentlemen, such is the impetuosity of our attack, such the ferocity of our blows that soon the blue lines break and in mad disorder routed the enemy flees, unable to face that irresistible torrent of Southern manhood."

From the audience spoke up a gray bearded listener.

"Say, looky here, Kurnel," he said. "I was in that there fight myself and whut really happened wuz that them plegged Yanks give us a fust rate lickin' and run us ten miles acrost country."

With a magnificent gesture of surrender the Colonel rose to his feet.

"Gentlemen," he said, "another instance of a good story spoiled by a damn eyewitness!"

§ 61   Solving a Dark Mystery

Achmed Abdullah, the novelist, is an Afghan, a descendant of an old and noble family of Afghanistan and a son of a former Governor of Kabul. He was educated in Europe, and he has lived and adventured pretty much all over the world. Being a natural linguist, he has picked up tongues as he went.

With the rank of captain he was on recruiting service once for the British army in Cairo. To him came an Egyptian officer of police to ask his aid. Two native constables had picked up in the bazaars a black man whose nationality was unknown and whose purposes were unfathomable, seeing that he could not be made to understand the questions put to him by his captors.

It seemed that for several days before his arrest the prisoner had been lurking about the bazaars, a butt for gamins and the despair of those who sought to interrogate him. As much for his own protection as for any other motive the police had locked him up. Now the assistance of Capt. Abdullah as translator was solocited.

Abdullah accompanied the puzzled functionary to the prison. In a corner of a cell crouched a huge black man staring with apprehensive, sullen eyes at the newcomers. It was evident that he was of some African stock; also it was plain that he was in a badly frightened state. He was clad in a nondescript costume of tatters which he had picked up somewhere—the sandals of an Arabian, a Turkish fez and the ragged remains of a donkey driver's robe.

Being admitted to the cell, the volunteer interpreter proceeded to fire simple questions at the captive, first in French, then in Afghan, and then in Ashantee, in Turkish, in Tibetan, in Greek, in Chinese, in Persian and in Batu. There was no response; the black merely continued to glower at him dumbly. So then Abdullah tried him in some of the tongues of the Sahara Desert and in the clucking dialects of one or two Congo tribes and finally in Zuluese, with which he was also more or less familiar. Still the hunched-up figure gave no sign of understanding.

In despair Abdullah gave it up. "I wonder," he said aloud to himself in English, "what in thunder you are, anyway?"

With a bellow of thanksgiving the prisoner leaped to his feet.

"Boss," he whooped, "I'se a Free Will Baptist!"

And so he was—a country darky from Alabama who had shipped on a tramp steamer out of New Orleans, had deserted off the African coast, swimming ashore naked, and had for days past been dodging about the native quarters, growing hourly more bewildered and more desperate in these strange surroundings.

§ 62   Enough of a Good Thing

In September of 1918 Col. Bozeman Bulger, in charge of the press bureau of the A. E. F., was driving in his car up toward the front on the afternoon of a day when there had been hard fighting with the stubborn Germans. Limping down the high road on the way from the forward trenches to rest billets came a company of infantry, or what was left of it, just relieved after more than a week of practically continuous service under fire.

The officer in command was a lanky youth of perhaps twenty-two whose face was gray with exhaustion. He hailed Bulger, asking for something to smoke. He had been without tobacco, he said, for four days—without food, too, for most of that time.

Bulger left his car and he and the youth sat down together in a convenient shell hole to pass the time of day. Between long, grateful puffs on a cigarette the youth discoursed of his recent experiences in the slow drawl of a Southwesterner.

"Major," he said, "we've had it pretty toler'ble tough these last few days—the Heinies shelling us day and night, communication interrupted and liaison broken, no chow to speak of, no makin's, no nothing except mud and wet and the chances of being blown into little scraps.

"As a matter of fact, I've had pretty rough sledding ever since I got over here, and that's more than a year ago. I haven't had any leave—they seem to have overlooked me when they were passing out the trips to Paris—and I've been working my head off when I wasn't in the line on active duty. And now finally, to top off with, we have this week up front."

"Where are you from?" asked Bulger.

"Texas," replied the youth. "Yes, sir, I was teaching school down there when we got into this war. I had a mother dependent on me, and while I wanted to go and do my bit I thought it better on my mother's account that I should wait until the draft took me. But while I was trying to decide Senator Morris Sheppard came to our town and made a recruiting speech. He said it was high time we were satisfying our national honor. Well, sir, that phrase hit me right where I lived. The next day I went in as a volunteer, and after a spell I got a commission—and here I am.

"Major, I don't regret having done what I did do. If it was to do over again I reckon I wouldn't hesitate. But, Major, as I look back on what I've gone through with ever since I landed, I don't mind telling you, in strict confidence, that my national honor is dern near satisfied!"

§ 63 Absolutely Bored by the Whole Thing

A youth in southeastern Missouri became involved in legal proceedings as the result of the mysterious disappearance of a neighbor's mare and the upshot was that a jury went so far as to find him guilty of horse-stealing and the judge gave him a sentence of five years at hard labor. A friend of mine defended him at his trial.

Some months after his late client had been taken away to begin serving his sentence this friend was sitting one morning in his office when the door opened and there entered the father of the youth, an elderly bearded hillsman.

"Hal," began the newcomer, "I come to see you to git you to do somethin' 'bout my boy Wesley Junior."

"Well, Uncle Wes," said the lawyer, "I don't believe there is anything I can do. You remember how hard I worked for him at his trial—how I sweated down two or three collars over yonder in that courthouse and how I wasted all the oratory I had in my system and how I snapped both my suspenders. But in spite of all I could say, you know as well as I do what happened. The case went against us and the Judge gave Wesley five years in the State penitentiary and there he is!"

"Yas, suh, Hal," said the father. "Wesley Junior, is up thar in that there penitentiary and that's jest the p'int! I got a letter frum him this mawnin'. And he told me to come to see you and to tell you to git him out of that place right-a-way—he's plum dissatisfied."

§ 64 The Question Categorical

There is a certain young actor in New York, a player of romantic swashbuckler parts who, when he is sober, is one of the gentlest and most companionable of men. But when he indulges in strong water his nature changes. He becomes dogmatic, disputatious, and occasionally quarrelsome. Such times he delights to corner some inoffensive acquaintance and pin him down to a definite position on this subject or that and then debate the point for hours on end.

One night, being in one of these alcoholically promoted moods, he trapped a friend against the bar of a certain club. The latter wished not to argue with any one on any topic whatsoever. But the actor would not have it so.

"You go 'round saying you know so mush, don't you?" he demanded belligerently. "You go 'round saying you know so many people in this town, don't you? Thatsh kinda fellow you are, ain't you—huh?"

"Not at all," protested the hapless friend, "I never———"

"Pleash don't contradict me," said the actor; "thatsh no way to carry on argument between gen'men. Lemme get through stating my side and then I'll lisshen to you. You go 'round saying you know more people in this club than I know, don't you? Just answer me that!"

"Why, I never said any such———"

"Kin'ly lemme get word in edgeways, if you please," said the actor with elaborate politeness. "You say you know more members of thish club 'en I do—more than anybody knows? A'right, then, you answer me thish: Do you know Jerome Lawrence—he'sh member here?"

"Certainly, I know him," said the badgered one, thinking he saw a loophole. "As it happens, I also know his brother, Oscar, who looks so much like him."

"Ah, hah!" exulted the intoxicated one, with the air of having led an unwilling witness into a damaging admission. "You say you know Jerome Lawrence and you say you know his brother Oscar that looks so mush like him? Well, then, if you know so mush, you tell me thish: Whish one of 'em looks the most alike?"

§ 65   Before or After Taking?

A well-dressed party, who was far overtaken in alcoholic stimulant, stumbled into a restaurant, slumped into a handy chair at a table and gave unmistakable evidence that he was about to enjoy a refreshing slumber. A waitress shook him by the arm.

"What is it you want?" she asked.

"Dearie," he said drowsily, "what have you?"

"Almost anything in the food line."

"Ver' well, then," he said, "bring me almost anything in the food line."

"How about a nice salad?" she asked, on a venture.

"That'd be lovely, dearie," he assented. "Glad you thought of it—shows you got a good mind—quick thinker, everything like that. Bring me nice salad."

"What sort of a salad?"

"That, dearie, I leave to your superior judgment," he said. "You been here longer than I have."

The girl went away, returning presently with a bowl of hearts of lettuce and sliced tomatoes, with an abundance of Russian dressing poured over the combination. The patron was now sound asleep. She slipped the order past his elbow and left it there where his eyes would fall upon it when he opened them.

Presently he did open his eyes. As though spell-bound he contemplated that which confronted him. He took a fork and gently he stirred the contents of the bowl. Then with his free hand he beckoned the young woman to his side.

"Dearie," he said, "drunk or sober or drinking, as is the case at present, my aim is ever to be a gen'man. Far be it from me to do anythin' which would bring reproach upon me as a gen'man or upon the fair and unsullied name of thish noble 'stablishment. But, dearie, in justish to all concerned, it becomes nes'ary for me to ash you a queshun."

"What's your question?" she said snappily.

"Well," he said, "I drift off in slumber. I wake up, and right here under my nose I find thish." And again with his fork he daintily agitated a frond of dressing-soaked lettuce. "So, therefore, dearie, the queshun is as follows: Do I eat this—or DID I?"

§ 66   A Time for All Things

It was an irate Iowa farmer of the old-fashioned type who sat him down, pen in hand, and wrote an indignant letter to a concern which made a specialty of selling plumbing supplies to rural patrons.

"I have got a kick to make,"—thus the farmer wrote. "Early last spring your agent came through this district taking orders for your patent porcelain bath tub. Some of the neighbors give him their names and so nothing would do but that my wife and daughter should have one for our house and they kept after me until I give your man my name too and told him to send me one of his tubs.

"Well, that was in the early part of April. April passed and also May and no sign of that bath tub. So I wrote to you telling you to hurry on up and deliver me that there tub. Nothing was done and so June went by and July and then August.

"And now here, when it's the middle of September and the bathing season practically over for the year, you people are trying to make me take that dern tub."

§ 67 Tuesday Would Be Just Like Sunday

On the occasion of a local election in a small Tennessee town an old colored man was the only member of his race who voted the Democratic ticket. It was felt that this devotion to the cause of the Caucasian—as it prevailed in that vicinity—was deserving of recognition.

Accordingly the incoming administration promptly created a department of street cleaning—something of which the municipality had never seriously felt the need before. This department was to consist of two members, namely, a foreman or superintendent and a staff of one. Naturally, to a white man went the job of foreman but upon the worthy old black man was conferred the honor of being the staff.

Now he had the idea, which is not uncommon among other political appointees, that holding a public office meant regular wages and considerable glory and no appreciable amount of manual exertion. Nevertheless on the Monday morning when he reported for duty, as a concession to the conventionalities, he did bring a shovel along with him.

But the white man who had been selected as superintendent had a very different idea of the obligations which he owed the municipality. No sooner had the old negro shoveled up one of the accumulated piles of vintage rubbish of the years from the public thoroughfare than the vigilant eye of the boss spied out at least half a dozen more similar mounds which to his way of thinking seemed to require immediate attention.

As a consequence it was 4 o'clock in the afternoon before the surprised and chagrined and pained old man had time to blow on the plump, new formed blisters in the palm of his hands or to rub the cricks out of his back. Finally in a lull in the operations he straightened his spine with an almost audible creak, and as he wrung the dew of unwonted toil from his forehead he inquired of his superior:

"Look here, mister, ain't you got nothin' to do 'ceptin' jes' to think up things fur me to do?"

"Yep," said the white man briskly, "that's all my job—just to keep you busy."

"Well, suh," said the old man softly, "in dat case you'll prob'ly be pleased to know dat you ain't goin' be workin' tomorrer."

§ 68 A Sort of Circulating Medium, as It Were

An auctioneer's man had been sent to a household to list its contents. Nothing of especial interest, either to himself or to others, marked the course of his labors until he had progressed so far as the dining room. Here, following his routine, he proceeded to enumerate the furnishings in proper order, item by item.

In his flowing professional script he set down the tally in his book:
One mahogany dining room table.
Six mahogany dining chairs.
One mahogany sideboard.
One bottle Scotch whiskey, full.

Seemingly, then, ensued a period when the appraiser was otherwise engaged and made no entries whatsoever. Then, in a somewhat struggling and uncertain handwriting, he scratched out the last item and concluded his labors for the day with the following notations:
One bottle Scotch whiskey, partially full.
One revolving Turkish rug.

§ 69 A Service to the Whole Land

In the early summer of 1918 three of us made a long trip by automobile to pay a visit to a colored regiment at the front in France. The results more than repaid us for the time and trouble. One of the main compensations was First Class Private Cooksey, who, because he had been an elevator attendant in a Harlem apartment house, gave his occupation in his enlistment blank as "indoor chauffeur." It was to First Class Private Cooksey that the Colonel of the regiment, seeing the expression on the others' faces when a shell from a German mortar fell near by on the day the command moved up to the front, put this question:

"Cooksey, if one of those things drops right here alongside of us and goes off, are you going to stay by me?"

"Kurnel," stated Cooksey with sincerity, "I ain't aimin' to tell you no lie. Ef one of them things busts clost to me I'll jest natchelly be obliged to go away frum here. But please, suh, don't you set me down as no deserter. Jest put it in de book as 'Absent without leave,' 'cause I'll be back jest ez soon ez I kin git my brakes to work."

"But what if the enemy suddenly appears in force without any preliminary bombardment?" pressed the Colonel. "What do you think you and the rest of the boys will do then?"

"Kurnel," said Cooksey, earnestly, "we may not stick by you, but we'll shore render one service, anyway: we'll spread de news all over France 'at de Germans is comin'!"

§ 70   Deportment Taught by Wire

There was a so-called financial wizard who advertised to give lessons by mail which would enable patrons to prosper in their speculations.

A subscriber down in the Southwest found himself in difficulties as a result of following the directions for playing the grain market as laid down by the expert. He wrote a letter to this effect:

"You told me if I got into trouble I was to communicate with you and you would tell me how to act. Well, I done just what you said about buying winter wheat and I am now busted. How shall I act? Please wire."

By wire promptly came back the answer:

"Act like you are busted!"

§ 71   Speaking of Carrier Pigeons

Speaking of carrier pigeons—although no one has done so—reminds me of a yarn that was related at the front in 1918. A half company of a regiment in the Rainbow Division, on going forward early one morning in a heavy fog for a raid across No Man's Land, carried along with the rest of the customary equipment a homing pigeon. The pigeon in its wicker cage swung on the arm of a private, who likewise was burdened with his rifle, his extra rounds of ammunition, his trenching tool, his pair of wire cutters, his steel helmet, his gas mask, his emergency ration and quite a number of other more or less cumbersome items.

It was to be a surprise attack behind a cloak of the fog, so there was no artillery preparation as the squads climbed over the top and advanced into the mist-hidden beyond. Behind, in the posts of observation and in the post of command, the Colonel and his aides and his intelligence officers waited for the sound of firing. When after some minutes the distant rattle of the rifle fire came to their ears they began calculating how long reasonably it might be before word reached them by one or another medium of communication touching on the results of the foray. But the ground telephone remained mute, and no runner returned through the fog with tidings. The suspense increased as time passed.

Suddenly a pigeon sped into view, flying close to the earth. While eager eyes followed it in its course the winged messenger circled until it located its portable cote just behind the Colonel's position and fluttering down it entered its familiar shelter.

An athletic member of the staff hustled up the ladder. In half a minute he was tumbling down again, clutching in one hand the little scroll of paper that he had found fastened about the pigeon's leg. With fingers that trembled in anxiety the Colonel unrolled the paper and read aloud what was written upon it.

What he read, in the hurried chirography of a kid private, was the following succinct statement: "I'm tired of carrying this damn bird."

§ 72   Total Loss!

For the first time in the history of the State—it was a Southern State—an electrocution took place within the walls of the State prison. The Legislature, keeping step with the march of progress and civilization, had ordered the installation of an electric chair to take the honored place of the old-fashioned slip-noose under the left ears of the fathers.

A negro "trusty" was an unwilling witness to the first performance under the new arrangement. The warden had detailed him as helper to the paid executioner. He issued forth from the lethal chamber with popped eyes and ashen face.

A group of his fellow convicts knotted about him, anxious to hear the grisly details. He proceeded to elucidate:

"Well, suhs," he said, with a shiver, "they teks an' strops you down, hand an' foot, in a big cheer. An' den they clamps some lil' things onto yo' haid an' yo' laigs. An' den one of de w'ite men he step over to whar they's a little jigger set in de wall an' he give it a lil' yank—zzz—like dat!"

Here he paused and fetched a deep breath.

"Whut den? whut den?" came the chorus.

"Nothin' but ruin—jes' absolute ruin!"

§ 73   With All Good Wishes

The colonel of one of our negro regiments serving in France during the world war impressed it upon the rank and file of his command that in the field a soldier addressing his superior officer invariably should have regard for correct military procedure and for correct military language. The lesson must have gone home, because now among the treasured possessions of that colonel is a certain document sent by runner from a forward trench to company headquarters back of the second line of defense.

On a scrap of paper, with a stub of pencil, the author of the communication, a much-harried black corporal then undergoing his baptism of shelling, wrote as follows:

"To Lieutenant Seth B. McClintock,
"Commanding Company F.—Blank Regimen'
"Blank Division, A. E. F., U. S. A.
"Dear Sir—I am being fired on heavily from the left. I await your instructions.
"Trusting these few lines will find you the same, I remain,
"Yours truly,
"James Jordon."

§ 74 A Start from Humble Beginnings

Mr. Campbell, who was a lawyer, felt somewhat irritated on reaching his office at 8:30 in the morning to find the fire in the grate unkindled and the floor unswept and the place generally in a state of disorder. It was nearly 9 o'clock before Ike, his black office servant, appeared.

"Good Lord, Ike," said Mr. Campbell petulantly. "What's detained you?"

"Mist' Campbell," apologized Ike, "you must please, suh, 'scuse me fur bein' late dis one time. I sort of overslept myse'f. De truth of de matter is dat I wuz kept up de best part of de night on 'count of j'inin' a lodge."

"It surely didn't take you all night to join a lodge, did it?"

"Naw, suh, not perzac'ly. De fust part of de evenin' they wuz 'niciatin' me into de membership an' de rest of de time dey wuz 'onductin' me into office."

"Isn't it rather unusual to confer an office on a member immediately after taking him in?"

"Naw suh, dat's de standin' rule in dat lodge—jes' soon ez you is 'niciated you gits a office."

"What office did they confer upon you?"
"Imperial Supreme King."
"What?"

A LAUGH A DAY KEEPS THE DOCTOR AWAY

"Dat's whut dey calls it—Imperial Supreme King of de Universe."

"Isn't that rather a high office for a brand new member?"

"Why, naw, suh, Mist' Campbell, dat's de lowes' office dey is in dat lodge. W'en I's been in a spell longer dey is goin' give me somethin' really wuth while."

§ 75   The Confusing Geography of Jersey

Years ago, when I earned my daily bread and occasional beer on Park Row, one Andy Horn ran a cozy bar in the shadow of Brooklyn Bridge. A grubby person known as Smitty was a fixture at Andy's. He cut up food for the free lunch counter, did odd jobs and in rush hours helped to serve the trade.

He had been born on Cherry Hill, right around the corner; he had been reared on the Bowery and he had never ranged farther than Coney Island or Far Rockaway. Greater New York city was all the world he knew or cared to know.

His sister married a market gardener over in New Jersey, and when his summertime vacation came Smitty went to visit her for two weeks. His new brother-in-law had bought a car and had promised to tour Smitty about the State and show him the sights.

At the end of a week Smitty was back at work. One of the regular patrons hailed him:

"Hey, Smitty, I thought you were going to stay longer. Didn't you care for country life?"

"Nix on dat stuff fur me," said Smitty. "I'm offen it fur life. Say, dat Joisey soitinly is one funny place. Why, all dem towns over there is got different names!"

§ 76   With Credit to S. Blythe

Sam Blythe claims this is a true one. Maybe he is right; Sam generally is.

He says a Washington wholesaler wished to learn the relative qualities of two brands of mucilage. He handed one bottle of each brand to his negro janitor.

"Henry," he said, "take these and test them and see which one is the stickier."

Hours passed before Henry reappeared. Wearing a somewhat unhappy, not to say distressed, expression, he entered his employer's office and placed the two bottles on the latter's desk.

"Well, Henry," said the jobber, "what's the result of your experiments?"

"Boss," stated Henry, "it's lak dis: Dis yere one gummed up my mouth the most; but dis yere other one, the taste lasted the longest."

§ 77   When the H. C. of L. Came Down

As I heard the tale it had to do with a small community in Texas where the railroad ran through the main street and on either side of the track stood a short order restaurant owned and operated by a colored man.

One night the official bad man of the vicinity came lurching into one of these rival establishments. The visitor was under the influence of strong drink—a circumstance calculated to make him slightly more dangerous than rattlesnakes.

While the uneasy proprietor made pretense at being glad to see him the bully flopped his long frame into a chair and demanded:

"Nigger, have you got a nice tender sirloin steak here?"

"Yas, suh!"

"All right, then; you cook it fur me and don't you cook it too long else I'll cook you. And along with it you better bring me some fried onions and fried potatoes and some celery and a mess of hot biscuits and green peas and roasting ears and pie and coffee and anything else tasty that you've got around this dump. Now jump before I start jumpin' you."

The black man jumped. In a miraculously short time, considering the magnitude of the order, he staggered in from his cubbyhole of a kitchen at the rear bearing a waiter tray piled high with dishes. He ranged the array of food in a half moon effect before his patron and then fluttered back a few paces.

When the bad man had eaten he leaned back in his chair, drew a spring-back dirk knife out of his pocket, flipped its five-inch blade out with a nudge of a practiced thumb and leisurely picked his teeth with its needlelike point. His caterer watched him as a fascinated bird watches a coiled serpent.

Suddenly he spoke and the negro jumped.

"What sort of a dump does that other nigger over acrost the tracks run?" he asked.

"Oh, you wouldn't lak dat place a-tall," stated the colored man. "Dat nigger natchelly thinks a fly is somethin' you cooks wid. He ain't sanitatious, lak I aims to be."

"Yes," said the bully, "and whut's more, he's a robber—he's a regular pirate."

"Is dat so, suh?"

"Well, judge for yourself. Last night I went into that nigger's joint and ordered just about what I've had here to-night—maybe a little more, maybe a little less. When I got through I asked him what the damage was and, do you know, that black scoundrel had the gall to ask me for a dollar and a quarter? Of course I oughter killed him. In fact, I got up intendin' to kill him. But something sort of stayed my hand. All I done to him was just to cut off both his ears with this here frog-sticker and feed 'em to him. By the way, what do I owe you for this mess of vittles?"

"Boss," said the darky, "I reckon a dime would be ample."

§ 78 How to Beat the System

The late "Tiny" Maxwell was a sporting writer in Philadelphia. He was called "Tiny" because he weighed nearly three hundred pounds. He had a ready wit.

Because he was an expert at football and also because back in his college days he was a gridiron star of magnitude, Mr. Maxwell frequently was called upon to referee games along the Eastern Seaboard.

One afternoon he was officiating at a match between Georgetown, which, as everybody knows, is a Catholic institution, and a team representing a Southern university. In an interval one of the Southern players limped up to Maxwell.

"Mr. Referee," he said, "I want to make a protest. There's one of those Georgetown men that seems to have a private grudge against me. Every time we two get in a scrimmage together he bites me. Yes, sir, he just hauls off and bites me. I don't want to start any rough house stuff, but I'm getting good and tired of having that big Irishman biting on me. What had I better do?"

"I should advise," said Maxwell, "that you play him only on Fridays."

§ 79 An Echo from 1865

I rather guess they have been telling this one ever since the War between the States. Indeed, for all I know to the contrary it may date back as far as the first and second Punic wars. For a good story never really dies. It merely goes into retirement for a season or a decade or a century and rises up again when occasion suits, with its youth miraculously restored.

The narrative runs that in the last days of the war a ragged, wornout, hungry, half-crippled, half-dead Confederate straggler was limping along a Virginia highway striving to catch up with his command. Where there was a puddle in the ruts he stopped to bathe his bruised and bleeding feet. As he sat at the roadside dabbling his swollen toes in the water a Union skirmisher, well fed and lusty, stepped from behind a tree with his musket raised to his shoulder and yelled out exultantly:

"Now I got you!"

"Yas," drawled the Southerner, "an' a hell of a git you got!"

§ 80   There'd Be a Popular Uprising

The revivalist was the mouthpiece of a new cult. In his interpretations of the Scriptures he saw no possible hope for any member of the human family who refused to accept his particular brand of religion.

Before an awe-struck congregation he was describing what would come to pass with regard to those stiff-necked and perverse nonbelievers who were found outside the fold on the day of judgment.

"My brethren," he clarioned, "there is no middle course. By the word of the Holy Writ I have proved to you that mankind either must take the true doctrine as it has been expounded here or accept the awful consequences. I can close my eyes and see the picture right now.

"Over there in shining robes stand the little group of the elect and the saved. And down below in the fiery pits of perdition millions of the unregenerate are roasting in the undying fires through all eternity while the minions of the Devil heap hot coals upon their heads and give them molten lead when they beg for water to cool their parched tongues. That, my brethren, is what will come to pass."

From the body of the house a small elderly gentleman rose up.

"Excuse me for interruptin'," he said, "but there ain't no chance fur sich a thing to happen. Why, the people jest natchelly wouldn't stand fur it."

§ 81   From the Book of Moses

Mose Morris used to live near Frankfort, Ky. He was a small, meek person of color who cultivated a truck patch for a living, and was generally liked by the white population. He remained a bachelor until he was nearing middle age.

Then, in an unthoughted hour, he suffered himself to be shackled in the holy bonds of wedlock with a large, truculent, overbearing black woman nearly twice his size. He led his bride away to his little house seven miles from town.

Within two weeks' time he came driving into Frankfort in a two-mule wagon, which was piled high with household effects. As he crossed the bridge over the Kentucky River a white gentleman hailed him.

"Why, hello, Mose! Where are you going with all that plunder?"
"I'se movin', Mist' Bob," answered Mose.
"Movin' where?"
"Movin' into town—done rented a lil' house down back behint de L. and N. depot."
"Why, I thought you liked the country?" said the white man.
"I used to lak it," said Mose. "I used to lak it powerful. But my wife she don't lak the country. An' yere lately I've tuck notice, Mist' Bob, dat w'en my wife don't lak a thing I jest natchelly hates it."

§ 82 Almost Startling, Really

In the days when Frank A. Munsey was in active editorial charge of his various publications he had a serious-minded office boy who took things literally—and with due deliberation.

One day Congressman Thomas B. Reed, then Speaker of the House, came from Washington to New York and dropped into the office of *Munsey's Magazine* to see its proprietor. Between the famous publisher and the famous statesman a close bond of friendship existed—they were both sons of Maine, and they had been intimate associates for years.

The bulky Reed stepped into the anteroom and without giving his name said he wished to see Mr. Munsey. The office boy told him Mr. Munsey was in conference and invited the caller to have a seat. More than half an hour passed before the caller was admitted to the inner room. Then he told Mr. Munsey how he had been kept waiting.

Indignantly the latter issued forth and descended upon the youthful keeper of the outer gates.

"Do you know who that gentleman is that you've kept dawdling about here?" he demanded. "That is the Hon. Thomas B. Reed of Maine!"

"I'm sorry, Mr. Munsey," said the youth. "I thought all the time it was Dr. John Hall."

"But don't you know that Dr. Hall is dead?" said Mr. Munsey.

"Yes, sir," said Truthful James, "that was what made it seem so strange to me that he should be calling."

§ 83   A Violent Indisposition

A colored man, on appearing for work one morning, wore a countenance so battered that almost one might have been pardoned for assuming that its owner had made a more or less successful effort to run it through a meat chopper. The white man for whom the scarred and bruised victim worked took one look at that disfigured face and threw up both hands in horror and sympathy.

"Great heavens, boy," he cried, "what have you been doing to yourself?"

"Me? I ain't been doin' nothin' to myse'f," explained the darky. "But somethin' is done been did to me, Mr. Watkins. It's lak dis, suh: Yistiddy evenin' I got into a kind of an argymint wid another nigger an' one word led to another, ez it will. An' purty soon I up an' hauled off an' hit at him wid my fist.

"Well, seemed lak that irritated him. So he took an' split my lip wide open wid a pair of brass knucks, an' he blacked dis eye of mine clear down to my armpit an' he tore one ear moughty nigh loose frum de side of my haid, an' den, to cap all, he knocked me down and stomped up an' down 'pun my stomach wid his feet. . . . Honest to Gawd, Mr. Watkins, I never did git so sick of a nigger in all my life!"

§ 84   The Simplest of Remedies

In Owen county, Ky., there formerly resided a self-ordained oracle on all questions pertaining to subjects of farming, horse raising and hog guessing. To him one day, as he sat on a horse block facing the public square at Owenton, came a pestered young husbandman from the knobs along the Kentucky River with this question:

"Uncle Hamp, how am I going to get shet of sassafras sprouts? The pesky dern things have jest about took an old field of mine. I've tried choppin' em out and plowin' 'em under and burnin' 'em over, but they keep on gittin' thicker and thicker all the time. It seems I can't git rid of 'em noway. Whut would you advise?"

"My son," said the wise man, "I don't want to brag, but I reckon you ain't made no mistake in comin' to me—you've struck on to one man that's fitten to advise you in this here matter ef anybody on this earth is. Man and boy, I've been givin' the subject of sassafras sprouts my earnest attention fur goin' on sixty years. And it's my deliberatic judgment that when sassafras sprouts starts to takin' a farm the only way you kin git rid of 'em is jest to pack up and move off and leave 'em."

§ 85 Proving There's Something in a Name

I once knew a colored child called "Exey" for short, whose real name was Eczema. The mother of the pickaninny had found the word in a patent medicine almanac and had fallen in love with its poetic sound. I also included in my acquaintance at one time a negro youth who answered to the title of Hallowed Harris.

"Yas, suh," stated his father on being pressed for his reason for choosing so unusual a baptismal prefix for his offspring, "I got dat name outen de Holy Bible. Don't you 'member, boss, whar it say in de Lawd's Prayer, 'Hallowed be Thy name'?"

But the Testamental name which struck me as being most interesting of all was worn by a dog—a mangy appearing, breedless, nondescript rabbit dog which trailed an old darky on a road in the piny woods of South Georgia. The dog ranged off into the thickets and his owner ordered him back.

"Did I hear you calling that dog 'Rover,' Uncle?" asked a white man.

"Naw, suh, I called him 'Over,' w'ich is short for 'Mo'over,' w'ich it is de dawg's right name."

"Where did you get that name and why?"

"Fur good reasons, boss," said the old man, with a chuckle. "W'en I gits dat dawg he's jest little scabby pup an' alluz 'nointin' of his-se'f wid his tongue. So I 'members whar de Good Book say, 'An' de dawg, Mo'over, licked his sores.' So I knowed den I had done hit on de right name fur dat pup of mine."

§ 86 Question: How Far Did George Go?

The white man was named Ferguson. He owned a string of two-room frame cottages and his tenants exclusively were colored. Very great was his chagrin when a negro man in a fit of pique cut a woman's throat in one of his houses so that she bled to death, leaving a large dark stain on the floor, because immediately the word spread among the black population that the building was haunted and thereafter nobody would rent it, even at reduced rates. For months the cottage stood empty. Then the owner had a bright idea. He went one evening and hunted up a large dark individual named George, upon whom, by way of beginning, he conferred a drink out of a bottle of corn spirits.

"George," said he, "these darkies tell me you know quite a lot about h'ants and ghosts and such things?"

"Well, suh, Mist' Ferguson," replied George modestly, "I does know a right smart 'bout sich."

"That's good," said the wily white man. "I'm rather an authority myself on such matters. Now, then, speaking as one expert to another, I want to tell you that shack of mine out here on Clay street, where that woman was killed, is not haunted. She died in a state of grace and her spirit rests in peace.

"But the trouble is that these colored people around this town don't know it and they've given the place a bad name. What I want to do is to prove to them that it's not ha'nted. And here's the way we're going to do it—you and me. I'm going to hire you to spend to-night in the room where the killing took place. Then, when you come out to-morrow morning and tell your people that nothing happened there during the night, I'll be able to rent the house again. I'm going to give you the rest of this bottle of liquor now and a fresh bottle besides. And to-morrow morning I'll hand you a ten-dollar bill. How about it?"

That slug of corn whisky already was working. It made George valiant. Besides, a white man had appealed to him for professional aid. He consented—after another lusty pull at the flask.

The crafty Ferguson took no chances. He escorted his newly enlisted aid to the house of tragedy, provided him with a pallet on the floor and left him there in the gathering darkness. But before departing he took the precaution of barring the two windows from the outside and securely locking the front and rear doors.

Next morning bright and early he came to release his brother expert. The windows still were shuttered, the doors still fastened tight; but the house was empty. Also it was in a damaged state. At one side the thin clapboards were burst through, as though a blunt projectile traveling at great speed had struck them with terrific force from within. The shattered ends of planking stood forth, encircling the jagged aperture in a sort of sunburst effect.

Upon a splintered tip of one of the boards was a wisp of kinky wool. Upon a paling of the yard fence was a rag, evidently ripped from a shirt sleeve. Otherwise there were no signs of George. He was utterly gone, with only that yawning orifice in the cottage wall to give a clue as to the manner of his departure.

Mr. Ferguson waited all through the day for the missing one to turn up. On the second day the white man gave the alarm. A search party was organized—men on horseback with dogs. Bloodhounds took the trail. They followed it from early morning until late that evening.

Just before dusk, in a swamp thirty miles away the lead-dog bayed exultantly. The pursuing posse, with Ferguson in the lead, spurred forward.

Here came the missing George. His face was set toward home. It was a face streaked with dust and dried sweat, torn by briers, wet, drawn, gray with fatigue. His garments were in shreds; his hat was gone. His weary legs tottered under him as he dragged one sore foot after the other.

Yet in the heart of Mr. Ferguson indignation was stronger than compassion. He rode up alongside the spent and wavering pedestrian.

"Well, by heck, you certainly are the most unreliable nigger in this State!" he said. "Here night before last I make a contract with you for a certain job. I leave you in one of my houses. I come there the next morning and not only are you gone without leaving any word, but one side of my house is busted out. And then I have to leave my business to come hunting for you. And after riding all over the country I find you here, thirty miles from home, in a swamp. Where in thunder have you been since I last saw you, forty-eight hours ago?"

"Boss," said George, "I've been comin' back."

§ 87   Natural Proof

When the weather gets unseasonably warm I deem the time suitable for reviving a story which I first heard at the Republican National Convention in Chicago in 1920. As may be recalled by those who attended that convention, the entire country from coast to coast sweltered through the week under a blanket of terrific heat.

A delegate from California, in a half fluid state, fell off of a transcontinental train. A Chicago friend met him at the station.

"Say, old man," said the friend when greetings had been exchanged, "is it as hot out West as it is here on the lake?"

"Is it as hot out West?" repeated the newly arrived one. "Say, don't make me laugh. You people here in the Corn Belt don't know what heat it. Listen, I'll illustrate to you just how hot it is on the other side of the Rockies. Coming across the Arizona desert day before yesterday I looked out of the car window and I saw a coyote chasing a jack rabbit—and they were both walking!"

§ 88   A Domicile for All Eternity

One of the surest tests of the excellence of a story is whether or not it speedily reaches the stage. Some stories no doubt originate there—born in the minds of patter-comedians or monologists; but the majority I think are built up on a foundation of fact elsewhere and then by adoption go into the theater.

Here is a sample. It had to do with a couple of darkies in Memphis.

One of them, who posed as bad, had just announced his intention of breaking into a chitterling supper where his presence was not desired. His companion followed him to the door.

"I'll be waitin' fur you outside yere," he stated.

"Ef you ain't gwine in wid me tain't no use fur you to be hangin' 'bout," said the truculent one.

"Oh, yas, dey is," said the friend. "I'll wait 'round to carry you to yo' home after dem niggers in dere gits through wukkin' on you."

"Not a chancet!" proclaimed the first negro, vaingloriously; "'sides w'ich I ain't got no home."

"Oh, dat's all right," murmured his friend softly. "I'm gwine dig you one."

§ 89   The Man Who Was Thursday

Two men, strangers to each other, but having something in common in that they had been indulging in potent home brews, fell into a hiccoughy conversation on the back platform of a suburban trolley car whizzing across the New Jersey landscape.

"Shay," inquired Number One, "whuz time is it?"

Number Two with difficulty extracted from his fob pocket a watch; but a temporary defect of vision prevented him from making out the position of the two hands. Nevertheless he did his best to oblige.

"It's izactly Thurshday afternoon," he said.

Number One gave a start.

"Iz tha's so?" he murmured in surprised tones. "Well, then, thish is where I hafter get off."

§ 90   The Least of His Worries

Down in southern Alabama a person of color was fetched into court to be arraigned for his preliminary hearing on a charge of wilful murder.

"Mose Tupper," said the judge, "you are accused here of one of the most serious crimes known to our laws—to wit, the taking of a human life. Are you properly represented by counsel?"

"Naw, suh," said the darky cheerfully.

"Well, have you talked to any one about your defense since your arrest?"

"I told de sheruff 'bout de shootin' when he come to my cabin to bring me heah," said the prisoner.

"And have you taken no steps whatever to engage a lawyer?"

"Naw, suh," said Mose. "I ain't got no money to be wastin' on lawyers. Dey tell me lawyers is mighty costive."

"If you have no funds," insisted the judge, "it lies within the power of the court to appoint an attorney to represent you without expense on your part."

"You needn't be botherin' yo'se'f, jedge," answered Mose.

"Well, what do you propose to do about this case?" demanded his Honor. "You must be properly defended—the law so provides."

"Jedge," said Mose, "ez fur ez I'se concerned you kin jest let de matter drap!"

§ 91   This One Stood the Test of Time

Here is one which at intervals I have been hearing for years. It seems to me it gets better with each time of telling. I wonder if the reader will agree with me that its antiquity does not affect its excellence.

The thing is supposed to have happened in a remote court house of Missouri. A resident of the Ozark Mountains whose reputation was none the best, had been on trial on the charge of horse stealing. The jury returned a verdict of guilty. Taking into consideration the past record of the offender, his Honor on the bench said:

"It is my intention to sentence you to at least eight years at hard labor in State's prison. Now, then, before sentence is formally pronounced, I shall listen to anything you may have to say in your behalf."

After a moment of consideration the offender spoke:

"Well," he said, "I don't know ez I've got ary thing to say only this—it strikes me that you folks 'round this here cote house air purty toler'ble dam' liberal with other people's time."

§ 92   The Prudent Bride

A comely colored girl was preparing for her marriage. Before the ceremony she hoarded her wages; but immediately after the wedding she hunted up her mistress and asked her to take charge of the fund.

"I'll take it, of course," said the puzzled lady; "but, Mandy, won't you be needing your money to spend on your honeymoon?"

"Miss May," said the bride, "does you think I'se goin' to trust myse'f wid a strange nigger an' all dat money on me?"

§ 93   As a Favor to the Railroad

A New Yorker had a bad attack of grippe and went South to recuperate. He stopped a few days in a small town in South Carolina. When he got ready to leave for the North he found the official bus had vanished; probably the driver had gone joy riding. There was no conveyance, public or private, to be had; in order to catch his train the Northerner was compelled to labor afoot over a mile and a half of dusty road, with a valise in either hand.

When he staggered up to the tiny station there was no one in sight except an old darky who was sitting on the platform.

"Uncle," inquired the New Yorker, "why in the name of goodness did they build this depot so far from town?"

The old man scratched his head.

"I don't know, boss," he said—"onless it wuz because dey wanted to git it closer to de railroad."

§ 94   Where the Real Fault Lay

The tourist was one of that type which for some mysterious reason are more numerously encountered abroad than at home. He was doing the cathedral towns of England, not because he particularly was interested in English towns, or in cathedrals either, but because the guide book advised him to do so.

Near the close of a glorious spring afternoon he stood on the greensward facing Canterbury cathedral with his legs planted far apart, his cap on the back of his head, his hands rammed deep into his trousers pockets, his cigar stuck into one corner of his mouth, and on his face an expression betokening profound boredom.

The celebrated Canterbury chimes were ringing for vespers, filling all the air with silver melody, when a side door of the cathedral opened and there issued forth a little, plump, pink-cheeked, benevolent clergyman. He approached the visiting stranger and in cultured tones said to him:

"I take it, sir, that you are a stranger?"

"Hey?" inquired the American, cupping one hand about his ear.

The clergyman raised his voice:

"I assume, sir, that you are not a resident of these parts?"

"Nope," said the American. "I hail from Wyoming. It's durned good State, too—best in the Union. You ought to come out there some time, Elder, and give us the once-over."

"Eh—quite so," said the reverend gentleman. "Then," he continued, "since you are newly-come to this place it must seem to you, even as it does to those of us who dwell in these cloistered and holy precincts, that the music of our glorious bells comes floating down to one almost like the voice of the Almighty Himself, seeking through the medium of their old brazen throats to communicate the message of peace on earth, goodwill to man, to us His children here below."

"Which?" inquired the visitor, inclining his head somewhat.

"Er—what I meant to say," stated the clergyman, "was that one must carry away from here, after hearing our chimes, the conviction in his soul that really he has been in communication with Deity itself —that the voices of the angels have cried out to him. Er—is it not so, my friend?"

The American shook his head.

"I'm sorry, parson," he said regretfully, "but them damn bells is makin' so much noise I can't hear a word you say!"

§ 95   An Appeal to the Senses

The editor of a New York evening newspaper has a little niece who, on her sixth birthday, received as presents a wrist-watch and a large bottle of perfumery. Having strapped on the watch, and copiously scented herself, the youngster spent the entire day proudly parading the apartment directing the attention of all and sundry to her new possessions. Eventually she became somewhat of a bore. For the evening some friends of her parents were coming in.

"Honey," said her mother, "I can understand why you should be proud of your birthday gifts, but grown people are not interested in such things. You may come to dinner to-night on condition that you do not once mention your wrist-watch or your bottle of perfumery."

The little one promised. At the table she sat, saying not a word, but from time to time sniffing audibly, and at frequent intervals raising her left wrist to her ear to catch the sound of the ticking. These tactics failed to attract attention. Toward the end of the meal, in a lull in the conversation, little Miss Helen spoke:

"Listen, everybody," she said. "If anybody hears anything or smells anything, it's me."

§ 96 The Truth from the Inside

The dining car waiter was one of those persons who feel a sense of personal proprietorship in the institutions they serve—a type not at all uncommon among members of his race. His manner, his voice, all about him, subtly conveyed the idea that here was one who took a deep pride in the undertaking of feeding people on a transcontinental train, and was determined that no blot ever should besmirch the fair name of the system.

So when the gentleman who was going to California gave a breakfast order of grapefruit, toast, coffee and soft-boiled eggs, he bent over the patron and in confidential tones whispered:

"Boss, I would not keer to reccermend the aigs this mawnin'! Naw, suh, I would suggest you tuck somethin' else on the bill."

"What's the matter with the eggs—aren't they fresh?" asked the customer.

The waiter's voice sank still lower.

"I don't know ef they's fresh or ef they ain't," he said; "but to tell you the truth, we ain't got none."

§ 97 The Fate of the Saloon

In the last months of the fighting in 1918, a draft regiment of colored troops from the Gulf States went in near the Flanders line, where the British held, to help mop up the retreating Germans. One morning three of my fellow-correspondents borrowed a staff car and rode up to an abandoned village where there had been sharp fighting, seeking for a forward dressing-station with intent to get stories from wounded men.

At an entrance to an improvised hospital in a dugout one of the group came upon a coal-black infantryman who, while not seriously injured, bore unmistakable signs of having come into abrupt contact with some form of high and violent explosive. He was wearing, for the moment, his belt and his boots and a part of his collar. The correspondent said to him:

"Soldier, how did you get hurt?"

"Well, mister," stated the victim, "it ain't altogether clear in my own mind yit, but I could mebbe tell you some of de things w'ich hez occurred."

"I should be very pleased to hear them."

"Well, suh, at daylight this mawnin' we fell into one of these yere lil' towns up yere jest 'bout the time dem Bush Germans wuz fallin' out of it. But even ef we did have de scoundrels on de run, dey didn't fergit to shoot at us ez dey went away. Dem big shells wuz whistlin' past over my haid, talkin' to demselves, an' ever' now an' then one of 'em would come by w'ich, it seemed lak, t'wuz speakin' to me pussonally. I could hear it say jest ez plain: 'You ain't never gwine *see-e-e-e-e* yore home in Ala-BAM!'

"So I sez to myse'f, I sez: 'Seein' ez dese Germans is all daid an' scattered an' ever'thing, 'twon't be any real harm ef I gets under cover myse'f!

"So I looks 'round fur a place to git at. 'Co'se, most of de houses in dat town hez done been shot down flat. But I sees one still standin', wid de roof on it, too—a lil' place called a *Taverne*. Dat's whut a Frenchman say, boss, w'en he means saloon.

"Natchelly, dey ain't nobody livin' thar no mo'. So I walks up an' I teks hold of de doorknob an' I'se jest fixin' to turn de knob an' shove open de do' an' step in w'en *BAM!* right 'long side of me one of dem German shells went off an' tuk dat saloon right out of my hand!"

§ 98   What the Case Called For

Gabe Thompson was a person of unrelieved color, the color being black. Always, until he reached middle age he had enjoyed perfect health. Suddenly he was stricken down with what seemingly was a grievous affliction. His complexion turned the color of wet wood-ashes and he moaned with pain. His wife, in alarm, summoned a friend from a near-by cabin.

"Gabe," said the neighbor, "You 'pears lak to me that you is powerful porely. S'posin' I hitches up an' goes to town fur the doctor?"

"All right," said Gabe, "but let de doctor w'ich you gits be a hoss doctor."

"Whu' fur you wants a hoss doctor?" asked the other in astonishment. "You ain't no hoss. Chances is you ain't got no hoss disease."

"Nummine," replied Gabe between gasps of agony, "you jest do lak I tells you. Ef I knowed whut ailed me 'twould be diffe'nt, but I ain't knowin'."

"Whut diffe'nce does dat make?"

"I'll tell you," said Gabe. "Ef a regulation doctor comes to see you he kin talk wid you. He kin ax you whar de pain is an' whut you been eatin' an' drinkin' an' you kin tell him. But a hoss doctor he can't talk wid his patients kaze de patients can't talk back. He's jest natchelly 'bleedged to know whut ails 'em.

"Nigger, you go git me de bes' hoss doctor you kin find!"

§ 99 The Light that Failed

An ambitious Chinaman secured a long time lease on a tiny island on the California coast. Here he built himself a simple shack and here he raised garden-truck. Because of the climate, which was generally damp, and because of the soil and most of all because of the tenant's industry, the venture prospered. Naturally, when a gentleman in uniform came along one day and suggested him that he should vacate the property and turn it over to the government, the Oriental protested. He wanted to know why Uncle Sam should covet his tiny possession.

The visitor said to him:

"Well, you see, John, it's like this: There's a lot of fog along this coast and Uncle Sam wants to put up a lighthouse here for the benefit of ships. Savee?"

The Chinaman shook his head.

"No glood," he said. "Lighthouse no glood for flog."

"What makes you think so?" asked the government agent.

"Listlen," said the Chinaman, "'fore I clumb here I live longtime in Oakland, acloss Bay from San F'lisco. Muche flog there. Uncle Slam plut up lighthouse and flog-whistle and flog-bell. Lighthouse he shine, flog-whistle he blow, flog-bell he ling—an' damn flog he come just same!"

§ 100 He'd Have Preferred Union Hours

Being seized with the fever for modern improvement, the legislature of a certain state in the South some years ago voted for the installation of the electric chair. At the same time the lawgivers tacked on a provision to the effect that no newspaper might publish the details of an electrocution but, on the contrary, should go no farther than to state that on such a date, at such and such an hour, the execution of the law was carried out upon the body of John Doe or Richard Roe, as the case might be, the purpose of this being to invest the entire proceeding with a mystery in the minds of those individuals most likely to come within the scope of its operations.

The first candidate for these lethal attentions in a remote county chanced to be a large, brawny negro. In passing sentence upon him the judge followed, in the main, the old and time-honored formula, merely altering it somewhat to conform to the new conditions. After reviewing the crime and the trial, His Honor spoke substantially as follows:

"It is the duty, therefore, of this court to charge that the warden of the state penitentiary shall closely hold you in confinement until the twenty-first day of August, next, when between the hours of sunrise and sunset he shall put you to death by the electric chair—and may God have mercy on your soul! Mr. Sheriff, remove the prisoner."

The sheriff took the condemned man away. Overnight, pending his removal to the place of execution, he was lodged in his old cell in the county jail. He sent a message to the commonwealth's attorney who had prosecuted him, asking that he might see that official immediately. The commonwealth's attorney went to the jail. The doomed darky was sitting on his cot with his face in his hands rocking himself back and forth while the tears trickled through his fingers.

"Mr. Corbett," he said, "I craves to ax a dyin' favor of you, please suh?"

"Well, Jake," said the attorney, "I'd do anything in my power, almost, to ease your mind. But if you are after a pardon or a reprieve I can't see my way clear to helping you. You killed that man in cold blood and you had a fair trial and you've got to die and, what's more, you've got to die on the date this judge has named."

"'Tain't dat, suh," bewailed Jake, "I ain't got no quarrel wid de date. I kin git all my worldly affairs settled up 'twixt now an' den an' mek my peace wid de Lawd, lakwise. But, Mr. Corbett,"—and here his voice broke sharply—"I p'intedly does hate to be settin' in dat dere cheer f'um sunrise plum' till sunset."

§ 101 The Perils of Pranking

There was a homicide trial going on in the mountains of West Virginia. A lanky native took the stand to testify to the good character and peaceful disposition of the prisoner at the bar. When he had given the accused a glowing testimonial the prosecuting attorney took him in hand for cross-examination.

"Look here," he demanded: "isn't that the mark of an old knife cut you've got across the lobe of your left ear?"

"Yas, suh; it is."

"Well, who inflicted that wound?"

"Bill, thar, he done it, one time."

"By 'Bill' you mean the defendant here?"

"Yep."

"I see you also have the scar of a bullet wound in your right cheek. Who made that?"

"Bill."

"On still another occasion didn't Bill, as you call him, gouge one of your eyes almost out?"

"That's a fact, too."

"Now, then, in view of the injuries you yourself admit having sustained at his hands, how do you reconcile your sworn statements of a minute ago that the defendant is an individual of peaceable and law-abiding nature, and a good neighbor?"

"Well, suh," said the witness, "Bill is one of the nicest fellers ever you seen in your life; but I must say this—he's a powerful onlikely pusson to prank with!"

§ 102 The Really Important Point

Among the writer's aquaintances is a well-to-do person who spends his summers cruising about in a private yacht. One afternoon near Cape Cod he dropped anchor just off a village for the night. While he was sitting on deck puffing a cigar before retiring, he saw one native approach another who was perched upon the dock and heard the newcomer say, in excited tones:

"I walked in my house awhile ago and the first thing I noticed was some blood spots on the kitchen floor. And then I seen how everything was mussed up, so that give me a kind of a start, and I dropped everything and went on into the settin'-room, and there was my wife stretched out on the floor, plum' unconscious, with a club layin' alongside her where somebody had knocked her cold. It certainly was a terrible surprise. Here I come home, tired out after fishin' all day long——"

"How was the fishin'?" inquired the friend.

§ 103 The Proper Remedy at Last

Possibly inspired by the missionary work of Pussyfoot Johnson, a Scotch Minister undertook a temperance crusade among the members of his flock. He announced that on a certain Sabbath he would deliver a sermon upon the evils of strong drink, with physical illustrations to prove his argument. Upon the appointed morning a congregation which crowded the kirk greeted him. The dominie lost no time in making his demonstration. Upon the pulpit he placed two glasses; one containing whiskey and the other spring water. Then in an impressive silence he brought a small box from his coat pocket, opened the box and produced a long wriggling worm.

First he dipped the worm in the tumbler of water, where it coiled and twisted happily. Then he dropped it into the whiskey. Instantly the hapless creature shriveled, and after a few feeble contortions became limp and lifeless. Hauling forth the dead thing and holding it in plain view of all present the minister said:

"Now then, my brethren, behold the effects of strong spirits upon this wee creature. In the water it took no harm; but the first contact with this foul stuff here instantly destroyed it. Need I say or do more to convince you of the effects of whiskey?"

From the body of the church there rose up a lantern-jawed person.

"Meenister," he said, "might I ask where ye got the whusky in that tumbler?"

"I'm glad you put that question," said the clergyman. "I purchased it at that den of iniquity, the public-house, which stands at the top of the street not a hundred yards from this place of worship."

"Thank ye," said the parishioner. "I'll be goin' there on the morrow. I've been troubled with worms myself."

§ 104   An Anniversary to Be Remembered

Differences of an acute nature arose in a crap game on the Nashville wharf. The dispute had to do with the ownership of a five dollar bill. For possession of it there were two claimants,—a resident roustabout and a truculent-looking stranger from up St. Louis way.

The argument reached a crucial and critical stage. The right hand of the visiting nobleman stole slowly back toward his hip pocket.

"Nigger," he inquired softly of his enemy, "whut date is dis?"

"I ain't payin' no heed to de dates," said the Nashville darky.

"Well, you better do so," said the stranger, " 'cause jest twelve months frum to-day you'll a'been daid perzackly one yeah."

§ 105   The Handiwork of the Amateur

Back about 1905, in the Dark Ages of automobiling a veterinary surgeon in my town, whom I shall call Dr. Jones, bought a second-hand car. It already was beginning to shake itself to pieces before it came into his possession. In fact, so loudly did it rattle, when in motion, that it was known affectionately throughout the county as Jones' Patent Pea-Huller. When the tires wore out the owner, who was by way of being a mechanical genius, equipped it with ordinary buggy-wheels.

One day an automobile run to a near-by town was organized. Every proud proprietor of a car joined in. As the procession headed out past the corporate limits it was met by a farmer, from the Massac Creek section on his way to the warehouse with a wagon-load of tobacco. His half-grown son rode with him.

As the head of the column loomed through the dust the farmer's two mules, unused to the sight of automobiles, showed signs of skittishness. The boy leaped down from his seat and held the heads of the team, the mules flinching and trembling as the cavalcade roared past.

Seemingly, the last car had gone by. The youth was in the act of climbing back to his place alongside his father when in the distance there arose a terrific clattering sound and over the crest of the hill appeared Dr. Jones, seated at the wheel of his machine and striving valiantly to overtake the tail of the vanished parade. On he came, with his gears grinding, the tormented vitals of his car shrieking, the wooden wheels clattering on the hard gravel of the turnpike and gusts of smoke issuing from beneath the body.

The astounded agriculturist caught one good look at the approaching apparition. Then as he set the brakes harder than ever and tightened his grasp on the lines he called out to the boy:

"Hold 'em, Wesley, for God's sake, hold 'em! Here comes a home-made one!"

§ 106   The Forethoughted Widow

In an unthoughted moment a colored woman in a North Carolina town contracted a matrimonial alliance. But the honeymoon ended tragically. Just two weeks after the wedding ceremony the happy bridegroom was fooling about the railroad yards and a switch engine ran over him—on the bias—and he, being of a fleshy build, was distributed for a considerable distance along the right of way becoming, to all intents and purposes, a total loss.

Yet it was immediately to develop that in a deceased state, he had a financial standing which had been denied him in the flesh. For, with that desire to do justice speedily which ever marks the legal profession, a claim agent of the railroad got hold of the widow before any other lawyer could reach her and hurried her to his office and there showed her five hundred dollars in shiny new bills, which was more money that she thought there was in the world. With one eager hand she reached for this incredible fortune and with the other, using haste lest the beneficent white gentleman should recover from his impulses of generosity, she signed on the dotted line A of the quit claim.

Another colored woman who had come with her to witness this triumph and who was standing behind her, perfectly pop-eyed with envy and admiration, said:

"Clarissa, whut you reckin you goin' do now, sence you had all dis luck?"

Before the widow answered she lifted a rustling twenty from off the top of the delectable heap and fanned herself with it and inhaled its fragrance; and then she said:

"I don't know ez I shall do anything—fur a spell. I got to wait till time is healed my wounds an' I's spent dis yere money. Of co'se in the yeahs to come I may marry ag'in an' then ag'in I may not—who kin tell? But, gal, I tells you right now, ef ever I does marry ag'in my second husband is suttinly goin' be a railroad mar

§ 107 Bumpy Times for the Late Lamented

The late Mr. Donovan had had a very close call from being a dwarf. Indeed, there are dwarfs in circuses not many inches shorter than he was. Despite his diminutive bulk and the handicap of lack of height he nevertheless had succeeded in the contracting business and when he died he left a tidy estate and his widow mourned him properly.

On the day before the funeral, having finished the preparations for the wake, she sat in the parlor of her home when Mr. McKenna, an old friend of the family, was announced. Dressed in his Sunday best Mr. McKenna entered and having shaken Mrs. Donovan's hand stated that he would be unable to attend the ceremonies that evening owing to other engagements. He asked, therefore, if he might be permitted to take a last look at the deceased.

"Help yourself," said the widow. "He's laid out upstairs in the front room. Just you walk up, Mr. McKenna."

So Mr. McKenna walked up. After the lapse of a few minutes he tiptoed down again, wiping away his tears.

The widow removed the handkerchief from her eyes.

"Did you think to close the hall door as you came down, Mr. McKenna?" she asked.

"I think so, madam," he said. "I was so overcome wit' me grief I didn't take much note. I think so, but I won't be sure."

"Would you make sure, thin," she said. "It's twice to-day already the cat's had him downstairs."

§ 108 The Genesis of an Old Favorite

There are several variations of this yarn but a Scotch friend of mine insists that the one which follows is the correct one and, by that same token, the proper ancestor of all the crop of differing versions. As he sets forth the original narrative it runs something like this:

An Aberdonian on his first visit to London got off the train at Euston station. While proceeding afoot along Euston Road on his way to his hotel he suffered a terrific misfortune. He dropped a sixpence and it rolled out of sight. The desolated victim put down his luggage and began a vigorous search for the missing coin. Presently a friendly policeman came along and having learned from the grieved Scot what the trouble was, proceeded to aid him in the hunt, but with no results, excepting the loss of fifteen minutes. Finally the Bobby said:

"You go along on your way and I'll keep my eye open for your money. If it turns up I'll have it for you, if you'll come back this way this afternoon."

All day the Scot was afflicted with distress. Promptly at four o'clock he was back on the spot where his sixpence had vanished. During the day the gas company had had a squad of men excavating in the street for new mains so that when the Aberdonian reappeared he found the paving torn up and a wide, deep trench extending from the house line to the middle of the road. He gazed at the scene for a moment and then remarked to himself:

"Weel, I must admit one thing—they are verra thorough here."

§ 109 "A Rose by Any Other Name . . ."

At a closely contested municipal election in New York the Tammany ticket seemed in grave danger. Accordingly steps were taken. Scarcely had the polls opened when a group of trained and experienced repeaters marched into a down-town voting place.

"What name?" inquired the election clerk of the leader of the squad, who was red-haired and freckled and had a black eye. The young gangster glanced down at a slip of paper in his hand to refresh his memory.

"Isadore Mendelheim," he said then.

"That's not your real name, and you know it!" said a suspicious challenger for the reform ticket.

"It is me name," said the repeater, "and I'm goin' to vote under it—see?"

From down the line came a voice:

"Don't let that guy bluff you, Casey. Soitin'ly your name is Mendelheim!"

§ 110   A Detail of Figures

Grand Central Pete was a noted bunco-steerer of the old days, but could neither read nor write. Once he fell upon hard times, and he and a younger but equally luckless confidence man undertook to beat their way on a freight train to Washington. A brakeman kicked them off at Trenton.

It was getting late and neither of them had a cent. Across the tracks from where they had landed was a hotel and right next door was an express office. Pete had an idea. He went into the express office, begged one of those large manila envelopes such as are used for transporting currency, filled the envelope with pieces of newspaper cut to the size of banknotes, and sealed it carefully.

"Now then," he said to his partner, "you take your fountain pen and write on the back of that there envelope '$9,000.' Then we'll go over to that hotel and explain that we've lost our baggage, and I'll hand this envelope to the clerk and ask him to lock it in the safe. He'll look at the figures on the back—and he'll take us for moneyed guys and give us rooms and grub until we can raise a stake."

The scheme sounded good to the younger man. He got out his pen and obeyed orders. Grand Central Pete took the envelope back in his hands and examined it carefully.

"Does that say nine thousand dollars?" he demanded.

"Yep," said his partner.

"Well, it don't look big enough to me," said Pete. "You'd better add on some more of them naughts."

The younger man protested, but Pete would have his way and kept after him until the educated one had tacked on three more naughts, making the grand total $9,000,000.

Then Pete marched grandly over to the hotel, registered for himself and his friend, passed the stuffed envelope across the desk to the clerk and called for the bridal suite.

The clerk took one look at the envelope, another look at the soiled faces and shabby apparel of the newcomers—and rang the bell for the bouncer. A minute later the discomfited pair were sitting on the sidewalk.

Grand Central Pete raised himself painfully and eyed his companion with a scornful, angry glance.

"There now,—dad-gum you!" he shouted; "I told you you hadn't wrote in enough of them naughts!"

§ 111 Provision for the Future

Nobody could tell a yarn of his own race better than the late Bert Williams could. I remember one story he used to tell. Hearing him tell it you felt, despite its gorgeous impossibility, that somehow it might have happened and that anyhow it should have happened. To the best of my recollection his version, delivered in his wonderful Afric drawl ran something like this:

"W'en I was a little boy I lived on the banks of a creek and I supported my whole family ketchin' feesh and peddlin' 'em off amongst the w'ite folks. Ever' mawnin' I'd ketch me a string of feesh and off I'd go wid 'em. I forgot to say that this yere creek run at the foot of a mountain seven thousand feet high and most of the w'ite folks lived up on the mountain-side.

"One hot mawnin' I ketches me a string of feesh and I teks 'em in my hand and I starts up the mountain. I comes to the fust house but they didn't want no feesh there; and I comes to the second house and it seems lak they don't crave no feesh neither, and so I continues till I reaches the plum top of that mountain seven thousand feet high.

"Now, right on the plum top, in a little house, live a little white man and he's standin' at his do' like he's waitin' fur me. I walks up to him and I bows low to him, ver' polite, and I sez to him I sez: 'Mister, does you want some fresh feesh?' And he sez to me, he sez: 'No, we don't want no feesh to-day.'

"So I starts back down that mountain, seven thousand feet high. And w'en I'm about a third of the way down I'm overtook by one of those yere landslides and under tons of rocks and dirt and soil and *daybris* and stuff and truck and things I'm carried plum to the foot of that mountain. So I digs my way out frum under all that there mess, still holdin' to my little string of feesh, and I wipes the dust out of my eyes and I looks back up the mountain to see what the landslide has done. And, lo and behole! The little man that lives in the little house on the plum top is standin' at his do' beck'nin' to me. So I sez to myself: 'Praise God, that w'ite man is done changed his mind.'

"So I climbs back ag'in up the mountain, seven thousand feet high, till I comes to the plum top and w'en I gits there the little w'ite man is still standin' there waitin' fur me. He waits till I'm right close to him befo' he speaks. Then he clears his throat and he sez to me, he sez:

"'And we don't want none to-morrow, neither!'"

§ 112 The Life of the Party, as It Were

Three aged Scots were in the habit of meeting on Saturday evening at the home of first one and then another of the group for social purposes. Their social demands were simple, just as their tastes were similar. All they craved was an opportunity to sit by a fire with their pipes lit and their whiskey glasses handy, in silence.

One evening there had been an especially enjoyable session. Two quarts of liquor had been consumed and hardly a word had been spoken. At the approach of midnight the two guests stood up to go. One of them, with difficulty focusing his vision upon his host, who sat in the inglenook, remarked to the third member of the party in an undertone:

"What an awfu' look Sandy has on his face."

"Aye," said his crony, "he's dead."

"How long has he been dead?" inquired the first speaker in shocked tones.

"The better part of twa hours."

"Why did ye nae tell me before?"

"Hoots, mon," said his crony, "I'm nae the one to brek up a pleasant evenin'."

§ 113   Something to Look Forward To

A hustling free-lance in the white goods business thought he saw a magnificent opening to buy up a stock of underwear and by a quick turnover among the jobbers to realize a handsome profit. He succeeded in inducing a Bowery bank to let him have a hundred thousand dollars in order to swing the deal. The deal was swung but for some reason or other the enterprising speculator was not able to move his newly acquired stocks as rapidly as he figured on.

One morning the president of the bank sent word to the borrower that he desired to see him immediately and the latter promptly answered the summons.

"Look here, Mr. Jacobson," said the banker, "I'll have to call your loan and I'll have to call it immediately."

"But Mr. Slocum," protested Jacobson, "you couldn't do that. Still I am all tied up with them goods und I must have more time."

"I'm sorry for you if you're going to be embarrassed," said Mr. Slocum, "but I can't help myself. The state bank examiner was in here yesterday going over our books and he tells me we must clean up a lot of our accounts. Now, your note for a hundred thousand dollars is a demand note, as you will recall, and not a time note, so I must ask you to be able to take up that note not later than Wednesday, the fifteenth of next month."

"Vell," said Mr. Jacobson resignedly, "that's the vay things go. Vot has to be has to be, I guess." He thought for a moment.

"Mr. Slocum," he said, "maybe you have yourself looked into the ins and out of underwear, eh?"

"Mr. Jacobson," said the banker, "I'm not interested in the underwear business."

"Vell," said Mr. Jacobson softly, "you should be. Because Venesday, the fifteenth, you're going to be in it."

§ 114 Me Lady's One Weak Point

Martin Green, one of the best-known newspaper men in New York, has remarkable memory for faces. Twenty odd years ago he was a reporter in St. Louis. At a summer park he became acquainted with a vaudeville team consisting of a brawny Irishman and the Irishman's equally brawny Swedish wife. The team had an act which was simple, and yet thrilling. Their stage props consisted of a sledge-hammer and a collection of paving-stones. The pair would come forth from the wings, and the lady would station herself in the centre of the stage and upon her head the gentleman would balance a large, jagged lump of limestone. Then, stepping back, he would swing his sledge-hammer aloft and bring it down with all the force of his mighty arms upon the stone, dashing it into scores of fragments. The lady would blink slightly, take her bow and the couple would back from sight to reappear an hour or so later and repeat the performance.

Two decades passed. In 1920 Green was reporting the National Republican Convention at Chicago. One evening he boarded a trolley car. The car was crowded and Green found standing room on the rear platform. Something about the face of the conductor stirred a memory long buried in his brain. He studied the countenance of the other for a minute and then the answer came to him.

"Say, look here," he asked. "Aren't you Brennan of the old team of Brennan and Swenson that used to do a turn at the summer park in St. Louis way back about 1900?"

"That's right," said the conductor. Then with a sigh he added, "Sure, but thim was the happy days."

"What made you quit the stage?" asked Green.

"It was on me wife's account," said the ex-Thespian. "She got so she couldn't stand it no longer, me bustin' thim cobblestones on her head."

"Gave her headaches, I suppose," said Green.

"No, not that," said Brennan. "It bruk her arches down."

§ 115 At the Crossing of the Ways

Beyond question his Honor on the bench was cross-eyed. Some persons went so far as to say that he was the crossest-eyed person or the cross-eyedest person, as the grammar may be, in the known world.

On a morning when for some reason or other his angles of vision seemed particularly out of alignment there were arraigned before him for preliminary examination three youths charged with hypothecating a stranger's automobile to their own use. The oldest of the trio, and the supposed ringleader, stood between his two alleged confederates. Addressing the middle one the judge said:

"Young man, you are accused here of grand larceny. How do you plead, guilty or not guilty?"

Instantly the one on the left said:

"Not guilty, Your Honor."

"I wasn't addressing you," snapped His Honor. "I was addressing this other accused. Wait until you're spoken to."

"Why, judge," protested the one on the right. "I ain't said a word."

§ 116 The Mysterious Stranger

The Scotch minister and his beadle, or sexton as we would call him, had attended a Masonic banquet and had done themselves, as the saying goes, exceedingly well. The dominie was a bachelor. His housekeeper was a very strict lady and he was a bit doubtful as to what his reception would be on his return to the manse. He considered the situation for a bit and then to his beadle he said:

"John, I think I'll slip in at the back door the nicht."

The beadle, who believed in upholding the dignity of the kirk, replied emphatically:

"You'll do naething o' the kind. Y're meenister o' this parish an' ye'll go in by your own front door."

"Weel, then," said the clergyman, "I'll walk in front o' you for a bit an' you watch how I get alang."

The minister proceeded ahead, striving to walk straight in the moonlight, and the beadle propping himself on his own unsteady pins, squinted his eyes in earnest observation.

Presently the dominie called back over his shoulder:

"How am I getting alang, John?"

"Ye're doing brawly," answered John, "but meenister, who is that ye have with ye?"

§ 117   A Chronic Loser

At Lynchburg, Va., a traveling-man climbed off the train in a hurry. He had but a few minutes in which to travel across town and make connections with a train for Roanoke. But the only rig in sight was an ancient carriage drawn by a scrawny, old crow-bait with an old negro man for a driver.

"Right this way, boss," shouted the old man as he ran forward to relieve the traveler of his hand-baggage. "Tek you anywhars in the city fur fifty cents. Hop right abode, suh!"

"I've got to rush over to the other depot," said the white man, "That mare of yours doesn't look very fast. Do you think she can make it?"

"Huh, dat mare?" proclaimed the old man. "She sholy kin. She's mouty deceivin' in her looks. They calls dis hoss Lightnin'."

Thus reassured, the stranger climbed in. The black Jehu mounted to his seat, snapped the lines and gave the word of command. Tottering on her shaky pins the venerable pack of bones ambled off.

"Say, look here, uncle," said the fare, "that nag of yours may be speedy when she's feeling right but it strikes me that she's lost her health or something. Why, she's almost weak enough to fall down in her tracks."

"Boss," said the old man, sinking his voice to a confidential undertone, "I'm gwine tell you a secret. Dat mare ain't sick, but yere lately, as you mout say, she's been kind of out o' luck."

"What do you mean—out of luck?" asked the passenger.

"Well, suh, ever' mawnin' I shakes the dice to see whether dat mare has a bait of oats or I has me a slug of gin. An' she ain't won fur goin' on mouty nigh a week."

§ 118   The Call of the Far East

Walter Kelly, famous in vaudeville, has an old friend at Buffalo who formerly was a Feinian and now is the most confirmed of Sinn Feiners. If there is anything on earth Kelly's friend doesn't like it's something English. His version of the British national anthem probably would run: "God Save the King Till We Can Get At Um!"

In 1921 Kelly was playing in vaudeville at Buffalo. As he sat in his dressing-room, awaiting his turn, his ancient acquaintance came to see him. When greetings had been exchanged Kelly said:

"Well, Dennis, it's a great day for all of us who are of Irish blood. Now that England has granted Ireland self-government, there's no reason, as I see it, why the Irish and the English should not try to forget their old feud and live hereafter at peace. The Irish have no further cause for a quarrel with the British!"

"Well, I don't know about that, Walter," said the unreconciled Dennis. "Don't ye think now we ought to be doin' somethin' fur thim poor Hindus?"

§ 119   He Wouldn't Commit Himself Yet

The conservation of the Down-East farmer is proverbial. Possibly this trait is a heritage of his Puritan ancestry.

Be that as it may, the fact remains that he is extremely careful to refrain from overstatement or exaggeration. A point in illustration is found in the story of the elderly Vermonter who was bringing in hay from his ancestral meadow. Seated upon a fragrant two-ton load he had guided his double team almost to the doors of his barn when one of the front wheels twisted on an outcrop of granite and the cargo capsized, precipitating the husbandman to the stony earth with great violence and entirely burying him under the mound of timothy.

The two hired hands leaped to the rescue. They forked away the hay and after several minutes of strenuous endeavor dug out their employer. He was speechless for the time being and half-suffocated. There was a bump on his forehead and one arm dangled to prove that his shoulder-blade had been snapped. As they propped the victim against the softer side of a handy boulder his son, who had been at work in the hayfield and who had been summoned by the cries of the rescuers, came running up. Filled with alarm and solicitude the younger man put a question which seemed somewhat superfluous but which, in view of his fright, was perfectly natural.

"Paw," he cried as he bent over his parent, "did it hurt you?"

"Wall, son," said the old man slowly, and measuring his words, "I wouldn't go so fur as to say it's done me any real good."

§ 120   A Seasonable and Timely Suggestion

It was in the old days up in the Klondyke. On a winter's night —a night destined to be remembered even in that land for its severity—the inhabitants of a mining-camp were gathered in the local dance hall for companionship and for warmth. It was too cold to play cards. Those present had huddled themselves about a huge, red-hot stove which stood in the center of the big room, when from without there came the sound of feeble cries.

The proprietor threw open the door and peered forth into the blizzard. The light from the coal-oil lamps behind him revealed a string of exhausted husky dogs and a sled upon which was huddled a human shape. Hardy spirits dashed forth into the storm and separated the form of the traveler from his sled to which he was frozen fast. They bore him inside, chafed his hands and thawed him before the fire, and by these means succeeded in restoring him his powers of motion and coherent speech. It developed that the rescued one was a green prospector who in his ignorance had undertaken to make the trip from a settlement ten miles below to a point considerably up country from the place where he now was. When he was almost spent from cold and exhaustion he had seen the lighted windows of the dance hall and had guided his staggering dog-team there in the nick of time.

Now that he was able to walk, two sympathetic Samaritans guided his footsteps to the bar where the barkeeper awaited them.

"Stranger," said the hospitable barkeep, "you've had a blamed close call and we're goin' to celebrate. This round is on the house. What are you goin' to have? I'd suggest a hot whiskey punch—or maybe you'd rather have a hot Tom-and-Jerry?"

The stranger considered for a moment.

"If you don't mind," he said, "I think I'll take a seltzer lemonade."

"What's that?" cried the stupefied barkeeper.

"I think I'd like to have a seltzer lemonade."

"Pardner," stated the barkeeper, "we're out of lemons and likewise we're shy on seltzer. But I want you to feel at home; I tell you what I'll do; I'll just run upstairs to my trunk and get you a nice pair of white duck pants to wear."

§ 121   Not Vouched For as Absolutely Authentic

This story probably isn't true. The more I think it over, the more am I convinced that somewhere it lacks plausibility. But in spite of this defect I deem it worthy to be included in this collection, because, if it serves no other good purpose, it may give the visiting foreigner and notably the visiting Briton an idea of the size of this country and the variations of weather to be found within our boundaries at one time.

As the story runs, a Galveston negro, born and reared on the Gulf coast, was offered a job one winter in St. Paul. Knowing nothing of the climatic changes he might, and undoubtedly would, encounter as he moved north, the colored man, attired in a cotton shirt and a pair of threadbare jeans overalls, boarded a through train for his future theatre of activities. By snuggling close up to the steam pipes he managed to remain fairly comfortable during the journey; but when he stepped off the cars at St. Paul things were different. For he stepped off into the swirling midst of the worst blizzard that had descended upon Minnesota in twenty years.

Bewildered by the screeching wind, blinded by stinging particles of snow, the stranger staggered a few yards from the station, growing more congealed every second. Within half a block, becoming absolutely rigid, he fell stiffly over in a snow bank. He was found by a policeman who called the patrol wagon and removed the unfortunate to the nearest police station. There a surgeon, after making a cursory examination of the stiffened frame, diagnosed the case as one of death by freezing. Since there was nothing by which the victim might be identified the desk sergeant entered him on the docket as an unknown person and the physician gave his sanction for the immediate disposal of the ill-fated one's mortal remains. As interment underground was out of question the police conveyed their burden to an improvised crematory, arriving about midnight.

Here an attendant lost no time in consigning the body to the flames and having closed the iron door of the furnace he called it a night and retired.

Next morning the authorities sent two more bodies to be consumed. As the functionary, wearing heavily padded gloves, unscrewed the caplike door of his little private inferno and involuntarily shrunk back from the blast of incredible heat which gushed out into his face, he was astounded to hear a querulous, plaintive, Afro-American voice uplifted from the very heart of the furnace, saying:

"Who is dat openin' dat do' an' lettin' all dat cold draft of air in yere on me?"

§ 122 One Time When the Colonel Balked

In his old age, after he quit the war-path, Quanah Parker, the famous chief of the Comanches, adopted many of the white man's ways; but in one important respect he clung to the custom of his fathers. He continued to be a polygamist.

He was a friend and admirer of ex-President Roosevelt. On

A LAUGH A DAY KEEPS THE DOCTOR AWAY 97

one occasion, when Colonel Roosevelt was touring Oklahoma he drove out to Parker's home camp twelve miles from Fort Sill to see the old warrior. With pride Parker pointed out that he lived in a house like a white man, that he was sending his children to the white man's schools and that he, himself, wore the garb of the white man. Whereupon, Colonel Roosevelt was moved to preach him a sermon on the subject of the moralities.

"See here, Chief," he said, "why don't you set your people a still better example of obedience to the laws of the land and the customs of the whites? A white man has only one wife; he's allowed only one at a time. Here you are living with five squaws. Why don't you give up four of them and remain faithful to the fifth? You could continue to support the four you put aside but they need no longer be members of your household. Then, in all respects, you would be living as the white man lives."

Parker, who spoke excellent English when he chose to do so, considered the proposition for a space in silence. Then, with a twinkle in his beady old eyes he made answer:

"You are my great white father," he said, "and I will do as you wish—on one condition."

"What's the condition?" asked the Colonel.

"You pick out the one I am to live with and then you go tell the other four."

§ 123   And No Steam Calliope, Either

There is a theatrical manager in New York who began his professional career as press-agent for a circus. A year or two ago he had occasion to believe that a bill-posting crew sent out by him to paper the territory for a big production in which he was interested had failed to live up to its contract. He decided to make a quiet trip over the itinerary and check up on the suspected shirkers. In a city just across the Canadian line in Quebec he hired a livery-stable rig with a driver for the purpose of riding through the adjacent country.

The driver of the rig he immediately recognized as a former boss-canvasman answering to the name of Saginaw Red. In the old days this Saginaw had been employed by one of the circuses for which the New Yorker also had worked. The recognition was mutual. Naturally the two of them renewed their ancient acquaintance and a flow of reminiscence started. As their buggy reached the edge of the town the driver halted it while a funeral procession bound for the cemetry passed through an intersecting street.

It wasn't much of a funeral procession. Behind the rusty, closed carriage containing the pall-bearers followed a dingy, glass-walled hearse and behind that, in turn, came four more closed carriages presumably containing mourners and friends of the deceased, and that was all.

Pointing to the cavalcade and employing the vernacular of their former calling, the manager addressed his companion:

"Well, Saginaw," he said, "what do you think of the grand free street parade?"

"It's a frost," said Saginaw; "only one open den."

§ 124 Absolutely Nothing to Debate

The official peacemaker, there is one in every community, and sometimes unthinking people call him a butter-in, was progressing on his homeward way. Of a sudden the loose prehensile ears of the pedestrian were assailed by sounds which to his eager perception betokened a bitter quarrel between a man and woman who stood on the porch of a vine-clad cottage. Without a moment's hesitation he opened the yard gate and hurried toward the seemingly belligerent pair.

"Tut, tut!" he cried. "Tut, tut, my friends, this will never do. Pray cease this unseemly argument."

The couple turned toward him. It was the man who spoke:

"What business of yours is it, comin' bustin' in here a-tut-tutting like a gas engine? Besides this here ain't no argument."

"Yes, but I heard——" began the peacemaker.

"Never mind what you heard," broke in the husband. "To be an argument there's got to be a difference of opinion, ain't they?"

"Yes, there has," conceded the peacemaker.

"Well, they ain't no difference of opinion here," said the man. "My wife thinks I ain't going to give her none of my week's wages and I know durned well I ain't!"

§ 125 Keeping It in the Family

The proprietor of a small general store in a remote New England district sat at the doorway of his establishment industriously whittling. A middle-aged native drove up in an antiquated car and halted.

"Hello, Eth," he said.

"Hello, Wes," answered back the storekeeper.

"Wall, Eth," said the newcomer, "you said I couldn't dew it, but, by Judas Priest, I done it!"

"You done whut?" asked the storekeeper.

"Sold that there old crow-bait mare of mine—that's whut I done," said Wes exultingly.

"Wall, you air the smart one!" cried the astonished Eth admiringly. "She wuzn't wuth nothin'. Whut did ye sell her fur?"

"She wuzn't wuth nothin', jest ez you say. But all the same I sold her fur a hunderd dollars—and I got the money right here in my pocket, too."

"I got to say it again," declared Eth. "You certainly air the smart one! A hundred dollars! Why that there old mare wuzn't wuth ten dollars. She wuz eighteen year old if she wuz a day and blind of one eye and spavined and wind-broke and all stove up. Who, in the name of Goshen, did you sell her to?"

"I sold her," said Wes, "to mother."

§ 126 Speaking, as It Were, with Frankness

Since an actor of distinction told me this story I take it that it may be repeated here without serious offence to the profession which he adorns and dignifies.

The proprietor of a small hotel of a small New England town was hunched behind the clerk's desk of his establishment when the door opened and there strode in a typical heavy man of a traveling repertoire company. The newcomer wore a mangy fur overcoat and a soiled white waistcoat and, as if to make up for his lack of baggage, bore himself with an air of jaunty assurance. He advanced to the clerk's desk and waited there as though expecting the innkeeper to rise and in accordance with the ritual, swing the register about for him and hand him a pen newly dipped in ink. If that was what the Thespian expected he was disappointed.

The prospective guest was not to be daunted by the lack of the customary evidences of hospitality and welcome. In his deepest and most impressive stage voice he said:

"I take it, my good man, that you are the Boniface of this hostelry."

"Wall, I'm runnin' this here tavern, ef so be that's whut you mean."

"Exactly so. It is even as I suspected. And what are your lowest terms for members of my profession?"

"Which?"

"I say, what are your lowest terms for actors?"
"Liars, loafers and dead-beats!"

§ 127   Glass of Fashion and Mould of Form!

In the last year of the Civil War a company of Federal soldiers were encamped in the Tennessee foothills. They had pitched their tents in a meadow belonging to a farmer whose log house stood in a grove at the edge of the field. Through the meadow ran a good-sized creek. The soldiers lost no time in pulling off their dusty garments and bathing in the stream.

That same evening the owner of the farm, a whiskered gentleman, called upon the young lieutenant in command of the detachment. He began by saying that his sympathies were with the Union and he felt upon this account if upon no other he was entitled to consideration. He had a complaint to make. He had no objection to the use of his meadow as a camp ground but he did wish to protest again the action of the men in swimming within sight of his domicile because, as he explained, he had two half-grown daughters.

The officer saw the point of the farmer's position and promised him that he would take steps. Immediately he issued an order that thereafter men wishing to bathe or swim should repair to a point at the far side of the meadow.

The next afternoon the farmer reappeared with a fresh protest. The lieutenant listened to him and then said rather impatiently:

"Say, look here, my friend, it strikes me you're somewhat fussy. The place where these men are now going into the creek is fully a quarter of a mile from your house if not farther."

"Yes, I know," said the farmer, "but you see, Mister, both of my gals has got spyglasses."

§ 128   Down to the Solid Portions

It seems the mother was determined her six year old daughter should learn table manners and especially that she should eat what was put before her without question or complaint. On a morning at breakfast the lady sat behind the coffee urn reading her mail. Little Mildred was perched upon a high-chair at the other end of the table. In front of the latter the maid put down a cup holding a soft-boiled egg.

"Please, mama," said Mildred. "I don't want an egg this morning. I had an egg yesterday morning."

"Never mind what you had yesterday morning," said the mother without looking up from her reading. "Eggs are good for you. Now you open that egg and eat every bite of it."

Mildred sniffled but obeyed. Presently her voice was again uplifted in protest:

"Mama, I don't like this egg. I don't think it's a very nice egg."

"It is a nice egg," contradicted the mother, still immersed in her correspondence. "Go right ahead."

Another pause ensued, punctuated only by muffled sobs and gulps from Mildred. Then:

"Mama, I've eaten nearly all of it. Can't I stop now?"

"Mildred, I don't want to have to speak to you again. I've told you what you had to do."

"But, Mama——" and now Mildred's voice rose to a wail—— "do I have to eat the bill and the legs, too?"

§ 129   An Anti-Expectoration Advocate

The young couple had recently moved to New York from the South and were living in an attractive but somewhat small apartment on Riverside Drive. One afternoon quite unexpectedly callers were announced from downstairs.

"Olga," the mistress said, turning away from the telephone after telling the telephone operator to send the party up, "guests are coming. I know they'll want to see Mabel. Please take her into the bathroom and slip a clean frock on her and tidy her up a bit and then send her back to the front room. Hurry now, they can only stay a little while."

So Mabel, the six-year-old daughter of the household, was gathered up by Olga and hurried out of sight. But Olga in her haste must have left the bathroom door ajar, for just as the visitors had been welcomed there came floating through the hall to them a protesting childish voice uttering the following ultimatum.

"Olga, company or no company, I ain't goin' to have my face washed with spit!"

§ 130   Putting Depew in His Place

There was a big dinner one night in London and Senator Depew, then at the head of the New York Central system, delivered the principal speech. Joseph Choate, our ambassador to the court of St. James, sat at the guest table flanked on either side by a serious-minded member of the British nobility, neither of whom had ever been to America.

As Senator Depew got into his swing one of Choate's neighbors said to him:

"Your fellow-American is a most captivating speaker, eh, what? Curious I never heard of him before. To what station in your American life would you assign him?"

Choate's gift of humor was brightest on the spur of the occasion.

"The Grand Central Station," he replied promptly.

"Ah, yes, I see," spoke up his neighbor on the other side, "what we call in England the great middle-class."

§ 131   How Larry Boosted the Game

"Larry," said the young man with the slicked-back hair. "I want you to do me a big favor. I've just met a girl who's visiting here and I've fallen for her strong. Now, I want to let her get the impression that I'm well-to-do. In fact, I don't care if she goes so far as to think I'm wealthy, but I don't want to do too much bragging in front of her. So that's where you fit in."

"How do I fit in?" inquired Larry, who was by way of being rather a rugged and untutored person.

"Easy enough," said the conspirator. "Tomorrow I've got a date to buy her a lunch at the Claridge. You drop in there as if by accident. I'll hail you and call you over to our table and introduce you to Miss Ferguson—that's her name, Gertrude Ferguson—and insist on you sitting down with us. Then I'll start in to talking about myself. I'll be sort of backward and diffident in referring to my own possessions but every time I mention anything that belongs to me that'll be your cue to interrupt and go the limit, swelling me. That's it, you boost and boost and keep on boosting until you make her believe that I'm a millionaire and all the time I'll be getting credit in her mind for modesty."

"I get you," said Larry. "Leave it to me."

The scene shifts to the following afternoon at Claridge's. The well-meaning Larry appeared. The chief plotter called him across the restaurant and he was duly presented to Miss Ferguson and by invitation took a seat. His friend took up the thread of his narrative.

"I was just saying to Miss Ferguson," he explained, "that last Sunday I was out at my little place in the country. . . ."

"Place in the country,—huh!" broke in Larry. "Listen to that, will you, lady, he calls it a place in the country. It's an estate, that's what it is—a regular estate, that's all.

The suitor smiled tolerantly and went on.

"Well, anyhow," he resumed, "I was out there at my shack. . . ."

"Ain't that just like you?" proclaimed Larry. "Shack, huh? It's a palace, that's all—a palace, I'll tell the world."

"No matter, old man," continued his friend. "What I was going to say was that I called the maid, and I told her. . . ."

"You called *the* maid?" clarioned the co-conspirator. "Why don't you say you called one of the maids. Near as I remember, you've got five or six maids hanging 'round that palace, not to mention a couple of butlers."

"Have it your own way, old chap," resumed the slick-haired one. "I called one of the maids, if you prefer to put it that way, and I told her to bring me some burnt sugar and some hot water and a little whiskey. You see, I've got a cold——"

"Cold?" whooped Larry. "Listen, lady, do you hear this guy sayin' he's got a cold? What he's really got is the gallopin' consumption!"

§ 132 When Goldstein Really Cut Loose

A jobber in the cloak and suit line suffered a bereavement. His wife up and died on him. Possibly because it was neighborhood gossip that the couple had not lived together very happily the bereft one felt it incumbent upon him to manifest an unusual degree of distress.

Two days after the interment the husband, dressed all in black and wearing a broad mourning-band on his left arm, was on his way to his place of business. A fellow-jobber halted him and without preamble spoke as follows:

"Honest, Goldstein, I got to say it—for you. I am ashamed that you should carry on so the way what you did at your wife's funeral. As a mark of respect for you I went by your house day before yesterday and the way you acted—well, I could only say again: As one business man to another I am ashamed for you that you should act so.

"A wife, yes? They come, they go; you get 'em, you lose 'em. That's life, ain't it? So why, then, when you lose one should you carry on so I positively absolutely could not understand."

"Did you maybe also come by the cemetery?" inquired the widower.

"Soitin'ly not," said his friend. "I'm a business man and it ain't that I could spare a whole day running way over on Long Island to a cemetery. I came by your house like I said before and when I seen how you carried on that for me was sufficient. Right off I came away disgusted."

"You think I carried on at the house, huh?" stated Mr. Goldstein. "You should a-come by the cemetery. That's where I raised hell!"

§ 133 Tired of Dealing with Crooks

A rugged person, who had acquired a considerable fortune in the wet-goods business in the old wideopen days in Denver, decided to invest some of his savings in oil and mining stocks. The venture, so far as he was concerned, did not prove a success. Between two suns both of his partners vanished and he was left to face a large deficit. While the wreckage was being cleared away by legal methods, the disillusioned ex-saloonist bared his inner feelings to his lawyer.

"Hal," said the old fellow, "I'm through with this game. I'm goin' to take what's left—ef so be there is anything left—and go back out west where I belong. This here stock-brokin' ain't for me. The trouble with it is that it's so full of crooks you don't know who to trust. You can't put no dependence in what these fellows tell you. They'll hand you what seems to be a straight line of goods and then turn right around and double cross you.

"Now, I ain't been used to doin' business that way. Before I came here I never traded with none but square guys. For instance, now, you take it when I was runnin' that bar in Denver. A fellow that I knowed would drop in to see me and show me some jewelry or silverware or somethin' and ask me what I'd give him for it. I'd ask him where he got it and he'd say to me: 'I lifted it tonight at Jones, the Banker's house.' 'All right,' I'd say, 'I'll give you so much for it.' He'd say that suited him and I'd hand him the money and he'd beat it out of town. Then, next mornin', sure enough there'd be a piece in the paper sayin' the residence of Mr. Jones the banker had been robbed the night before, and I'd know I'd been doin' business with a square guy."

§ 134 By Way of Compromise

Up in Minnesota a railroad train killed a cow belonging to a Scandinavian homesteader. The tragedy having been reported at headquarters a claim-agent was sent to the spot to make a settlement of damages.

Now, the claim-agent was a plausible and persuasive person, else he would not have been a claim-agent. Having found the Scandinavian and introduced himself by his official title, he proceeded to make out as strong a case in rebuttal as was possible under the circumstances, with the hope of course, of inducing the injured party to accept a moderate sum.

"Mr. Swanson," he said with a winning smile, "the company wants to be absolutely fair with you in this matter. We deeply regret that your cow should have met her death on our tracks. But, on the other hand, Mr. Swanson, from our side there are certain things to be considered: In the first place, that cow had no business straying on our right-of-way and you, as her owner, should not have permitted her to do so. Moreover, it is possible that her presence there might have caused a derailment of the locomotive which struck her and a serious wreck, perhaps involving loss of human life. Now, such being the case, and it being conceded that the cow was, in effect, a trespasser on our property, what do you think, as man to man, would be a fair basis of settlement as between you and the railroad company?"

For a space Mr. Swanson pondered on the argument. Then, speaking slowly and weighing his words, he delivered himself of an ultimatum:

"I bane poor Swede farmer," he said. "I shall give you two dollars."

§ 135 The Lady Made Good at Last

There was a Down-East housewife who, for years, was troubled with heart seizures. At the most inopportune times she would drop unconscious and after appearing for awhile to be at her last gasp would rally, and after an hour or so, seemingly would be as well as she ever had been.

The frequency of these attacks naturally interfered with her husband's labors and also was highly disturbing to his peace of mind. As he worked in his woodlot, or his hay meadow or about his barn he never knew when the hired girl would be coming at full speed breathlessly to tell him his wife had suffered another stroke and surely now was on the point of death. If his patience frayed under repeated alarms of this sort the worthy man gave no outward sign. Whenever the summons came—and it came very often—he would drop whatever he was doing and hasten to the house, invariably to find the sufferer on the way back to consciousness.

One hot day he was hoeing his potato patch when word arrived by messenger that the invalid had just had an especially violent attack. He lumbered to the cottage.

The form of his wife was stretched upon the kitchen floor where she had fallen. A glance told him that this time she had made a go of it. Beyond question, life was extinct.

"Wall," he said, *"this* is more like it!"

§ 136 The Low-Down on the Saw-Milling Business

An office-man for a Chicago lumber concern decided to get into the business on his own account. Sight unseen, he purchased a milling property in the White River bottoms of Arkansas at a figure which seemed to him highly attractive. He settled up his affairs in the city and caught a train for the South to take over the bargain.

At a way-station on the edge of a swamp he left the cars. The man from whom he had purchased, a lean, whiskered individual, met him with a team and a buckboard, and together they started on the long drive back in the country. As they bumped along over the corduroy road the Northern man turned to his companion and said:

"I'm hoping to make a good deal of money out of this new line and I'm trusting to you to put me onto the ropes. I know something about the selling end of the game but this is going to be my first experience in the actual getting out of the raw stock."

"Well, suh," said the late proprietor, "I'll give you my own experiences in the saw-mill business and then you kin draw yore own conclusions. This yere mill I sold you didn't cost me nary cent to begin with. When my father-in-law died he left it to me all complete and clear of debt.

"Labor ain't cost me nothin' because my two boys and me do all the work and we ain't never had to hire no outside help. And the timber we've cut ain't cost nothin' neither 'cause, just between you and me, we been sort o' stealin' it off the land of a rich Yankee who owns a big stretch of the bottoms and ain't got nobody watchin' it.

"I've also been kind of favored in the matter of shipments, seein' that my cousin is district freight-agent for the railroad and he fixes up things so our freightin' don't amount to nothin' at all.

"That's the way she stands—no wages for outside hands, no cost for timber, and practically nothin' for freight bills.

"And last year I lost twenty-five hundred dollars."

§ 137 There Spoke a Sympathizing Soul

In the latter years of his picturesque career Colonel Eph Lillard was warden of the state prison at Frankfort. It was no more than natural that the Colonel should be a sincere lover of good horseflesh. To him, a thoroughbred was almost the noblest work of God.

In his conduct of the prison he applied some of the kindly principles which actuated him in his private life. It was his boast that no penitentiary in the South was run on more humane lines. One morning, though, word spread through the town that during the night a convict up at the Colonel's big, stone-walled establishment had hanged himself to the bars of his cell. In a body, the correspondents of the Louisville and Cincinnati papers waited upon the warden to learn the details of the suicide. They found Colonel Lillard in his private office wearing upon his genial face a look of genuine concern.

"Colonel," said the spokesman for the group, "it begins to look to us as though some of your pets were not so well satisfied as you've been letting on. How about that fellow who killed himself last night?"

"Boys," said the Colonel, "I've just been conductin' an examination into the circumstances of that most deplorable affair. The situation with regards to the late deceased prove to be mighty affectin'. It seems he was sent up the first time to serve two years for stealin' a horse. When he got out he went back home and stole another horse. They caught him before he'd gone more than half a mile and the jury gave him five years and back he came again. After he'd served his second term he went into an adjoinin' county to the one where he'd formerly lived and slipped into a stranger's stable and stole a mighty likely blooded mare, but was overtaken at daylight next morning and inside of three months was back here again doin' an eight-year term. The way I look at it, the poor fellow took to broodin' and just naturally despaired of ever gettin' hisself a horse."

§ 138 The Inevitable Consequences

Martin Littleton was born in East Tennessee. When he was a boy he moved to a community in Texas, largely settled by people from his own part of the country who had carried with them to their new home the customs and traditions of their native mountains. There he studied law and presently he opened a modest law-office.

Almost the first person who called upon him in a professional way was a gaunt Tennesseean whom he had known as a child. The visitor stated that he wished to bring a lawsuit against a neighbor, also a transplanted Tennesseean, to decide a dispute which had arisen over a line fence.

"Now see here, Uncle Zach," young Littleton said, "it's too bad that two old friends from the same part of the world should be lawing each other. Isn't there some way you men can settle this thing out of court?"

The old fellow shook his grizzled head.

"Martin, I'm afeard not," he said. "When this yere row first got serious betwixt us I made him a proposition. I suggested to him that we should decide it the same way we used to decide sich arguments back home. I told him if he'd meet me at sun-up in my pecan grove, bringin' his squirrel rifle with him, we'd stand up back to back and each one would step off twenty steps and swing around and start shootin'. But Martin, the low-flung craven, he couldn't stand the gaff when the shootin' time came. He didn't have the sand. When I'd stepped off twenty steps and whirled around you kin believe it or not, but the cowardly dog had done jumped behind a tree."

"What happened then?" asked Littleton.

"Well, natchelly, Martin, that th'owed me behind a tree."

§ 139 Not Listed among the Leading Ones Anyhow

A youth from the slums attained fame as a prize-fighter. With prosperity and prominence, he turned arrogant.

One day he openly snubbed a companion of his earlier days. The snubbed one presently sent an emissary to reproach him for his snobbishness.

"Jim says you ought to be ashamed of yourself for throwing him down now when you two used to be such good friends," stated the intermediary. "He says he's done you a whole lot of favors in the past."

A LAUGH A DAY KEEPS THE DOCTOR AWAY

"Aw, tell him to forgit it!" growled the pug. "Dat guy never done nothin' for nobody. Whut did he ever do for me?"

"Well, all I know is he told me to ask you if you'd forgot that hotel episode in Toledo when you were there together the time of the Willard-Dempsey fight?"

"He's a liar," said the pugilist. "To begin with, they ain't no Hotel Episode in Toledo."

§ 140 A Warning to the Yanks

When Sherman, after his march from Atlanta to the sea, turned his columns northward he was temporarily halted just below Fayetteville, North Carolina, while his engineers threw a temporary bridge across a swollen creek, the Confederates in falling back having destroyed the only bridge which spanned the stream. The retreating Southern army had left behind in Fayetteville a population made up almost altogether of women, children, boys too young to fight and men too old for service.

In response to a call, practically all of these older men gathered at the courthouse to discuss such measures as might be taken for the protection of the town in view of the approach of the invaders. Various expedients for saving the place from the fate which already had overtaken Atlanta and Columbia were discussed. But none of them seemed feasible, inasmuch as the community could muster no adequate defending force.

Finally an aged veteran of the Mexican War rose from his seat and caught the eye of the presiding officer.

"Mister Chairman," he quavered, "I make a motion that we collect a fund and have a lot of dodgers struck off at the printin' shop and circulated amongst the Yankee Army, warnin' them that they enter Fayetteville at the peril of their lives."

§ 141 In the Nature of a Shock

Riley Wilson is one of the best story-tellers who ever came out of the South. He loves to go to horseraces when he is not playing politics in his own state of West Virginia. Indeed he owns a string of race horses.

At the Latonia track once Riley ran into a rural friend of his from Tennessee and in the goodness of his heart gave him a tip on a horse which he had entered for one of the events. The friend excused himself and went away for a few minutes, and when he returned to where Wilson sat in the grand stand he confessed that he had wagered practically ever cent he had on Wilson's entry; which admission might be taken as evidence of sporting blood, inasmuch as it developed that he had never before seen a running race and never before had wagered money on one.

The gee-gees were off. At once Wilson's horse and another contender took the lead. Together the pair of them fought it out all the way. Neck and neck they swung into the home stretch, and neck and neck they thundered toward the goal. A scant ten feet from the wire the rival horse gave a convulsive leap and won by half a nose from Wilson's colt.

As this dreadful thing happened, the Tennesseean fell back in his seat, pawing at himself with both hands.

"Was it much of a shock to you?" asked Wilson.

"Much of a shock?" echoed the loser. "I ain't been all over myself yet, but as fur as I've gone here's what's happened to me: My watch is stopped, both my suspenders is busted, and my glass eye is cracked right through the center."

§ 142 His Worst Fears Confirmed

An elderly English actor came over to take his first American engagement. He had never visited the country before but he had strong—not to say fixed—prejudices touching on the United States, as compared with the British Isles.

The voyage across was a rough one and the visitor's disposition did not sweeten by reason of it. On landing he started for an English boarding house uptown, where he had been told he could get English food uncontaminated by base Yankee notions. To keep down expenses he elected to repair thither by a street car instead of using a cab.

He emerged from the pier laden with his hatbox, his umbrella, his makeup tin, his grips—two in number—his steamer rug, his tea caddy, his overcoat, his framed picture of the Death of Nelson, and other prized personal belongings, and climbed aboard a car.

Just as he got fairly upon the platform the car started and he fell through the open door into the aisle, scattering his goods and chattels in every direction. As he got upon his knees he remarked in a tone of conviction:

"There now! I knew I shouldn't like the blarsted country!"

§ 143   Only Three Had Remained

From where he lived high up on a ridge of the mountains along the boundary between Kentucky and West Virginia, an elderly hillsman came down to the general store at the cross roads for provender. There he met a lowland acquaintance who asked him whether there was any news up in the knobs.

"Well, son," said the mountaineer, "I don't know as there's any neighborhood gossip stirrin' without you'd keer to hear about my affair with them dad-fetched Hensley boys."

The visitor professed a desire to know the details.

"Well," said the old gentleman, "off and on, here lately, I've been havin' a right smart trouble with them Hensleys. The whole passel of 'em live right up the creek a little piece above my place, and they tuck a sort of a grudge ag'inst me. Every night when I went out to feed the stock they'd be hid in the brush-fence at the lower end of my hoss-lot and they'd shoot at me with them high-powered rifles of their'n. It pestered me no little!

"Finally I got plum' outdone over it. Of late years I've tried to live at peace with one and all; but there's a limit to any man's patience. Besides, I'm gittin' along in years and I can't see to aim the way I could oncet, on account of my eyesight; but I jest made up my mind the other night that I wouldn't stand it no more.

"So that night when I went out to feed I taken my old gun along with me. Shore enough, they was ambushed in the same place, and they cut down on me jest as soon as I came into sight.

"So I up with my gun and I sort of sprayed them bushes with bullets. That seemed to quiet 'em down, and I went on with my feedin'; but after I'd got through I felt sort of curious and I walked down to that there brush fence and taken a look over on the fur side of it. And, son, all of them Hensleys was gone but three!"

§ 144   She Who Sought for Peace

Young Mrs. Smith was in need of a domestic for general housework. She inserted a notice in the local paper. In answer to the advertisement a rather slatternly-looking colored girl applied for the job.

"Where did you work last?" asked Mrs. Smith.

"I wukked fur de Jones fambly right down de street yere a piece," said the candidate.

"Do you mean the Herbert Joneses who live in the white house on the corner?" inquired Mrs. Smith.

"Yassum, they's the ones."

"When did you leave their employment?"

"Las' Sad'day night."

"Did you quit or were you discharged?"

"I quit. Yassum, of my own free will I up and quit."

"Why did you quit?"

"Me, I likes peace—tha's why! I couldn' stand it no mo' to be stayin' in a house whar they's always so much quollin' goin' on."

Now the Joneses were friends of Mrs. Smith, and, to her always, they had seemed a happy couple, ideally mated. Naturally this disclosure shocked her greatly. She hardly could believe it. Still, she shared with the rest of us an almost universal trait—she had a natural curiosity. If the household of her neighbors was rent by internal dissensions here was a chance to find out the true state of affairs.

"Do you mean to tell me that Mr. and Mrs. Jones have been quarreling?"

"Yassum. All de two months I stayed there they was quollin' constant."

"What did they quarrel about?"

"Diffunt things, ever' day. Ef 'twasn't Mrs. Jones quollin' wid me 'bout somethin' or other I'd done, 'twas Mr. Jones."

§ 145   An Exception for a Native Son

The clannishness of the rural Vermonter is proverbial. In illustration of this trait a distinguished citizen of the Green Mountain state told me a story. He said that on a rather cloudy day a typical group of natives sat on the porch of the main general store in a town on the shores of Lake Champlain. Among them appeared a youth citified as to dress and having rather an air of assurance about him. In silent disapproval the company took in his belted coat, his knickerbockers and golf stockings and, most disapprovingly of all, the confident manner of the alien.

"Good morning, everybody," he said breezily.

The elder of the group, a venerable gentleman, made answer for the rest:

"How' do," he said shortly.

Somewhat abashed at the coolness of his reception, the young man tried again:

"Looks rather like rain," he said.

" 'Twon't rain," said the old man in a tone of finality.

"But I rather thought from the looks of these clouds——"

" 'Twon't rain," repeated the ancient in the voice of one who is not used to being argued with.

A daunting silence ensued. The stranger fidgeted in his embarrassment. The old man fixed him with a cold and hostile eye.

"What mout your name be?" he inquired, as though desirous properly to classify a curious zoölogical specimen.

"My name is Nelson—Herbert Nelson," stated the youth.

"Nelson, hey?" said the patriarch. "There used to be some Nelsons out in the Kent neighborhood. Don't s'pose you ever heerd of them."

"I've been hearing of them all my life," said the young man. "I come from New York, but my father's name was Henry Nelson and he was born out near Kent in this county."

"Then you must a-been a grandson of the late Ezra Nelson," said the aged Vermonter. His manner perceptibly had warmed; indeed, by now it was almost cordial.

"Yes, sir," said the youth. "Ezra Nelson was my grandfather."

"Dew tell, now!" said the patriarch. "So you're a son of Henry Nelson and a grandson of Ezra Nelson? Well, in *that* case it may rain."

§ 146   Without Professional Assistance

A lady who lives on a plantation in the southern part of Alabama went up to Birmingham on a visit. Upon her return an old negro man who occasionally did odd jobs for her dropped by to welcome her home and to tell her the news of the neighborhood.

"Whilst you wuz gone Aunt Mallie died," he said. Aunt Mallie was a poor old black woman who lived in a tumbledown cabin half a mile away.

"Oh, that's too bad," said the white lady sympathetically. "How long was she sick?"

"Jes' three or fo' days," he said.

"What ailed her?"

"They didn' nobody know. One mawnin' she up and fell sick and she kep' on gittin' wuss and wuss 'twel de fo'th day come and den, all of a suddenlak, she hauled off an' died."

"Who was the doctor?"

"She didn' have no doctor—she died a natchel death!"

§ 147   Making It Harder Than Ever

There was a complaint in a small village a few miles from Edinburgh regarding the trolley fare. For four rides into the city the company charged a shilling. This, in the opinion of many of the villagers, was much too much.

A delegation was chosen to visit the offices of the line and make representation in favor of a lower rate. The arguments advanced by the plenipotentiaries prevailed. The company decided that thereafter six tickets might be had for the former price.

The townspeople returned home rejoicing, but there was at least one of their fellow-citizens who did not share in the view that a wise step had been taken. This was an elderly gentleman renowned for his frugality even in a community where frugal folk are common.

"It's all dam' foolishness," he declared. "Now we've got to walk to town six times instead of four-r times to save a shillin'!"

§ 148   Why They Called Him Speedy

Bert Swor, the minstrel man, is something more than a mere black-faced comedian. He was born and reared in a Texas town and he probably knows as much about the true delineation of certain negro types as any living man.

One of his most popular wheezes is a rendition of something which a colored man at Fort Worth said years ago. Two negroes were talking together. As Swor passed by he gathered that the subject under discussion was the relative fleetness of foot of the pair. One of them said:

"You claims you is fast! You says you's so fast folks calls you Speedy! Jest how fast is you, nigger?"

"I'll tell you how fast I is," said the other. "De room whar I sleeps nights is got jest one 'lectric light in it w'ich dat 'lectric light is forty feet frum de baid. W'en I gits undressed I kin walk over to dat 'lectric light and turn it out and git back into baid and be all covered up befo' de room gits dark."

§ 149   There Would Be Three in All

Out on the Pacific Coast, where the Japanese question and the prospect of a war with Japan are ever-living issues, a group of the hands at a canning factory were spending part of their lunch hour discussing these vital questions. Sitting on a packing case was a lank Oregonian munching the last bites of his sandwich and taking no part in the discussion. The foreman addressed him.

"Look a-here, Jeff," said the foreman. "How do you feel about it? If the Japs were to land an invading army in this country I suppose you'd go to the front, wouldn't you?"

"Yes, I'd go," said Jeff. "Me and two others that I knows of."

"What two others?" inquired the foreman.

"Why, the two that'll drag me there," said Jeff.

§ 150   The Colonel's Checking System

One of the most widely known railroad men on the Western hemisphere has for many years handled the publicity for a Canadian system. He is as popular in the States as he is in the Dominion.

Having so many friends and being of so social a disposition, it is almost inevitable that he must do his share of drinking. A few years ago he suffered an attack of illness and the physician who attended him put him on a diet. One of the regulations was that, until further notice, he must take no more than one high-ball every twenty-four hours. A few months later he ran down to New York. He called upon a friend and the friend opened a bottle of prime Scotch. As the Canadian refilled his glass for the third time the friend said:

"Look here, Colonel, I thought by the doctor's orders you were allowed to take only one drink for each day."

"Yes, that's right," said the Colonel, "and I'm following instructions. This drink here, for example,"—and he raised the tumbler and gazed upon its delectable amber contents—"this is my drink for August the twenty-first of next year."

§ 151   The Reunion of the Aged

There is a certain musical comedy star who is not quite so young as she once was. During the season of 1923 she headed a road show. Business at times was not especially good and the tempers of the troupers suffered. Relations became somewhat strained between the prima donna and certain members of the chorus.

This friction was at its height when the company began a week's engagement in a middle Western city. The theatre was old-fashioned and somewhat primitive in its appointments behind stage. For example, the dressing-rooms were no better than overgrown stalls.

The walls between them ran up only part way toward the ceilings so that voices in one of these cubicles might plainly be heard by those beyond the separating half-partitions.

For the opening performance the house was no more than two thirds filled, and the audience, for some reason or other, seemed rather unresponsive. The leading lady was not in a particularly happy frame of mind as she sat in her dressing-room after the final curtain, removing her make-up. Next door several members of the chorus were shifting to street dress.

There came a knock at the star's door.

"Who is it and what do you want?" she demanded sharply.

"It's the house manager, Miss ———," came the answer "There's a lady out front who'd like very much to see you."

"I'm not receiving visitors to-night," said Miss ——— rather acidly. "Who is this lady?"

"She tells me that she thinks you'll be glad to see her. She says that she was a chum of yours when you were at high school. Shall I show her in?"

Over the dividing wall came floating the voice of a catty chorus-lady:

"Wheel her in!"

§ 152 Probably Stewed Kidneys Ran Third

Back in the days when crowned heads were more numerous in Europe—and more popular—than at present, Carlos of Portugal paid his first visit to the British Isles. At the conclusion of his trip King Edward, so it is said, asked young Carlos what, of all things in England, he liked best.

Now, Portugal's king was by way of being a consistent and sincere trencherman. He thought for a moment and made answer:

"The roast beef," he said.

"Is that all that has impressed you?" inquired His Majesty of England.

"Well," replied Carlos, "the boiled beef is not so bad."

§ 153 Pretty Pol!

It will be recalled that it was necessary for the Wright brothers to go abroad in order to secure proper recognition for their first aeronautic inventions. The French government welcomed them and gave them proper opportunity to demonstrate what they had done;

but as a group, the French aeronauts were disposed to show jealousy for the two Yankees.

Following the successful proof by the Wrights of their ability actually to fly and, what was more important, to guide their machine along a given course, a banquet at Paris was arranged in their honor.

Naturally, there was a deal of speech-making. The chief orator was a distinguished Frenchman who devoted most of his remarks to claiming that France had led the world in the new field of endeavor—or so he insisted—and to proclaiming that future developments ever would find Frenchmen at the forefront. Curiously enough, he had very little to say in compliment of the two chief guests of honor.

Wilbur Wright was next called upon by the toastmaster. Slowly he rose to his feet.

"I am no hand at public speaking," he said, "and on this occasion must content myself with a few words. As I sat here listening to the speaker who preceded me I have heard comparisons made to the eagle, to the swallow and to the hawk as typifying skill and speed in the mastery of the air; but, somehow or other, I could not keep from thinking of the bird which, of all the ornithological kingdom, is the poorest flier and the best talker. I refer to the parrot."

And down he sat amid tremendous applause from the Americans present.

§ 154   The Unforgivable Sin

A year or two before his death, Booker T. Washington made an address in a small town in Georgia. When he had finished, an old Confederate soldier, white-haired and white-moustached, pushed forward to the platform, his face aglow with enthusiasm.

"Professor Washington," he declared, "I want to do now what I never thought I'd be doing—I want to clasp your hand and pledge you my support for the great work you are doing. And furthermore, I want to tell you this: that was the best speech I ever heard in my life and you are the greatest man in this country to-day!"

"I'm afraid you do me too much honor," said Washington. "Wouldn't you regard Col. Roosevelt as the greatest man we have?"

"Huh!" exploded the Southerner. "I've had no use for him since he invited you to eat a meal with him at the White House."

§ 155 The Burden of the Black Brother

I just told a story relating to Booker Washington. Here's another. It was a favorite anecdote of the great negro educator. He said that the citizens of a remote Southern community got interested in a project to import some Europeans to the neighborhood and colonize them.

A meeting was held at the courthouse to discuss ways and means. In the audience sat an elderly and highly respected colored citizen.

After the meeting adjourned the chairman of it hailed the old negro.

"Hello, Uncle Zack!" he said. "I was glad to have you with us to-night. I take it that you endorse the project we've put under way?"

"Well, Kunnel, I wouldn't go so fur ez to say dat," stated the old man. "To tell you de Gawd's truth, they's already mo' w'ite folks in dis county than us niggers kin suppo't."

§ 156 Openings in the Higher Branches

Fourth of July was supposed to be a holiday in a certain garrison of the regular army out West, but a grizzled old sergeant named Kelly, in charge of the guard house, had his own ideas about this holiday notion. After breakfast he ordered all his prisoners to line up outside their prison quarters, and he made a short speech:

"There is no doubt in me own mind," he said, "but that a good many of you men should not be prisoners at all. You've neglected your opportunities, that's all. Some here has had educations and should make good company clerks. Maybe there's some others amongst you who'd like to be company barbers and earn a little money on the side."

A murmur of assent ran through the lines.

"Now, thin," went on Sergeant Kelly, "all you men who are educated or who think ye cud learn to do paper work, step two paces to the front."

About half of the prisoners came forward.

"Now, thin, all who'd like to learn the barberin' business advance two paces."

All save two moved toward him with alacrity.

The sergeant addressed the remaining pair:

"What did the two of you do before you joined the army?" he asked.

"We was laborin' men," answered one.

"Very well, thin, all you educated guys take these here gunnysacks and pick up every scrap of paper around the parade grounds. And the rest of you, who want to learn barberin', you grab these here lawn mowers and cut grass until I tell you to leave off. You two laborin' men kin go back inside the tent and take a nap."

§ 157   A Distinction and a Difference

On the Congressional Limited a passenger who, to judge from the visible evidences, had been patronizing a bootlegger, hailed the Pullman conductor as the latter passed through the car.

"Shay, conductor," he inquired rather thickly, "how far is it from Wilmington to Baltimore?"

The conductor told him the distance, and passed on. On his next appearance the inebriated one halted him again:

"How far is it," he asked, "from Baltimore to Wilmington?"

"I told you just a few minutes ago," said the Pullman man.

"No, you didn't," said the traveler. "You told me how far it was from Wilmington to Baltimore. What I want to know now is how far is it from Baltimore to Wilmington."

"Say, listen," said the irate conductor. "What are you trying to do—make a goat of me? If it's so many miles from Wilmington to Baltimore, isn't it necessarily bound to be the same number of miles from Baltimore to Wilmington?"

"Not nesheshar'ly," said the other. "It's only a week from Christmas to New Year's, but look what a devil of a distance it is from New Year's to Christmas."

§ 158   The Prediction That Came True

A young woman in the confessional confided that she was afraid she had been spending some of her money foolishly.

"Spending your money foolishly calls for penance," said the priest sternly. "How have you been spending yours?"

"Well, Father, I went to a fortune teller," admitted the penitent.

"Oh, ho, so you went to a fortune teller, eh? Well, that's wrong to begin with. In the first place, professional fortune tellers are most of them frauds, and in the second place, they pretend to deal with the supernatural. And what did you do for this fortune teller?"

"I gave him two dollars, Father."

"Worse and worse—wasting your hard-earned wages on a fakir. And, in exchange for your two dollars what did he do for you?"

"He told me a pack of lies, Father, about my past and my future."

"What did he say about your past?"

"Only a pack of lies, as I was just afther tellin' you."

"And what did he tell you about your future?"

"He said, Father, I would shortly be goin' on a long, hard journey."

"Well," said the priest reflectively, "he may have lied to you about your past, but when he predicted that you would be going on a long, hard journey in the near future he was not far wrong, after all. You'll do the Stations of the Cross twelve times!"

§ 159 It Wasn't His Move, Either

A venerable mountaineer residing near the boundary between Tennessee and North Carolina sat one bright afternoon on the stile in front of his cabin, busily engaged in following his regular occupation of doing nothing at all. At the edge of the clearing, fifty yards away, suddenly appeared an individual in flannel shirt and laced boots who aimed at the old gentleman a round-barreled instrument mounted on a tripod, which the native naturally mistook for a new kind of repeating rifle. Up went both his hands.

"Don't shoot!" he shouted. "I surrender."

"I'm not fixing to shoot," said the stranger, drawing nearer. "I belong to an engineering crew. We're surveying the state line."

"Shuckins, son," said the old man, "you're away off. The line runs through the gap nearly half a mile down the mounting below here."

"That's where it used to run," said the engineer, "but it seems there was a mistake in the original job. According to the new survey it'll pass about fifty feet from your house, on the upper side of the hill."

"Say, look a-here, boy," stated the old man, "won't that throw me from Tennessee clear over into North Carolina?"

"Yep, that's what it'll do."

"Well, that won't never do," demurred the mountaineer. "I was born and raised in Tennessee. I've always voted thar. It looks to me like you fellows ain't got no right to be movin' me plum' out of one state into another."

"Can't help it," said the surveyor. "We have to go by the corrected line."

"Wall," said the old man resignedly, "come to think it over, I don't know but what it's a good thing, after all. I've always heered tell North Carolina was a healthier state than Tennessee anyhow."

§ 160   Spreading the Feast for the Stranger

When Sam Blythe was a Washington correspondent he went into New England to sound out public opinion on one or another of those crises which, politically speaking, are forever threatening the liberties of the people.

He called upon the retired political leader of New Hampshire, who lived in a small but comfortable cottage in a little town. The old gentleman felt a deep concern in the vital question of the hour, whatever it was. Noontime approached and still he was nowhere near through with what he had to say. So he insisted that Blythe should remain with him through the afternoon.

Having sampled the cuisine of the local hotel at breakfast, Blythe promptly consented. The old gentleman excused himself in order to inform his wife that there would be a guest for the midday meal and also to get some important papers bearing on the subject which were stored away, he said, in a room upstairs. Going out, he left the parlor door ajar.

Through the opening Blythe heard a voice, evidently one belonging to the mistress of the household.

"Samantha," the lady said, raising her tone in order that she might be heard by the cook in the kitchen, "my husband has invited a gentleman to stay for dinner. Take those two large potatoes back down cellar and bring up three small ones."

§ 161   A Very Natural Request

A certain captain of the regular army was on trial before a court-martial for alleged intoxication. His orderly, whose name was McSweeney, appeared as a witness for the defence.

"What was the condition of the accused on the date in question?" asked the judge advocate.

"He was sober, sor," said McSweeney.

"It has been reported," stated the judge, "that he was in such a condition that you had to help him to his quarters and undress him and put him in bed."

"No, sor," said Private McSweeney, "I just wint to quarters with the captain—that's all, sor."

"Did he say anything that would lead you to think he was intoxicated?"

"No, sor."

"Did he say anything at all?"

"Well, he did say wan thing."

"What was that?"

"Well, sor, just as I was leavin' he sez to me, he sez, 'McSweeney, if you're wakin' call me early. For I'm to be Queen of the May.'"

§ 162   The Voice of a Prophet

A company of a division of colored troops were in heavy marching order awaiting the word to start for the front. It was to be their first actual contact with the enemy. One of the privates had somewhere picked up a copy of the Paris edition of the New York *Herald*.

"Does dat air paper say anything about us boys?" inquired a sergeant.

"It sho' do," answered the private, improvising. "It sez yere dat twenty-five thousand cullid troops is goin' over de top to-night, suppo'ted by fifty thousand Frenchmen."

From down the line came a third voice, saying:

"Well, I knows whut to-morrow's number of dat paper's gwine say. It's gwine say, in big black letters, 'Fifty thousand Frenchmen trompled to death by twenty-five thousand niggers.'"

§ 163   The Trifles of an Earlier Day

In the great Meuse-Argonne advance two doughboys were squatted in a shell hole for shelter. In another minute or two they expected an order to go forward again against the German positions. The enemy was pouring everything he had in their direction. Machine-gun bullets were whining by just above their heads. High explosives and shrapnel shells were bursting about them. Hundreds of guns, big and little, roared and thundered.

One of the soldiers turned his head toward his companion.

"Buddy," he said, "I've just been layin' here thinkin'."

"Hell of a time to be thinkin'," said his pal. "What were you thinkin' about?"

"I was thinkin' how a fellow's feelin's get changed in this war."

"What do you mean—get changed?"

"Why, once upon a time, back home, a fellow with a thirty-eight calibre pistol run me plum' out of town."

§ 164   In Accordance with the Ritual

Archie Gunn, the artist, is a Scot who was educated in England and who still has a great love for the national game of the British Isles, to wit: cricket. Will Kirk, the verse-writer, is a product of Wisconsin and until one day when his friend Gunn took him over on Staten Island had never seen a game of cricket.

Teams made up of English residents were playing. The spectators, almost exclusively, were their fellow-countrymen.

A batsman dealt the ball a powerful wallop.

"Well hit, old chap!" cried Gunn. And "Well hit! Well hit!" echoed others in the crowd.

An opposing player made a hard run to catch the ball as it descended into his territory. He almost got under it—almost, but not quite. It just eluded his clutching fingers.

"Well tried, old chap! Well tried!" called out Gunn.

Kirk figured this sort of thing must be in accordance with the proper ritualism of the game. He decided that, to show his approval, he would at the next opportunity speak up, too.

Once more the batsman smote the ball. It rose high in the air. A fielder for the rival club ran to catch it. His toe caught in a clod of upturned turf and he tumbled forward on his face, and the ball, dropping, hit him squarely on the top of his head.

Kirk's yell rose high and clear above all lesser sounds.

"Well fell, old chap!" he shouted. "Well fell, by gum!"

§ 165   A Customer Who Wasn't Wanted

Almost invariably, when men fall to discussing examples of business sagacity, someone present is reminded of the illustrative incident of the white tramp and the colored saloon-keeper.

The colored man sat behind his bar in a moment when trade was slack. Through the swinging doors entered the ragged Caucasian.

"Give me a good five-cent cigar," he ordered.

The proprietor produced a box containing a number of dangerous-looking dark-brown rolls. The patron made a discriminating choice and then in the act of putting the cigar between his lips checked himself.

"Say, I've changed my mind," he said. "Believe I'll take a glass of beer instead."

The negro returned the cigar to its box and drew a glass of beer. The customer drank it, wiped his mouth on the back of his hand and started to withdraw.

"Yere, hol' on, w'ite man," said the negro, "you forgot to pay fur dat beer."

"Why, I give you a cigar for it."

"Yes, but you ain't paid fur de cigar, neither."

"But you've still got the cigar, ain't you? What's the matter with you, anyhow?"

The colored man scratched his head.

"Lemme see, boss," he said, "ef I gits dis thing straight: You don't owe me for de beer, 'cause you give me de cigar fur it; and you don't owe me fur de cigar, 'cause you handed it back to me. Is dat right?"

"Certainly, it's right," said the crafty white.

"Ver' well, then," agreed the colored man; "but say, mister, I wants to ax you a favor: Next time you feels lak smokin' or drinkin' please tek yo' custom somewhars else."

§ 166   The Surest System Yet

This story has to do with a man describing a poker game which he was invited to join while visiting in a strange town.

"The first hand that was dealt," he says, "I had threes. I opened the pot and one other man stayed. He drew one card. We bet back and forth for a while and finally he called. 'I've got three of a kind,' I said, and showed down my three nines. 'I've got a straight—ten high,' he says, and pitches his hand in the deck and reaches for the chips. 'Hold on,' I says, 'I didn't see what you had.' He looks at me sort of surprised and the fellow who's givin' the party speaks up and says to me: 'This is a gentleman's game. If a man wins a pot here we never ask him to show his hand. We just take his word for it that he holds the winning cards and we let it go at that. That's our rule.'"

"Did you keep on playing after that?" asks a bystander.

"Certainly I did," says the first speaker.

"And did you win?"

"Did I win? Huh—the first pot was the only one I lost!"

§ 167   All According to Specifications

"Now, then, children," said the Sunday school teacher in her best Sunday school teacher's manner, "the lesson for to-day is about the Prophet Elisha. Can any little boy or little girl here tell us anything about Elisha?"

"Me," answered a ten-year-old urchin, holding up his hand.

"Very well, then, Eddie," answered the teacher. "Now, then, all the rest of you be nice and quiet while Eddie, here, tells us about the Prophet Elisha."

"Well," said Eddie, "Elisha was an old bald-headed preacher. One day he was goin' along the big road and he came past where some children were playin' in the sand, and they laughed at him and poked fun at him and called him names and hollered, 'Oh, look at that old bald-headed man!' That made Elisha hoppin' mad and he stopped and turned around and shook his fist at 'em and he said: 'Don't you kids make fun of me any more! If you do I'll call some bears out of them woods yonder and they'll shore eat you up.'

"And they did and he did and the bears did."

§ 168   The Reason the Artist Quit

This is in explanation of why a rather well-known New Yorker gave up free-hand drawing. Although without any artistic training, he rather fancied himself a pretty fair amateur sketch artist.

In company with a newspaper man he was touring Spain. One morning in Malaga the two Americans dropped into a little café for breakfast. They knew no Spanish and their waiter knew no English. Largely by signs they made him understand that they wanted coffee and rolls. But when the newspaperman decided that he wished also a glass of milk difficulties arose.

Singly and in chorus they pronounced the word "milk." Then they spelled it out. Then they shouted it loudly as one always does, somehow, when using one's own language, one is dealing with a stranger who doesn't understand that language. The waiter merely shrugged his shoulders and spread his fingers in a gesture of helplessness.

The man who wanted milk imitated the action of one milking a cow, meanwhile mooing plaintively, and then, to round out the illustration, went through the pantomime of emptying an imaginary glass. Still the waiter stared at him uncomprehendingly.

"Hold on," said the artist, "I've got an idea. I can draw about as well as the next one. Lend me a pencil; it won't take me a minute to make this fellow understand."

With the pencil, on the table cloth, he sketched rapidly what seemed to him a very graphic likeness of a domestic cow, and, squatted down alongside the cow, his conception of a conventional milkmaid engaged in the act of milking.

As he made the finishing strokes the waiter, who had been watching the operation over his shoulder, burst into a delighted cry of "Sí! Sí! Señor!" and, tucking up his apron, dashed from the restaurant and ran across the street into the shop of a tobacconist.

"Now, then," said the artist to his friend, "see what a knack with the pencil will do for a fellow when he gets into difficulties in a foreign country? I'll venture I could go all over the world, making my meaning clear by dashing off these little illustrations."

"Maybe so," said the newspaper man, "but why in thunder did the waiter go to a cigar store for milk?"

"Probably a custom of the country," said the artist. "The main point was that just as soon as he'd had a good look at my drawing he was on his way. He'll be back here in a minute with your glass of milk."

The prediction was only partly true. The waiter was back again in a minute or less, but he brought no milk. Triumphantly, he laid down in front of his patrons two tickets for a bull-fight.

§ 169 To the Depths of Dogology

It was back in 1899 that State Senator William Goebel seized the Democratic nomination for Governor of Kentucky and, so doing, split the party in the state to flinders. The feuds born of that fight are still alive to-day after the lapse of more than twenty-three years. It was my fortune as a reporter from a Louisville paper to follow the story of the conflict.

Theodore Hallam, perhaps the greatest orator in a state of orators, and almost the quickest-thinking man on his feet, I believe, that ever lived anywhere, having bolted the nomination of Goebel, took the stump against him. The seceding wing of the party picked on Hallam to open its fight, and chose the town of Bowling Green as a fitting place for the firing of the first gun, Bowling Green being a town where the rebellion inside the Democratic ranks was widespread and vehement. But Goebel had his adherents there, too.

You could fairly smell trouble cooking on that August afternoon when Hallam rose up in the jammed courthouse to begin his speech. Hardly had he started when a local leader, himself a most handy person in a rough-and-tumble argument, stood upon the seat of his chair, towering high above the heads of those about him.

"I want to ask you a question!" he demanded in a tone like the roar of one of Bashan's bulls.

One third of the crowd yelled: "Go ahead!" The other two thirds yelled: "Throw him out!" and a few enthusiastic spirits suggested the expediency of destroying the gentleman utterly.

With a wave of his hand Hallam stilled the tumult.

"Let it be understood now and hereafter that this is to be no joint debate," he said in his rather high-pitched voice. "My friends have arranged for the use of this building this afternoon and I intend to be the only speaker. But it is a tenet of our political faith that in a Democratic gathering no man who calls himself a Democrat shall be denied the right to be heard. If the gentleman will be content to ask his question, whatever it is, and to abide by my answer to it, I am willing that he should speak."

"That suits me," proclaimed the interrupter. "My question is this: Didn't you say at the Louisville convention not four weeks ago that if the Democrats of Kentucky, in convention assembled, nominated a yaller dog for Governor, you would vote for him?"

"I did," said Hallam calmly.

"Well, then," whooped the heckler, eager now to press his seeming advantage, "in the face of that statement, why do you now repudiate the nominee of that convention and refuse to support him?"

For his part Hallam waited for perfect quiet and finally got it.

"I admit," he stated, "that I said then what now I repeat, namely, that when the Democrats of Kentucky nominate a yaller dog for the governorship of this great state I mean to support him—but lower than that ye shall not drag me!"

§ 170 Time Was No Object

A colored man was idling along the sidewalk on the opposite side of the street from where the county jail stood. From a barred window high up in the structure came the voice of a member of his own race:

"Say, nigger," called the unseen speaker.

The pedestrian halted and faced about.

"Whut you want?" he demanded.

"I wants to ax you a question," said the invisible one.

"Well, ax it. I's listenin'."
"Is you got a watch on you?"
"Suttinly I's got a watch on me."
"Well, den, whut time is it?"
"Whut is time to you?" answered the man in the street. "You ain't fixin' to go nowheres, is you?"

§ 171 A Diagnosis Made Offhand

Puffed with pride, a colored man returned to his native town in North Carolina after a season spent with a traveling circus. He was recounting his experiences in the great world at large to a fellow Afro-American.

"I started out," he said, "ez a roustabout, but de boss man w'ich owned de show he right away seen dat I had merits above my station an' he permoted me to be a lion tamer. So dat's whut I is now—a reg'lar perfessional lion tamer."

"Is dat so?" said his townsman. "Tell me, boy, how does you go 'bout bein' a lion tamer?"

"It's ver' simple," said the returned one. "All you got to have is bravery an' de dauntless eye. Fust you picks out yore lion—de best way is to pick out de fiercest one. Den you walks up to de cage whar he is wid a club in yore hand an' open de do' and jump inside an' slam de do' shut behind you. Natchelly, de lion rare hisse'f up on his hind laigs an' come at you wid his mouth open an' his teeth all showin'. You waits till he's right clost up to you an' den you hauls off an' you busts him acrost de nose wid yore club. Den you backs him up into a corner an' you beats him some mo' till he 'knowledges you fur his master. Den, w'en he's plum' cowed down, you grabs him by de jaws an' twists his mouth open an' sticks yore head down his throat an' after dat you meks him jump th'ough a hoop an' lay at yore feet an' sit up an' beg fur raw meat an' teach him a few more tricks such as dem. Tha's being a lion tamer."

"Huh, nigger," grunted his audience, "you ain't no lion tamer—you' a lyin' scoundrel!"

§ 172 Remodeling the Calendar

August Winestopper ran a family liquor store in the day when there were family liquor stores. Mr. Winestopper's knowledge of

A LAUGH A DAY KEEPS THE DOCTOR AWAY

English was somewhat circumscribed but, as events were to prove, his business sagacity was profound.

In the early part of the summer business, for some reason or other, fell off considerably. While Mr. Winestopper, was canvassing in his own mind the possible causes for this shrinkage in normal neighborhood consumption of wet goods other discomfiting things began to occur. The agent for the owner of the premises waited upon him and told him that, beginning the following month, the rent would be advanced $600 per annum. The two barkeepers notified him that the barkeepers' union had passed a rule calling for an increase in the wage scale. He got a summons for an alleged violation of the Sunday closing law and was confronted by the prospect that, if found guilty, he would pay a heavy fine. The brewery sent him word that the price of beer shortly would go up.

Mr. Winestopper considered the situation in all of its various and disturbing phases. Then he took a piece of chalk and on the mirror behind the bar he wrote, where all might read, the following ultimatum:

"The first of July will be the last of August!"

§ 173   Of a Careless Nature

A colored man owned a mule which, for reasons best known to himself he desired to sell. He heard that a neighbor down the road was in the market for a mule. So he put a halter on the animal and led her to the cabin of the other negro.

At once negotiations were entered into. The owner had delivered himself of a eulogy touching on the strength, capacity for hard work, and amiable disposition of his beast, when the prospective purchaser broke in with a question:

"Is dis yere mule fast?"

"Fast?" the proprietor snorted. "Look yere!" He gave the mule a kick in the ribs, whereupon she bucked sideways, tore down a strip of fencing, galloped headlong through a week's washing, butting against the side of the barn, and then caroming off, tore across a garden patch and vanished into the woods beyond the clearing.

"Look yere, nigger," said the owner of the damaged property, "dat mule must be blind."

"She ain't blind," said the owner; "but she jest natchelly don't keer a damn!"

§ 174 The Light That Failed

An old colored man, who had been crippled in the railroad service, served for many years as a watchman at a grade crossing in the outskirts of an Alabama town. By day he wielded a red flag and by night he swung a lantern.

One dark night a colored man from the country, driving home from town, steered his mules across the track just as the Memphis flier came through and abolished him, along with his team and his wagon. His widow sued the railroad for damages. At the trial the chief witness for the defence was the old crossing watchman.

Uncle Gabe stumped to the stand and took the oath to tell the truth, the whole truth, and nothing but the truth. Under promptings from the attorney for his side, he proceeded to give testimony strongly in favor of the defendant corporation. He stated that he had seen the approaching team in due time and that, standing in the street, he had waved his lantern to and fro for a period of at least one minute. In spite of the warning, he said, the deceased had driven upon the rails.

Naturally, the attorney for the plaintiff put him to a severe cross-examination. Uncle Gabe answered every question readily and with evident honesty. He told just how he had held the lantern, how he had swung and joggled it and so forth and so on.

After court had adjourned the lawyer for the railroad sought out the old man and congratulated him upon his behavior as a witness.

"Gabe," he said, "you acquitted yourself splendidly. Weren't you at all nervous while on the stand?"

"I suttinly wuz, boss," replied Uncle Gabe. "I kep' wonderin' whu wuz gwine happen ef dat w'ite genelman should ax me if dat lantern wuz lighted."

§ 175 Sir Izaak Walton in Black

Captain George Walker, of Savannah, used to have a hand on his Georgia plantation who loved ease and fishing. When he wasn't fishing he was loafing.

One night there was a rain almost heavy enough to be called a cloudburst and the next morning all the low places on the plantation were flooded two feet deep. Passing his tenant's cabin, Captain Walker found him seated in any easy chair at the kitchen door fishing in a small puddle of muddy water that had formed there.

"Henry, you old fool," said Captain Walker, "what are you doing there?"

"Boss," said Henry, "I's jes' fishin'."

"Well, don't you know there are no fish there?" demanded Captain Walker.

"Yas, suh," said Henry; "I knows dat. But this yere place is so handy!"

§ 176   Doing Something for the Patient

Frank McIntyre, the plump comedian, played vaudeville dates one season. One night after his turn he dropped into a short-order restaurant near the theatre for a bite, before going to bed. Sitting next to him was a former circus acrobat, who did a horizontal-bar act on the same bill with McIntyre.

The acrobat was sawing away at the sinewy knee-joint of a fried chicken leg. Though the knife was sharp and he was athletic, he made but little headway.

He waved his arm toward a bottle of ketchup which stood upon the counter near McIntyre's elbow.

"Say, bo," he requested, "pass de liniment, will you? De sea gull's got de rheumatism."

§ 177   The Real Point of the Joke

Two American performers, filling vaudeville engagements in London, took lodgings together in a house on a side street back of Covent Gardens. Late at night, following the first day of their joint tenancy they left the theatre in company and, having had a bite and a drink at a chophouse set out afoot for the new diggings. One of the pair undertook to show the way. The trouble was, though, that for the life of him he couldn't recall the name of the street where the house stood nor the number of the house. For nearly an hour they wandered through deserted byways seeking their destination. Finally they happened upon a street which wore a familiar look. Sure enough, half way down the block stood the house where they were quartered.

With glad cries the tired pair hurried to it. Here a fresh difficulty arose. They had no latch keys. Coming away that afternoon neither had thought to ask their landlady for a key. However, the second man figured he could pick the lock. He worked at it vainly for another half hour while his companion fidgeted about. Finally in disgust and despair he gave it up as a bad job, and the two of them went to a hotel where they spent the remainder of the night.

Now comes the point of the story: The man who could not remember the name of the street, nor the number of the house, was Barton the Memory Wizard. The man who could not master the lock was Houdini, the Handcuff King.

§ 178   The Mystery of Wednesday

A Broadway actor got carried away by the spirit of the prohibition times and remained carried away for several days. He came to himself in his own room without knowing exactly how he got there. A friend sat beside him.

"Hello," he said, as he opened his eyes, "what day is this?"

"This," said his friend, "is Thursday."

The invalid thought it over a minute.

"What became of Wednesday?" he asked.

§ 179   The Cockney and the Lady

Mrs. Pat Campbell has rather a caustic wit, as her friends—and more especially her enemies—can testify. On one occasion an interview with her was besought by a London playwright for whom personally Mrs. Campbell did not care very deeply. The playwright was a self-educated cockney. Sometimes in moments of forgetfulness he lapsed into the idioms of his youth.

He desired an opportunity to tender Mrs. Campbell a play he had just completed and in which he hoped she might consent to take the star rôle. She sat in silence while he read the script, act by act.

When he had finished he looked up, expecting some word of approval or at least of comment from his auditor. Mrs. Campbell, with a noncommital look on her face, said nothing at all. An awkward pause ensued.

"Ahem," said the dramatist at length, "I'm afraid my play seemed rather long to you?"

"Long? Well, rather!" drawled the lady. "It took you over two hours to read it—without the h's."

§ 180 Neither Here Nor There

Two French Canadians were traveling down a Quebec river in a houseboat. One of them knew the river and the other did not.

They anchored for the night on a bar. During the night the river rose and along toward daylight the craft went adrift. Three hours later the motion awoke one of the travelers. He poked his head out of the door. An entirely strange section of scenery was passing.

"Baptiste! Baptiste!" he yelled. "Get up! We ain't here some more."

"No, by gar!" said his companion after a quick glance at the surroundings—"we are twelve mile from here!"

§ 181 One of the Marvels of Science

On a hotel porch at a summer resort a visitor approached, in the dark, the spot where a beautiful young thing with bobbed hair and melting baby-blue eyes was sitting with an adoring youth.

As he neared the pair the newcomer heard her say: "Aren't the stars just beautiful tonight? I love to sit and look at the stars on a night like this and think about science. Science is so interesting, so wonderful; don't you think so? Now you take astronomy: Astronomers are such marvelous men! I can understand how they have been able to figure out the distance to the moon and to all the other planets, and the size of the sun, and how fast it travels and all. But how in the world do you suppose they ever found out the right names of all those stars?"

§ 182 The Proper End of a Caddy

In a Southern town is a lady, socially prominent, who enjoys the reputation of being a modern Mrs. Malaprop. The latest speech attributed to her had to do with the ancient game of Scotia.

"I've often thought," she said to a friend, "that I'd like to go in for golf, but somehow I have never gotten 'round to it; and, besides, I don't understand the first thing about playing it. Why, if I wanted to hit the ball I wouldn't know which end of the caddy to to take hold of."

§ 183 One Way to Beat the Game

Those who in their youth were addicted, or subsequently have been addicted to the good old American game of Seven-up will appreciate a little tale which Frank I. Cobb, of the New York *World*, told.

Cobb, who was born in Kansas and reared in Michigan, went to a town in the former state to call upon an elderly uncle. He arrived about suppertime. His aunt received him and welcomed him, telling him that her husband would probably be along shortly.

Time passed and still the old gentleman did not appear.

"I wonder," said Cobb, "whether Uncle Henry has been detained at his shop?"

"Oh, no," said his aunt in a resigned tone. "He's down at Number Two Engine House, claiming Low."

§ 184 Absolutely No Reason for It

Harry Beresford, the actor, was born in England but has lived long enough in America practically to have recovered from it. One fall a friend sent him two tickets for one of the World's Series ball games at the Polo Grounds, and he took with him to the game a newly arrived Englishman, a distant kinsman.

The stranger sat patiently enough through seven innings. The riotous proceeding was a puzzle to him but he was too polite to mention it. Then, when the mighty crowd, following the baseball custom, stood up to stretch, he rose, too, and started for the aisle.

"Hold on!" said Beresford. "It isn't over yet."

"I was only going to get a cup of tea, old chap," explained his guest.

"You can't get tea now," said Beresford; "the game goes right on."

"You mean to say there is no tea being served?" demanded the Englishman in amazement.

"Certainly not!" said Beresford.

"Well," demanded the other, "what, then, is the purpose of the damned game?"

§ 185 The Withdrawal of the Candidate

When Miss Annie Oakley, the famous rifle shot, was traveling through the country giving exhibitions of her skill at theatres, she reached a small town in Texas; and her manager inserted an advertisement in the home paper for a smart colored boy to assist in the performance. Applicants were instructed to apply at the stage door of the local opera house at one P. M. sharp.

When the manager arrived he found the passageway congested with little negroes, each eager to testify to his smartness. He made a selection, picking out a spry boy of about twelve. He took his applicant inside and stationed him near the wings.

"You will stand right here and not move," he said. "When the curtain goes up, Miss Oakley will come out and talk to the audience for a few moments. Then I will balance a small apple on your forehead and the lady will go over on the other side of the stage yonder and shoot it off.

The candidate grabbed for his hat, his eyes wildly rolling in search of the nearest path to safety.

"Mistah," he demanded, "who's goin' to shoot whut apple offer whose haid? Me, w'y I wouldn't let mah own mammy shoot no apple offer mah haid, let alone it's some stranger!"

And he was gone.

§ 186 A Peacemaker Who Blessed Himself

The proprietor of a drug store in a small Indiana town was issuing from the front door of his place when a small boy came tearing 'round the corner at top gait with his head down and butted squarely into him.

"Hey, kid!" demanded the druggist. "What's the matter?"

"I'm tryin' to keep two boys from gittin' into a fight," panted the youngster.

"Who are the boys?" asked the druggist.

"I'm one of 'em."

§ 187 The Long Wait at Burlington

Included in my list of acquaintances is a gentleman who promotes sporting events. Originally he promoted foot-races, later he conducted balloon ascensions and parachute drops at county fairs and carnivals. Still later, he turned aviator himself and bought an early model aeroplane with which, in the period when flying was more of a novelty than it is at present, he gave exhibitions.

The members of a Catholic congregation in a suburb of New

York City were striving to raise funds for a new rectory. They rented an old driving-park and gave a fair. For the crowning attraction on the final afternoon my friend was engaged to make a flight.

Now, the weather was lowering and the winds were capricious. Feeling a natural reluctance to trusting himself aloft under such circumstances the performer had recourse to an expedient he had employed on similar occasions. He sparred for time in the hope that darkness would come and so save him from taking the risk. He tinkered with his engine. He fiddled with the planes. He unscrewed this bolt and he screwed up that one.

The assembled crowd, grew impatient over the delay. Finally the parish priest, who was acting as master of ceremonies, approached the aeronaut and to him he said:

"My son, can't you go ahead and give us the exhibition you promised us and for which we already have paid you in advance? These people have already been waiting more than an hour and a half for you to go up."

"Father," said my friend, "there's a bunch of folks out in Burlington, Iowa, that have been waiting more'n eighteen months for me to go up."

§ 188 Where Jimmy's Education Really Was Shy

After a twenty years' absence a gentleman returned to the little New England town where he had been born and where he spent his boyhood. In the neighborhood in which he had been reared he found but one of the original residents remaining, an elderly Irish lady. She welcomed him back home again, and they fell to talking of the boys and girls with whom he had grown up. Finally he asked:

"Tell me, Mrs. Daly, what ever became of poor little Jimmy McKenna who used to live in the shanty right down the street here?"

"Poor, is it?" echoed Mrs. Daly. "Poor nothin'! Jimmy McKenna had no schoolin', as you may remember, but when he grew up he got into the truckin' business and from that he turned to contractin', and though he couldn't read and write, he made a million."

"Bully!" said the returned one. "And where is he now?"

"As to that," said Mrs. Daly, "I couldn't say. I hope, though, he's in Heaven. You see, sor, here about two years ago, Jimmy went down to the gravel pit where some of the byes was in swimmin', an' it bein' a warm day he took off his clothes and waded in, and he waded out too far and he got over his head and was drownded."

"Oh, that's too bad," said the visitor. "To think of a boy who had no better start than Jim McKenna had doing so well in the world, and then meeting an end like that! And he made a million, you say? And yet he couldn't read nor write."

"No," said Mrs. Daly, "nor swim."

§ 189   The Made-in-England Substitute

An American actor with a reputation for wit went to a luncheon given by a famous actress to several members of her supporting company. Among the guests of honor was an English leading man, who rather fancied himself—and showed it. He monopolized the conversation, speaking copiously and feelingly of himself, his personality and his merits.

From his place across the table the American eyed him with an enhancing disfavor. At length he turned to the man sitting next him on the right.

"Our British friend over there is by way of being a regular ass, isn't he?" he asked in a whisper.

"Oh I'd hardly go so far as to say that," answered his neighbor.

"Well, he'll do, won't he, till one comes?" said the American.

§ 190   Practically Destitute

Tilted back in his chair on the boatstore porch overlooking the river sat Cap'n Joe Fowler, as typical a Kentuckian as the fag end of the last century produced. A packet bound from Cincinnati to New Orleans, landed. Up the steep slope of the wharf came a tourist lady from up North somewhere. In the crook of her arm this lady bore the first Mexican hairless dog Cap'n Joe had ever seen. The animal was no larger than a full grown rat; in fact it rather resembled a rat. It seemed a miserable, naked, sickly little thing which shivered even though the air was balmy and flinched with vague uneasiness at every sound.

As the lady drew close Cap'n Joe stood up and made a low bow to her.

"I beg your pardon, madam," he said in his best company drawl, "but might a total stranger so far intrude upon you as to ask you a question?"

"You might," she said, her sharp accents in strong contrast to his deeper yet softer tones.

"Thank you, madam," he said. "The question, madam, relates to the dog you air carrying. Is that your own dog?"

"It is," she said.

"Is that the only dog you've got?"

"It is."

"Madam," said Cap'n Joe, "ain't you mighty nigh out of dog?"

§ 191   Assigning G. B. S. to His Place

When George Bernard Shaw, as a young man, emerged from his native Ireland and moved to England he began writing a column for a London weekly publication.

At that time Oscar Wilde was enjoying his vogue as a wit and an epigram-maker. One evening an acquaintance, calling upon Wilde, happened upon a copy of the paper to which Shaw was a contributor and reading therein one of Shaw's characteristic articles which was signed with the author's initials, said to his host:

"I say, Wilde, who is this chap G. B. S. who's doing a department for this sheet?"

"He's a young Irishman named Shaw," said Wilde. "Rather forceful, isn't he?"

"Forceful," echoed the other, "well, rather! My word, how he does cut and slash! He doesn't seem to spare any one he knows. I should say he's in a fair way to make himself a lot of enemies."

"Well," said Wilde, "as yet he hasn't become prominent enough to have any enemies. But none of his friends like him."

§ 192   A Voice from the Void

A group of big leaguers on their spring training trip were marooned by rain one morning so that they could not go to the ball field for practice. They sat under the portico of the Texas hotel where they were quartered and swapped small talk. An admiring ring of villagers surrounded them.

A languid, ragged negro drew near, anchoring himself at the outer edge of the audience. He laughed with loud appreciation at every sally from this or that visiting notable. He had the look about him of one seeking a suitable opportunity to solicit the gift of a small sum from some generous white stranger. But hour after hour passed with no proper opening until the forenoon was spent.

Suddenly the whistle on the canning factory across the street from the hotel let go with a blast and the hands came trooping out, bearing their lunch pails.

"Uh uh, dar she goes," said the darky, as the siren voice died away. "Hit's dinner time fur some folks—but jes' twelve o'clock fur me."

§ 193 Taking Nothing from Nothing

It was a striking coincidence that the new clerk at the soda-fountain was locally regarded as being a half-wit, and that the individual who approached him also happened to be the possessor of one of those fractional intellects.

"What'll it be?" inquired semi-idiot number one.

"A glass of plain soda without flavor."

"Without what flavor?"

The customer pondered this for a brief space.

"Without chocolate flavor," he said.

"You can't have it without chocolate flavor," answered the soda-jerker. Because we ain't got no chocolate. You'll have to take it without vanilly!"

§ 194 The Fate of Poor Harry

A cockney music-hall performer, to a congenial group of performers in London, was describing what had happened the night before to a brother actor whom he spoke of affectionately as "'Arry."

"Poor old 'Arry, 'e 'ad a most awful time. They wouldn't even let 'im finish. Before 'e was 'arf through with the first verse of 'is opening song they began giving 'im the rarsberry proper. And w'en 'e quit, them blokes in the gallery 'issed 'im right off the stage. They 'issed and 'issed and kept on 'issing even after 'e was out of sight. Right after 'im I 'ad to go on."

"How did your act go?" inquired one of the listeners.

"'Ow, I got over fine," said the modest vaudevillian. "But right in the middle of my act they starts 'issing 'Arry again."

§ 195 A Wholesale Order

The late Sam Davis, editor of the Carson *Appeal,* was known as the Oracle of the Nevada sage-brush. Once upon a time he was instructed by the San Francisco *Examiner* to meet Mme. Sarah Bernhardt at Reno and bring her over the mountains of California on her first tour of the Western Slope.

Davis was a most likable person. The great French actress became so fond of him that thereafter she declined to be interviewed by any other newspaperman during her sojourn on the Coast. If she had anything to say for publication, he said it for her.

The day came when the train bearing her private car was about to start on the long journey back East. As the locomotive bell was ringing, she put her hands upon his shoulders, kissed him upon either cheek, and then squarely upon the mouth, remarking, as she did so,

"The right cheek for the Carson *Appeal,* the left for the *Examiner,* the lips, my friend, for yourself."

"Madam," said Davis, without the slightest sign of bashfulness. "I also represent the Associated Press, which serves 380 papers west of the Mississippi River."

§ 196   This "Yes" and That "Yes"

A distinguished French diplomat lately put into a few words what I think is the best possible explanation yet offered as a reason for the failure of his countrymen to perceive what our national attitude is, touching on the post-war issues which so deeply concern France and, by the same token, the failure of our countrymen to make out what the people of France want and what they are striving for.

"To begin with," said the distinguished visitor, "the two races speak separate languages—always a bar to the adjustment of contrary points of view. But even where you find a Frenchman who speaks your tongue or an American who speaks mine, there still remains an obstacle.

"For example:

"When you set forth a proposition to an American and he says 'Yes,' he means, 'I'll do it.'

"But when you state the same thing to a Frenchman and he answers 'Yes,' what he really means is 'I understand what you are saying.'"

§ 197   Satisfactory in Every Respect

A Jewish friend of mine told me of a co-religionist of his who had acquired a fortune. This gentleman had a daughter of whose talents he was tremendously proud. The young woman sang. The father sent her to Europe to study voice culture under the best Continental teachers. Upon her return home he arranged that she should give a recital at Carnegie Hall. To the recital all his friends were invited.

In celebration of the event he decided also to give a banquet to a chosen group of some ten or fifteen at the Waldorf. But even in the heights of his parental enthusiasm prudence guided him. He summoned the prospective guests together and to them he said this:

"If Miriam should make a big hit I gif you fellows all vot you can eat und drink—the very best of everything, disregardless of expense. But of course there's a chance maybe she vont make a hit. She iss young und berhaps she gets scared ven she sees so many beeple all vaiting to lissen at her und, possibly, in that case, she might not go so vell. So, if she should fall down, ve vouldn't feel like a celebration, und there vould be no dinner, understand?"

At Carnegie Hall the father's fears were justified. The young woman immediately on her entrance was seized with a terrific attack of stage-fright. She uttered plaintive bleating sounds, then burst into tears and fled into the wings.

Almost before she vanished, her father had seized his hat, had dashed from the box where the family were seated, and, in a taxi-cab was hurrying down town to countermand the order for the spread. He reached the hotel, ascended in the elevator to the floor where he had engaged a private dining-room and ran through the hall to notify the head-waiter that there would be no feast.

But as he neared the door the sounds of brisk knife-and-fork play gave him added speed. He burst open the door and stood transfixed on the threshold. Only the place which had been reserved for him at the head of the table was vacant. At every other place sat one of his friends, stowing away expensive victuals and costly wines at tremendous speed.

"Vait!" shouted the agonized father. "Vait! Didn't I say only ve should have a dinner if Miriam was a success?"

A spokesman for the others raised his face from the terrapin stew.

"Vell," he said, "ve liked her!"

And went right on eating.

§ 198   Precisely the Right Word

Sometimes a speaker, casting about for exactly the right word, hits on the wrong word and yet, paradoxically, the wrong word seems exactly to sum up the situation which the orator has sought to describe.

Down at Whitehall, which is in the state of Virginia not many miles from Richmond, a negro farm-hand, whose first name was Levi, met a violent and sudden death. He was ploughing a corn patch when a thunder shower came up. In the midst of the storm, a bolt of lightning struck the tree under which he had taken shelter and scarcely enough of him was left for purposes of burial.

Nevertheless, his family and friends did give him an elaborate funeral. A colored minister, with a reputation for eloquence, was imported at considerable cost to preach the sermon.

The preacher very soon got into his swing while the congregation swayed and moaned and gave vent to muffled hallelujahs and amens. He came to his climax:

"De call fur our pore brother wuz swift an' suddin. He did not linger fur long months on de bed of pain an' affliction. He did not suffer an' waste away. No suh, de Lawd jest teched an electric button in de skies an' summarized Levi!"

§ 199   Touching on London Weather

The other day *Punch* had a picture of an old gentleman about to climb into a taxi to escape a terrific snowstorm.

"Cabby," he says, "it's a miserable winter day, isn't it?"

"Guvinor," answers the frost-bitten taxi driver, "I pass you my word I've been out since early mornin' and I ain't seen a single butterfly."

But, offhand, I'd say the prize under this heading goes to Fred Greig, the New York art critic, for his telling of a personal experience.

At the age of twelve he was riding on the front seat of a Fleet Street bus. Although the month was July, rain had been coming down, practically without cessation, for more than a week. An East Indian, garbed all in white, went past, slopping along the sidewalk under an umbrella.

The driver aimed his whip at the dark stranger.

"Wot's that?" he asked.

"That," said Young Greig, who at school had been studying up on Oriental history and customs, "is a Parsee."
"And wot's a Parsee?"
"A sun-worshipper."
"Well," said the driver, "'e must be 'ere on a blinkin' vacation."

§ 200   The Detour in the Bridal Path

A young couple, on their honeymoon, spent two days in a small Southern city. When they got off the train an old negro man, who served as porter, runner, chief bell-boy and general factotum for the hotel greeted them at the depot. He took charge of their hand-baggage and led the way for them to an ancient vehicle.

As he drove them along the street the young husband took him into their confidence:

"Now, look here, Uncle," he said, "we don't want anybody here to know that we've just been married. Probably some of the other guests will speak to you about us and we count on you to throw them off the track."

"Boss," said the old man, "don't you an' the young lady worry. Jest trust me. 'Taint nobody goin' fin' out by axin' me questions."

But when the pair came down from their room that evening for supper, they found themselves a target for the interested stares of everyone else in the dining room. All eyes were turned in their direction. At the conclusion of a somewhat hurried and decidedly embarrassed meal, the young man hunted up the old negro.

"Say," he demanded, "I thought you promised not to give us away, and yet everybody around this hotel is looking at us and grinning."

"Boss," said the old negro fervently, "ef dey's learned the truff, dey didn't none of 'em learn it frum me—naw, suh!"

"Well, did anybody speak to you about us after we registered?"
"Yas, suh, sevr'l."
"Did any of them want to know whether we were on our wedding trip?"
"Yas, suh, they did."
"Well, what did you say to them?"
"I sez to 'em: 'Naw, indeedy, them young folks ain't no bridal couple—they's jest a couple of chums.'"

§ 201 Tuesday May Have Been Worse

Out in Australia two Cockneys were sentenced to die for an atrocious murder. As the date for execution drew nearer the nerves of both of them became more and more shaken. Dawn of the fatal morning found them in a state of terrific funk.

As they sat in the condemned cell waiting the summons to march to the gallows one of the pair said:

"Me mind's all in a whirl. I carn't seem to remember anything. I carn't even remember what dye of the week it is."

"It's a Monday," stated his companion in misfortune.

"Ow!" said the first one, "wot a rotten wye to start the week!"

§ 202 A Touch of Summer Complaint

A small negro boy went to a physician in Natchez to be treated for a painful sensation in one of his ears. The doctor examined and found the ear was full of water.

"How did this happen," he asked after he had drained the ear—"been going in swimming?"

"Naw, suh," said the little darky—"been eatin' watermelon!"

§ 203 He Never Went There Anyhow

A chronic imbiber in a New England city was clinging to a lamppost one Sunday morning when a stranger came along and addressed him.

"Sir," inquired the stranger, "can you tell me where the Second Presbyterian Church is?"

"Mister," answered the weary one, "I don't even know where the first one is!"

§ 204 Where Republicans Are Scarce

That famous wit, the late Private John Allen of Mississippi, while a member of Congress used to tell a story illustrative of political conditions in his home state.

According to Allen, there was a man in his county who hankered to hold public office. "Every time we had a Democratic primary," said Allen, "this fellow turned up, seeking the nomination for one job or another. But always he was turned down—he never made the grade.

"Finally, he just naturally abandoned the Democratic party. He said the Democrats didn't appreciate true worth; that they didn't know real merit when they saw it. So he turned Republican.

"At the next election he entered himself as a candidate for sheriff on the Republican ticket. Well, sir, that fellow certainly made a spirited campaign. If ever a man worked to bring out the full strength of the white Republican vote he was the man. He canvassed the county from end to end. He spoke at every cross-roads blacksmith shop and every country schoolhouse. He left no stone unturned.

"Well, election day came. He got exactly two votes—and was arrested that night for repeating!"

§ 205 The Sole Drawback to Utter Success

Probably there are a dozen differing versions of this story but the one I like best of all is the one I heard some twenty-five years ago. Mandy, the cook, left her employer's kitchen early one afternoon to attend a marriage ceremony in the colored quarter of the town.

The high contracting parties to the union were to be distinguished members of local Afro-American Society, and Mandy, as one of the invited guests, anticipated an enjoyable evening. Nor, as it would appear, was she disappointed. For, when she appeared at 8 o'clock next morning she gave her mistress an enthusiastic account of the affair.

"Miss May," she declared, "dat suttinly wuz a scrumptious weddin'! I reckin very few w'ite folks an' no niggers at all in dis town ever did have a weddin' dat wuz de beat of dish yere one. I only wisht you mout a' seen de bride yore own se'f. My! My! Dat gal suttinly wuz got up regardless. Her weddin' gown wuz all hollered out at de top an' 'twuz trimmed 'round de aidges wid rows of w'ite vermin. An' her hair wuz done up high on her haid in a pampydo, an' right in de middle of it wuz stuck one of dese yere w'ite regrets. And de contras' betwixt dat black pamp and dat w'ite regret—*Ump huh!*

"Dat wuz only jest de beginnin'. De parlor wuz all trimmed wid smileaxes an' de ushers dey all wore w'ite gloves an' swaller-tail coats. An' they wuz a string band of eight pieces to play de weddin' march.

"Miss May, you sho'ly also an' likewise should a' seen de table whar de bridal feast wuz spread. Dey had chicken croquettes at ever' plate an' ice-cream 'twell you couldn't rest, an' punch made out of gin an' a whole soup-syringe full of simon salad.

"De weddin' feast lasted all night an' tain't finished 'till yit. Dem niggers is still over dere dancin'. I jest stole away to cook you up a lil' breakfust an' den, befo' I washes de dishes, I aims to run on back fur to tek a hand in de las' quodrille."

"But Mandy," said her mistress, "you haven't said anything about the bridegroom?"

"Nome, I lef' him out a-puppos. He wuz de only drawback dey wuz to dat weddin'."

"Oh, I'm so sorry. Was he drunk?"

"I don't know ef he wuz or ef he wuzn't; but Miss May, wid dat gal got up de way she wuz an' wid all dat music an' all dem vittles, dat nasty, low-flung, kinky-haided nigger, he never did come."

§ 206   Sure Damnation for Somebody

As a boy, I had this one from my father. I seem to recall that he said it actually had happened before the Civil War in the remote Southern settlement where my forbears lived for upwards of a hundred years.

Into the community there came a dashing stranger. He had no visible means of support, but such was his ingratiating personality that speedily he became a favorite among the simple pioneers. Shortly after this advent the local Methodist circuit rider organized a protracted meeting.

The last night of the meeting was devoted to foreign missions. The preacher rose to inspired heights of eloquence. In vivid colors he painted the forlorn and ignorant state of the heathen and the crying need of funds with which to spread the Christian doctrine in far-off pagan lands. At the psychological moment, when the assemblage had been worked up into a fit frame of mind for contributing heavily, the preacher called upon the fascinating stranger to pass the hat. It developed later that upon that very day the latter had gone to the minister and volunteered for this service.

He passed the hat. He passed it until it was filled to the brim with the offerings of the multitude. When his round of the pews was completed, instead of marching up to the pulpit and depositing the funds there, the newcomer began to edge toward the door of the church, and, incidentally, toward where his horse was tethered outside. Observing this suspicious maneuver, the preacher was filled with a horrid dread.

"My brother," he called out, "if you go away from the house of God with that there money you will be damned!"

On the words, the stranger vanished out of the door. The voice of a resident in a back pew broke the horrified hush which followed.

"Well, parson," he said, "ef he ain't went, I'll be damned!"

§ 207   The Final Smash

There was company at the farmhouse that evening and Mrs. Purdy, who had her share and more of New Hampshire thrift, was moved through hospitality to offer the suggestion that possibly the guests might like a glass apiece of fresh apple cider. There was unanimous endorsement of the idea. So Mr. Purdy got a china pitcher from the pantry and started for the cellar where the cider was stored.

The cellar was dark and the steps leading to it were steep. Half day down he stumbled and dropped with a resounding thump upon the brick floor six feet below, where he lay half-stunned.

Upstairs in the parlor they heard the sound of his fall. With alarm and wifely solicitude writ large upon her face Mrs. Purdy ran to the head of the cellar steps.

"Paw," she called down, "did you break the pitcher?"

From the void below a determined voice answered her back:

"No, I didn't, but by Judas Priest, I'm goin' to now!"

§ 208   Making It Unanimous

A few years ago Colonel Hal Corbett, one of my oldest friends, came up from the South to stay a week with me in New York. Three of us, all old cronies of his but all living in the North, met him at the train.

At his suggestion we dropped into the café of the Imperial Hotel on Broadway. Hotels had cafés in those days, and Corbett was thirsty, he said. We lined up at the bar, facing a genial gentleman in a white jacket and a white apron.

Now it so happened that at the moment all three of us, for one reason or another, were riding on the well-known water wagon—a circumstance of which Corbett was not aware and probably one which he had never dreamed could be possible.

He turned to me:

"What's it going to be?" he asked genially.

I said:

"A glass of buttermilk."

He gave a start of surprise. But, like a true Kentucky gentleman, he did not voice his emotions. He turned to the second member of the group.

"And what do you take?" he inquired hopefully.

"Oh," said Number 2, "I don't want anything except a plain lemonade."

Corbett's eyes widened as he waved his arm toward the third man.

"And yours?" he inquired.

"Mine is a ginger ale," was the answer.

Corbett faced front:

"Mr. Barkeeper," he said, "I'm going to be in the fashion while I'm here if it kills me. Give me a quart of blueing."

§ 209 Advice from Expert Sources

There used to be a ticket seller with the old Yankee Robertson circus who owned a big green parrot. The parrot's perch swung from the roof of the ticket wagon and there the bird would sit just above her owner's head.

The ticket man had a line of patter which he constantly chanted as the patrons surged in front of his wicket twice on each week day of the season—before the afternoon performance and again before the evening performance.

"Don't shove, friends!" he would say. "Don't crowd! Take your time. Give everybody a chance!"

The parrot memorized this speech. She even learned to mimic her master's exact tone. Repeating his admonition was a favorite part of her repertoire.

One afternoon when business was over he went away, forgetting to close the slide on his window. When he returned a little later his pet was gone. Immediately he organized a search party to look for the truant bird.

Half a mile distant from the show lot, in a field, he found Poll. She was reared back on the ground, practically featherless. About her circled and swirled a great flock of crows, cawing joyously. Every instant nearly, one of the crows, twisting out of the circle, would dart down and pluck a souvenir of green plumage from the disheveled alien.

And each time this happened Poor Poll, in a beautiful imitation of her owner's voice and accent would shriek out:

"Don't shove, friends! Don't crowd! Take your time! Give everybody a chance!"

§ 210 A Seeker after Hidden Facts

When the New York Central inaugurated its fast service between New York and Chicago there was a great pother along the main line. Employees of whatsoever rank were instructed that the paramount consideration was to get the Twentieth Century Limited through on schedule. If the slightest mishap occurred to the train all hands were charged to forward prompt reports to headquarters, giving the complete details.

At a small flag-stop west of Albany, the station-agent was a callow youth. By enthusiasm and a sense of his responsibilities he made up, though, for what he lacked in experience. In addition to being the ticket-seller he also was the despatcher.

One wintry evening just at dusk he caught, passing over the wire, word that the Twentieth Century Limited was two hours behind time. What had retarded her he did not learn, but he knew wherein his duty lay.

He lit his lantern, sharpened a pencil, and got out a notebook, then sat him down to bide his time. Ten minutes before the belated Limited was due to whiz past he left the station, walked eastward along the tracks a quarter of a mile and posted himself between the rails.

Soon the headlight hove into sight. In an effort to make up the precious lost minutes the engineer was driving his locomotive at tremendous speed. Suddenly far ahead he saw the dancing signal of a lantern. He gave her the brakes; he gave her the sand. Passengers in the coaches behind were slammed up against the end bulkheads of their berths. With sparks flying from her wheels, the snorting mogul stopped not fifty feet distant from where the youth stood. The engineer and his fireman dropped down from the cab and ran forward, sputtering questions.

The station-agent stilled them with an authoritative gesture. He put down his lantern on the right-of-way, braced his pad in the crook of his elbow, poised his pencil ready to record their answers and said briskly:

"Now then, boys, tell me—what detained you?"

§ 211   The Curfew in Nebraska

Of course, in these days, when no community is so small or so obscure or so old-fashioned that it lacks service stations and jazz orchestras and schemes for a proposed Civic Center, this story no longer could be made to apply in any American town.

As the tale runs, a man who had been born and reared in a remote Nebraska country-seat moved to New York where he succeeded in business. Years later a friend from his former home came to see him. Naturally, talk drifted back to childhood scenes and memories.

"I guess the old town hasn't changed much, has it, Jim?" asked the New Yorker.

"Not much," said Jim. "She's pretty much the same."

"I presume they still blow the curfew whistle at nine o'clock every night just as they started to do shortly before I moved East?"

"Naw, they had to quit that after a few months. It woke everybody up!"

§ 212   The Reward of the Early Riser

In a small New England town, there used to be an Irishman of convivial habits. He *convived* in season and out of it. In fact, he was in a fair way to qualify as the village drunkard.

Late one night—perhaps I should say early one morning—half a dozen natives were on their homeward way after a social evening at the groggery. At the foot of the main street they stumbled upon the recumbent form of the inebriate, whose name was McGuire. Now, they were what used to be known in the old pre-Volstead days as "pickled." But he was absolutely petrified. At sight of their friend peacefully asleep, thwartwise of the sidewalk, one of the party had an inspiration.

"Here," he said, "is a beautiful chance to cure old McGuire of boozing. Let's carry him out to the cemetery and stick him in an open grave, if we can find one. Then we'll hang around and wait until he comes to. He'll think he's been buried alive, and the shock will be a lesson to him."

The suggestion met instantaneous approval. The slumberer was picked up by his arms and legs and borne to the burying-ground. Circumstances and chance favored the conspirators. In an ancient vault from which the roof was missing they found an abandoned coffin. Into the empty box they snuggled their victim and, placing the crumbling lid over him for a coverlet, they hid themselves behind adjacent tombstones to await the climax of their plot.

The wait was a long one, but all of them stayed on, allured by the prospect that patience eventually would be rewarded. At length dawn showed in the east. Daylight broke; the sun came up and presently it was six o'clock. Prompt on the hour the whistle of a near-by shoe-factory cut into the morning calm with a shrill siren whoop.

At this blast Mr. McGuire stirred. He threw up his arms, displacing the lid, sat up in his narrow form-fitting casket, and blinked in the rosy light. Then, as he comprehended where he was, a triumphant smile split his face.

"By cripes!" he said exultantly, "'tis the Resurrection Day and I'm the first son-of-a-gun up!"

§ 213   A Competition Which Was Open to All

Two gentlemen connected with the cloakings and suitings trade went to the Catskills on their vacations. Shortly after their arrival they took a tramp among the hills.

"I wish," said one, "that I owned that tallest mountain yonder and that it was all solid gold."

"That's a lovely thought," said the other approvingly. "Say, Ike, if that mountain was solid gold and you owned it all by yourself would you give me some of it, huh?"

"Certainly I wouldn't!" said Ike. "Wish yourself a mountain."

§ 214   Not the Order of the Bath

In a small city which we will not name, there lived a maiden lady who, for convenience, shall here be called Miss Henrietta Blank. She was of an old family and she was prominent in club life. In fact, so constantly was she engaged by her communal activities that, according to local rumor, she rarely found time for applying soap and water to her neck and ears.

On a certain occasion a patriotic organization, of which she was a member, was holding a session. Miss Blank was not present. The presiding officer, a lady civically celebrated for her ready wit, was delegated to choose the members of a special committee.

After deliberation she made this announcement:

"For the members of this committee I shall name Mrs. Major Jones, Mrs. Dr. Robinson and Miss Henrietta Blank."

"Oh, Madam Chairman," put in a member, "I'm sure I do not wish to be unkind, but this is really a very important matter where decision is needed and prompt action. Don't you think you should substitute someone else for dear Miss Henrietta—she's so wishy-washy!"

The presiding officer's retort was instantaneously delivered:

"The person in question may be wishy," she said, "but the Lord in Heaven knows she is not washy!"

§ 215   The Embarrassing Broad A

A Chicago man visiting in London was invited to a ball where everybody except himself talked with an exceedingly broad *a*, as people will do in England—and Boston, Mass. The accent was puzzling to his Chicago ears but he did his best.

He danced with the wife of his host. The lady spoke with an especially broad accent; also she ran somewhat to flesh. When they had finished the round of the floor she was panting in a repressed and well-bred way.

"Shall we try another whirl?" inquired the Chicago man.

"Not now," she said; "I'm darnced out."

"Oh, no," said the Chicago man, "not darn stout—just nice and plump, ma'am."

§ 216   Tributes to the Late Lamented Ones

Out West a dump car broke its couplings and went on a wild trip down grade. At a switch it was derailed, turning over on its side and instantly crushing to death a Mexican laborer.

It fell to the lot of the foreman of the gang to which the victim belonged to render a report of the tragedy. This foreman, whose name I believe was Cassidy,—at any rate, it was a good Hibernian name,—got along fairly well with his literary labors until he came to the final space in the printed form, opposite the question: *Remarks?* Mr. Cassidy studied awhile and then inserted these words:

"He never made none!"

The companion-piece to this has for a setting a stretch of a Southern line whereon a freight train had killed a cow, the property of a farmer. Mr. Dugan, the resident section boss, interviewed the owner of the slain animal and then proceeded to fill out a blank for the subsequent use of the claim agent.

Painstakingly Mr. Dugan entered references relating to the circumstances under which the fatality occurred, also the age, color and presumed value of the lately deceased cow and other particulars, as gleaned from eye-witnesses and from the bereft farmer. But he was stumped when he came to the words: "State disposition of the remains?"

He was stumped, but not for long; he set down this:
"She was kind and gentle!"

§ 217 And the Point of Order Was Sustained

Back in 1890 George Clark, of Waco, and James S. Hogg, of Tyler, were candidates for the Democratic gubernatorial nomination in Texas. At the convention, Hogg won.

Clark, the defeated aspirant, was not satisfied with the methods used to bring about his opponent's nomination. He and some of his followers bolted the convention and he ran as an independent candidate. In this emergency, both he and Hogg sought the endorsement of the Republican organization.

In 1890 the Republican party in Texas was even more of a minority party than it is to-day. Its leaders mainly were white men, but the rank and file overwhelmingly was black; so that when the Republican state convention met at Fort Worth the delegates nearly all were negroes.

The Clark people controlled the preliminary organization. The temporary chairman called upon the Reverend Sin Killer Griffin to open the proceedings with prayer. Sin Killer was a famous revivalist hailing from near the border between Texas and Arkansas. He was fat and black and had a mighty voice. In thunderous tones he invoked the blessings of the Almighty upon the assemblage. And just before he concluded, he roared out these words:

"An' finally, Oh Lawd, bless thy sarvant, George Clark, an' mek 'im gov'ner of de great state of Texas." Instantly a roar of mingled protest and approbation arose. The tumult continued for several minutes. Finally down in the body of the hall a bullvoiced black politician obtain recognition from the presiding officer.

"Mista' Cheerman!" he shouted, "I teks de floor to mek a motion:

I moves dat de name of George Clark be oxpunged from dat air prayer an' dat de name of de Honor'ble Jeemses Stephens Hogg be substituted therefur."

The Sin Killer was still upon his feet.

"Mista' Cheerman," he proclaimed, "I speaks to a p'int of order."

"State the point of order."

"De genelman's motion is pintedly out of awder fur de reason dat de prayer in question done went to Heaven more'n five minutes ago!"

§ 218   The Light That Lies in Bankers' Eyes

This offering has to do with a leading financier of a Middle Western city—a gentleman renowned for his personal vanity as well as for his cold-blooded sagacity in financial matters. The gentleman in question had a glass eye; but, so well did it match its fellow, that it was a point of pride with the owner that no one, lacking full information on the subject, could tell at a glance the artificial from the real one. His name was Oliver. One day, a citizen of the community, who was a chronic borrower, emerged from Mr. Oliver's bank after an unsuccessful effort to negotiate a loan, and on the sidewalk met a friend.

"Say," he said, "you know a lot of people in this town have never been able to tell which one of old Oliver's eyes was his glass eye. Well, I know. I found out awhile ago when I was in there trying to get him to let me make a ninety-day note. All the time we were talking I was watching him and I finally caught onto the secret. It's the left one."

"How do you know it's the left one?" asked his friend.

"Because it was the one that seemed to have a kindly human gleam in it."

§ 219   A Call for the Prohibited Stuff

A hand-picked group of American bankers went to France to study financial and economic conditions with a view to pooling a large loan on some Continental industrial properties. Naturally, the prospective borrowers exerted themselves to win the favor of the distinguished visitors.

The hosts labored under the impression, seemingly, that, because America has in force a Prohibition law, their guests must be exceedingly thirsty. Accordingly, in whatsoever part of the republic the party stopped, the pick of the vintages of that particular district was served. There was wine for breakfast, wine for luncheon, wine for dinner, wine for late supper and unlimited wines between meals.

Now, one of the group from the States was a native son of the far West. Through his life he had been an imbiber but an exceedingly moderate one. Howsomever, if his gorge rose and his palate grew jaded because of the irrigating facilities constantly provided by his hospitable French friends, he gave no sign, for he was a polite man.

At length the expedition arrived in Paris, after a tour of what seemed to the Westerner all the vineyards in France. On the day of his arrival he met an old acquaintance now residing abroad.

"Say," declared his friend, "this reunion calls for a celebration. You've got to dine with me tonight at the Golden Snail. I'll order some food there that'll make your eyes bug out.

"As a further inducement, I might add that the Golden Snail restaurant has as good a cellar as there is in this town. You can have whatever you want to drink and as much of it as you can hold. Now, there's a Burgundy——"

"Hold on!" said the Californian. "Do you mean that? Can I really have what I crave most in this world? It may be hard to find in this town—I warn you of that."

"You name the brand and I'll engage to find it."

"All right, then. You look up a good reliable local bootlegger and see if you can get me about two quarts of drinking water."

§ 220   The Perfect Introduction

In his second race for president W. J. Bryan was beaten. In fact, it will be recalled that in all his races for the presidency Mr. Bryan has been beaten. But in the 1900 campaign, while Democracy lost nationally, certain local triumphs were here and there achieved. A city in northern New York which usually went Republican by an overwhelming majority reversed itself and elected for Mayor a German flour miller.

It was felt that the victory deserved suitable celebration. The local Democrats organized a monster rally. The Great Commoner accepted an invitation to attend the jubilation and deliver the principal address. It was deemed fitting that the newly chosen Mayor should sponsor the distinguished guest. Now, the Mayor was a good citizen and his flour was above reproach, but he was no orator; indeed, until this occasion came, he had never in all his life formally addressed a public assemblage.

The great evening came and a great host gathered. Side by side on the platform sat Bryan and the Mayor-elect. The latter's secretary had written a suitable speech for His Honor's use, and His Honor laboriously had memorized it. But as he waited the cue to launch himself in his new rôle it was plain to be seen that the gentleman was in a distressful state. He was deathly pale. Perspiration rolled down his face in streams, wilting his collar; and when finally he stood up, all present could tell from his expression that the last shreds and remnants of the carefully rehearsed oration treacherously had departed from him.

He choked and gulped. Then, seizing inspiration out of sheer desperation he made what Mr. Bryan subsequently declared to be the most complete speech of introduction that Bryan in all his long career on the stump and the rostrum ever has heard or ever expects to hear.

"Ladies und chentelmen," said the Mayor, "I haf been asked to bresent to you Mister Vilhelm Chenninks Bryne, who vill speak. I haf now done so! He vill now do so!"

§ 221   An Answer Right Off the Ice

Just before he started on that famous Arctic expedition of his which was crowned with success, the late Admiral Robert E. Peary boarded a train at New Orleans. He settled down in the smoking compartment to enjoy a cigar. Presently there entered a rather self-sufficient young man who took the seat adjoining and engaged Peary in conversation.

"Well," he began, "I'm off on a long hard trip."

"Yes? Is that so?" said Peary, politely.

"Yep. I go clear through to Louisville. Traveling far yourself?"

"Yes, a fair distance," said Peary.

"Well, I'm bound clear through to Louisville, as I was saying. Pretty tiresome trip, too—all the way through from New Orleans to Louisville."

"Probably so," agreed Peary.

"By the way," said the young chap, "you didn't tell me where you were going?"

"No," said Peary, "that's a fact, I didn't."

"Well, I don't suppose you're as used to traveling as I am," said the young fellow. "Whereabouts are you headed for, anyhow?"

"Me?" said Peary. "Oh, I'm only going to the North Pole."

§ 222 Where He Could Go for Thirty Cents

"About three months ago," so a friend of mine said, "fourteen of us were waiting in a line at the Grand Central Station to purchase fares on outgoing trains. Some among us had but a few minutes to spare. All of us, naturally, were in a hurry to transact the business and get ourselves and our luggage aboard the cars.

"All of a sudden an inebriated person burst like an alcoholic bombshell among us. Ignoring the rules of procedure, he shoved his way to the front, elbowing and jostling those already in line, until he reached the ticket window. Upon the shelf he slammed down a quarter and a nickle and in a loud voice stated his wishes.

" 'Gimme a ticket for San Francisco,' he said.

" 'You can't go to San Francisco for thirty cents,' stated the ticket-seller.

" 'Well, where can I go, then?' he asked.

"And with one voice, all fourteen of us told him."

§ 223 Overlooking No Side Bets

Jimmie and Arthur, aged respectively six and ten, were spending a week with their grandmother, who was wealthy and generous, while their parents were away from home on a visit.

A few nights before Christmas the youngsters were getting ready for bed. Their grandmother was in an adjoining room waiting for them to retire so she might turn out the light.

Arthur said his prayers and crawled under the covers. Jimmie, still on his knees, proceeded to petition Heaven for an extensive line of Christmas presents. As he progressed, his voice rose louder and louder. Also he began to repeat himself. He spoke somewhat after this fashion:

"And, Oh, Lord, please send me a soldier-suit, and a tool-chest—a big tool-chest, Lord—and a watch and a drum and a horn and a toy wagon and——"

Annoyed, the older brother raised up and interrupted:

"Say," he demanded, "you needn't be praying so loud; the Lord ain't deaf."

"I know he ain't," said Jimmie, "but Grandma is."

§ 224 The Lick That Won the Victory

There was a Scotchman who had a wife and she had strong views upon the subject of strong drink. One night he came home late and badly befuddled. He managed to get inside the house without awakening her, but, in order to reach his own sleeping quarters, it was necessary for him to pass through her room.

On its threshold he had an inspiration. He got down on his hands and knees and started to crawl across the intervening floor-space. But when he was just alongside of her bed he chanced to brush against the coverlids and the lady was aroused.

In the darkness, mistaking the dark bulk that was in arm's reach of her for the family house-dog, she said. "Come, Jocko, Jocko!"

"Whereupon, at that verra moment," said the husband next day when recounting the event to a crony, "I had the rare intelligence to lick her hand."

§ 225 No Closed Season on Fanchon

When a Frenchman goes hunting he takes the sport rather seriously. In certain districts there isn't much in the way of game for him to kill. So the native makes up for this by wearing a most elaborate and fanciful costume.

An American, visiting in the château country, was invited by his host to go for a rabbit hunt. With a borrowed gun in his hands and wearing his oldest clothes, the American went. Alongside him, as they trudged through the cover, walked the Frenchman, gorgeous in gaiters and belted jacket, with a pheasant's feather curling from the brim of his hat.

Presently a bunny darted from a thicket. The American raised his fowling-piece.

"Don't shoot!" cried out his host. "That's Armand, a great pet of ours. We never shoot at Armand."

A little further along a second rabbit hopped into view. Again the visitor made ready to fire and again his host detained him with:

"That one is Pierre. We never shoot at Pierre, either."

Almost immediately, a third rabbit, a long rangy animal, came bouncing into sight.

"Shoot! Shoot!" cried the Frenchman, throwing his own gun to his shoulder. "That is Fanchon. We always shoot at Fanchon."

§ 226 Down and Out for the Count

Dr. Jones, a young physician with a growing practice, had been going night and day for the better part of a week. If it wasn't the stork busy in one part of the town it was the malaria microbe busy in another. He kept up his round of visits until exhausted nature demanded a respite.

He staggered into his house in the evening completely fagged out, and tumbled into bed, telling his wife that, excepting upon a matter of life and death, he was not to be called.

At two o'clock in the morning she came to his bedside, shook him, pinched him, slapped him in the face with a wet washrag and finally roused him to a state of semi-consciousness. Mrs. Smith, physically the biggest woman in town, had been seized with a heart attack at her home on the next street and he was wanted immediately.

He struggled to his feet, threw a few garments on over his night-clothes, caught up his emergency kit and in a sort of walking trance made his way to the Smith residence. A frightened member of the household led him to the sick-room. There the patient lay, a great mountain of flesh, her features congested and her breath coming in laborious panting. Dr. Jones took her pulse and her temperature and examined her eyes, her lips and her tongue. Then he perched himself in a half recumbent attitude upon the side of the bed, put his right ear against her left breast and said:

"Madam, will you kindly start counting very slowly? Now then, one-two-three and so on. Go on until I tell you to stop."

Obediently the sufferer began.

The next thing Dr. Jones knew was when a shaft of bright morning sunlight fell upon his face, and, drowsily, he heard a faint, weak female voice saying:

"Nine-thousand-seven-hundred and one, nine-thousand-seven-hundred and two———!"

§ 227 The Plan of the Shut-In

A gentleman who resided in the heart of the Corn Belt paid his first visit to Chicago. With him came two friends. The three of them occupied one large room in a Loop hotel.

On the second day of sight-seeing the Corn Belter's feet gave out on him. Leaving his companions to finish out the evening at a theatre, he returned to the hotel and went to bed. When the other two arrived, shortly before midnight, they found the door of their room locked. They pounded on the panels until the sleeper awakened.

"Let us in, Zach!" said one of them impatiently.

"Let yourself in," he answered. "The key is outside there in the hall."

"How does it come to be outside when you're inside?" demanded one of them.

"Oh, after I got undressed I throwed it over the transom so's you fellers could git in without no trouble. It must be layin' on the floor."

They found the key and admitted themselves. As they entered one of them asked:

"Say, Zach, what would you have done, locked in here this way, if there'd been a fire?"

"Why, I wouldn't have went."

§ 228 The Quick-Thinking Referee

In the ninth inning the score was a tie, with two men on bases for the home team and one out. Naturally the excitement was intense — for this game was for blood money and the Afro-American championship of the county. The umpire, a small, dapper man, a barber by profession and naturally mild-mannered, was filled with regret that the opportunity for prominence had lured him into taking this job. He had a sincere conviction that, no matter what decision he made next, somebody would feel aggrieved.

The manager of the side at bat sent in, as an emergency hitter, a large, broad-shouldered person with a reputation for being very touchy on matters affecting his personal interests or his personal honor. As this individual moistened the bat after the approved manner he cast a glowering look upon the umpire who crouched back of the catcher.

"Jedge 'em an' jedge 'em right, lil' nigger," he growled, "else six of yore friends 'll be wearin' w'ite gloves 'bout dis time day after to-mor'."

The pitcher wound up and sped the ball across.

"Strike one!" shrilled the umpire.

As the batter turned his head to scowl at the referee the pitcher shot another across—a perfect one, waist high and right over the center of the plate. *Plunk!* it landed in the catcher's mitt.

"Two!" chanted the umpire.

The big darky dropped his bat. He fixed both brawny hands

on the throat of the umpire and squeezed hard. There was murder in his eyes.

"Two whut?" he demanded as though he could not believe his outraged ears.

"Too high fur a strike!" quavered the umpire with magnificent presence of mind. "Yas, suh, entirely too high fur a strike."

§ 229 George, the Forbearing

When Millie came on a Saturday night to bring the week's washing her comely, pleasant brown face was disfigured by a swollen black contusion which began at her left eye and extended downward until it covered her cheek.

"Oh, Millie," said her distressed employer, "what a dreadful bruise! How did it ever happen?"

"A nigger man hit me," explained Millie simply.

"Oh, that's terrible!" exclaimed the white lady. "I hope—I hope it wasn't your husband that struck you?"

"No'm, Mizz Harrison, 'twuzn't him. Gawge, he don't never hit me. He treats me mo' lak a friend than a husband."

§ 230 An Old One and Its Younger Half-Brother

Everybody does know—or should know—the ancient wheeze of the theatre manager who posted a sign in his house: "Don't Smoke—Remember the Iroquois Fire," and of the wag who wrote under this the added warning: "Don't Spit—Remember the Johnstown Flood." A half-brother to this yarn, of somewhat newer vintage, however, comes from a regular army post.

A newly enlisted private, still unskilled in military etiquette, flung a lighted cigarette end on the parade ground. The first sergeant of his company saw the crime committed. He made the offender pick up the smouldering butt and then stand at attention while being scolded at length.

When mess call sounded, the new hand was tardy for his meal.

"What made you late?" demanded the sergeant.

"Oh," said the private, "I walked down to the river to spit."

§ 231 Corroboration from On High

Little Florence was inclined to over-exaggeration; also she was overly timid in some regards. Her mother was striving to rid her of both faults.

One afternoon Florence was playing in the front yard. A fox-terrier, belonging to a neighbor, darted at her playfully. With a shriek of fright Florence fled indoors and never stopped running until she had reached the room upstairs where her mother sat.

"What's the matter?" asked Mrs. Marshall.

"Mamma," said Florence, "a great big bear came through a crack in the fence and chased me in the house; he almost caught me, too."

"Florence," said the mother sternly, "aren't you ashamed of yourself to be so frightened of Mr. James' little pet dog and then to tell a deliberate falsehood? I was sitting here at the window and I saw the whole thing. Now I'm going to punish you. You go in your own room and get down on your knees and confess to the Lord that you're a naughty little girl and that you told your mother a deliberate lie. I want you to stay there, too, until you feel sure that you have obtained forgiveness for your sin."

The sunshine outside was alluring and there was a mud-pie in a half finished state in the yard. Florence reluctantly withdrew herself to the privacy of the nursery. In a surprisingly short time she opened the door and poked her head out.

"It's all right, mother," she said. "I told God all about it and He says He didn't blame me a bit. He thought it was a bear, too, when He first saw it."

§ 232   Suffering from a Relapse

In those wicked days before the Eighteenth Amendment and the Volstead Act put an end to all liquor-drinking in America there were two actors in New York who sometimes carried their social inclinations to an extreme. To put the matter brutally, they occasionally had attacks of what were known in the vernacular as the "willies." While recuperating from these seizures they customarily patronized the same sanitarium. Let us, for convenience's sake, call them A. and B.

It befell one day that A. felt himself to be acutely in need of a period devoted to rest and restoration. As he approached the door of the sanitarium he met his friend, B., rather white and drawn-looking, just coming out.

"'Lo, old man," said A. somewhat thickly, and with difficulty repressing a hiccup, "whaz mazzer wiz you? Same ol' complaint, eh?"

"I'm all right now," said B., "but I've had an awful time. Never again for me—I'm through. You may think I'm a little bit shaky and nervous now, but you should have seen me last week before I began to get over it. Why, man, for ten days, little red lizards with green eyes and purple tails were crawling all over me."

With his horrified eyes starting from his head, A. aimed a tremulous forefinger at B.'s coat collar.

"My God, man!" he cried. "You—you ain't well yet! There's one of 'em on you now!"

§ 233 One Old Enough to Merit Respect

I venture to present here and now the famous and deservedly immortal tale of the Educated Flea. At a theatrical hotel a vaudeville performer was stopping. He was the owner of a troupe of performing fleas. One evening, at dinner, he was telling his fellow-lodgers how he went about the job of training his tiny pets. To demonstrate, he cleared a space on the table, took one of his fleas, an especially intelligent and gifted insect, out of a small box, and proceeded to put the lively little chap through his paces.

"Hop East!" he commanded, and the flea hopped.
"Hop West!" The flea obeyed.
"Forward!" The flea marched.
"Face about!" And the flea whirled into the air to execute the command. But one of the lady boarders, in the intensity of her interest, was bending close and the flea landed in her hair and was instantly lost from view.

Confusion followed. After much searching the lady produced the truant and the performance was resumed.

"Hop East!" the man commanded, but the flea refused to move.
"Hop West, then!" The flea remained stationary. Surprised, the owner leaned over and scrutinized the performer more closely. Then, sitting up with a start and staring at the lady, he said in a stern, accusing voice:

"Madam, there has been a mistake—this is not my flea!"

§ 234 The Retort Courteous

There was once a boy who grew up in the village of Weeping Willow, Nebraska, with the persisting idea in his head that railroading offered the best career for an ambitious and energetic youth. When he was eighteen his opportunity came. He got a job as helper to the local station agent at forty dollars a month.

Years passed. The youth was a youth no longer; he was nearing his fortieth birthday but still he served the railroad at Weeping Willow. So well and so truly had he served it that, step by step, the management had widened the scope of his duties until now he was the entire resident staff of the great transcontinental system which passed through Weeping Willow. He was station agent, dispatcher, ticket-seller, train-caller, express-agent, baggage-handler, janitor and porter, all rolled into one. As a further mark of the esteem in which it held him and of the confidence it reposed in him, the railroad had never seen fit to reduce his wages by a single penny. He still drew down his forty a month just as regularly as pay-day came around.

Yet there were people in Weeping Willow who could not understand why it was that, holding so many responsible positions and receiving so steady an income, the man sometimes should show signs of broodiness and irritation verging upon outright melancholy. But such was the case. At times his peevishness was most marked.

On a broiling July day he sat in his small cubby-hole of an inner sanctum manipulating the key of his telegraph instrument. It was one of his gloomy days. As he sat with the perspiration coursing down his nose and his black calico sleeve protectors growing damp and soggy upon his wrists, the local Baptist minister, whom he disliked excessively, poked his head through the ticket window and in his best pulpit voice said:

"Brother, what tidings of the noon train?"

Without lifting his head the dripping misanthrope made answer: "Not a gol darn tiding!" he said.

§ 235 The Proper Point of View

There was an Englishman who made a tour of this continent. The tourist was a fit type of a certain group of Englishmen who think that nothing is worth while unless it is to be found on British soil, or at least under the protecting shadow of the Union Jack.

When he got back to New York after his swing across the land, an American asked him what he thought of our country.

"Oh, on the whole, rather tiresome," said the visitor.

"Didn't you see anything out of the ordinary?" asked the American.

"Cahn't say that I was especially impressed."

"Well," said the American, "you astonish me. We rather thought there were a few interesting sights over here. Did you, by any chance, see Niagara Falls?"

"Oh, yes. Spent half a day there."

"Well, isn't Niagara Falls worth looking at?"

"From the Canadian side—yes!"

§ 236 Between the Cloves and the Hiccough

Before prohibition the bar in the Lambs' Club—now given over to soft drinks, confectionery and vain regrets—was a famous place. I think more quick humor originated there than on any other spot of similar size on this hemisphere.

I remember one night when a distinguished comedian in a groggy condition was clinging to the rail. Only a few days before, he had announced that he was off the stuff forever. A fellow-actor entered.

"Why, Jack," he said, "I thought you'd taken the pledge and now here you are with a bun on. How did you get it?"

The inebriated one raised his head, revealing a happy, dreamy smile.

"Drink by drink," he murmured softly. "Drink by drink."

But, to my way of thinking, the honors for repartee at the Lambs' bar should go to Hap Ward, of the old team of Ward and Vokes. Hap, one day, was acting as host to a group of thirsty Lambs. A newcomer joined the party, bringing with him as a guest a gentleman of a serious aspect. When introductions had been completed, Hap addressed the stranger.

"What will you have, sir?"

The visitor drew himself up.

"I have never indulged in the habit of imbibing strong drink in my life," he said.

"My friend," said Ward, "I can teach you in three easy lessons."

§ 237 War Upon the Reptiles

Messrs. Cohen and Shapinsky retired from the white-goods business to devote themselves to lives of leisure. They took up golf.

Mr. Shapinsky sliced his drive and the ball, flying off at a tangent, descended in a bunker. Over the parapet of the bunker there came to the ears of the waiting Mr. Cohen muffled sounds as Mr

Shapinsky with his niblick dug into the sand. Finally he emerged.

"Vell," he said, "not so bad, huh? It only took me three strokes to get out of that pit."

"Vat do you mean three strokes?" demanded Mr. Cohen. "Myself I stood here und counted und I distinctly heard you hit the ground mit your iron nine times."

"Oh," said Mr. Shapinsky, "I vas killing a snake."

§ 238 One of Those Nature-Faking Yarns

A gentleman of social habits came home one evening to be confronted by a wife bristling with indignation. No sooner had he opened the front door of the apartment than she fired a blast at him.

"Why, my dear," he said, "what's the matter?"

"Matter enough," she answered. "I thought you told me that you were going down to Belmont track yesterday afternoon with a party of men!"

"That's right," he said, "what of it?"

"Then perhaps you can explain this," she said. "This morning I sent the suit you wore yesterday out to be pressed. But first I went through the pockets and in one of the pockets I found a card and on the card was written in your handwriting: 'Evelyn, 2161 Fitzroy.' Now then, what does this mean?"

Without a moment's hesitation the husband answered.

"My dear child," he said soothingly, "the thing is simplicity itself. 'Evelyn' is the name of a racehorse—a friend gave me a tip on her. And '2161' were the odds on her for first and second place. 'Fitzroy' is the name of the jockey. Surely you've heard of Fitzroy, the famous jockey? Now then, aren't you ashamed that you suspected me?"

The lady admitted that she might have been a bit hasty in jumping at conclusions. She dried her tears and peace descended upon the household.

On the following evening the husband entered the flat at peace with the world and whistling a merry catch. An ominous silence greeted him.

"Hello, dearie!" he hailed. "How do you feel?"

"I'm quite all right, considering," answered his wife frigidly.

"Any mail here for me?"

"You might look and see."

A LAUGH A DAY KEEPS THE DOCTOR AWAY

"Anybody drop in today?"

"No."

"Has anything happened at all?"

"Well," she said, "about three o'clock this afternoon your race-horse called up and asked for you."

§ 239 The Unaccommodating Kansan

Our country was enjoying one of its regular Japanese war-scares. I forget, now, whether it was the fifteenth or the sixteenth Japanese war-scare. A Congressman, representing a Kansas district, felt that a crisis impended.

On the floor of the House he made a speech pointing out the need of preparedness, and having done this, he took the train for his district with a view to sounding out his constituents upon the advisability and wisdom of the measures he so strenuously had advocated.

However, upon his arrival home, he was pained to note that the voters seemed strangely apathetic as regarded the prospect of an invasion by the Mikado's armed forces. By a personal campaign the Representative undertook to arouse his people to the seriousness of the situation.

The first prospective convert he encountered was an elderly farmer, who listened as the statesman expounded his views and then slowly shook his head, in seeming dissent.

"But look here, John," protested the Congressman. "If this war comes it may be necessary to call every able-bodied man in America to arms. You even may be called. Wouldn't you fight the Japs if they set foot on the soil of this country?"

"I reckon I wouldn't do that," said the farmer. "From what I kin understand, most every Japanese is what they call a fatalist."

"What has their fatalism got to do with your duty as a patriot?" asked the Congressman.

"Well," said the honest Kansan, "it looks to me like I couldn't derive much nourishment from fightin' with a lot of fellows that think you're doing 'em a personal favor every time you kill one of 'em."

§ 240 The Happy Return

Egbert, aged seven, went to the Sunday-school picnic. For days he had been looking forward to the event; but, as in the case of so many other things, realization hardly measured up to anticipation.

In the wagon on the way to the picnic ground, Egbert had a personal difference with a fellow-passenger. He came out of the altercation second best. Shortly after his arrival at the scene of festivities he sat down on a bumble-bee, with the result that he was painfully stung. Then he fell in the creek. A little girl took offence at a perfectly innocent pleasantry on his part and smacked his face and pulled his hair. He got badly sunburnt.

Late in the afternoon Egbert, in a disheveled state, reached home. As he limped up the front steps his father, glancing up from the evening paper, said:

"Well, son, what sort of a time did you have at the picnic?"

"Papa," said Egbert, "I'm so glad I'm back I'm glad I went."

§ 241   Bringing in the Sheaves

This story may or may not be true, but in view of the drops in the currencies of certain European countries which suffered heavily in the Great War, I am inclined to thing it at least has a plausible sound to it.

It is said that a Swiss hotel-keeper made an announcement which was calculated to bring him the patronage of refugee notables from other lands. He gave it out that at current rates of exchange, he would accept money of any Continental nation in settlement of accounts. As a consequence, his establishment was at once filled up with distinguished exiles.

An Austrian asked for his bill. He glanced at the figures and then heaved a heavy suitcase upon the desk of the proprietor.

"You will find enough money in this bag to pay you," he said.

Next to come was a German nobleman. Upon learning the amount of his indebtedness he produced a yellow slip and put it into the hand of the Swiss.

"This," he said, "is the bill of lading for a carload of marks which arrived yesterday, consigned to me. The car is now at the station. Go there and get as many bales as you need."

The third patron was a Russian prince. After a glance at his bill he drew from an inner pocket a flat thin heavy package which gave off a metallic sound as he deposited it upon the desk-top.

"What's this?" asked the hotel-keeper.

"These," said the Russian, "are the engraver's plates. Kindly take them and print as many million-ruble notes as may be required."

§ 242 Regarding the Brooklyn Boys

It would seem that a person named George customarily patronized a certain bar wherein gathered nightly a group of men whose highest ambition was to be on their feet when all the others were under the table, and whose proudest boast was that they had never been known to "pass out of the picture." To these ambitions George subscribed.

One night they missed George. Nor did he come the next evening, nor the next, nor the next. It was a month before he reappeared; and then he was so swathed in bandages, so painfully hopping on crutches, that they swarmed around him with excited questionings.

"How did I get this way?" said George. "Well, I'll tell you. Y' remember that las' night I was here? Drinkin' pretty heavy that night, but you know how it is with me. . . . When I left, the ol' bean was as clear as a bell. Actually, I might just as well not a' had anything. Well, somehow I knew the Brooklyn Boys were going to show up that night: I sort of felt it. And when I turned out the light an' hopped into the ol' bed, sure enough there was two of them—one on each corner, down by my feet."

"The Brooklyn Boys?" somebody queried.

"Yeh, sure," said George. "You know 'em, don't you? Little men about so high"—with his hands he indicated a span of four or five inches—"in bright yellow shirts.

"Well, as I said, there they were, two of 'em. I laid still for awhile, pretendin' I was asleep, an' watched 'em lookin' at me and then at each other, and noddin' their heads an' sayin': 'That's him. That's the guy.' Then all of a sudden I made a spring at them. But they got away . . . one hopped over the transom and one oozed out through the keyhole.

"'Well,' I said to myself, 'that settles 'em for tonight.' An' I got back in bed.

"D'ye know, I hadn't been there a minute when I looked around and saw, there in the middle of the floor, *seven* of those Brooklyn Boys, all lookin' up at me and noddin' among themselves and sayin': 'That's the guy there—that's him.'

"Well, I jumped out of bed like a flash but they were too quick for me. They all scooted—under the door, over the door, through the keyhole an' everywheres.

"Well, I thought I'd sure finished 'em for a while. But I'd no sooner got back in bed when I heard a sound and I looked around and there was *sixty* Brooklyn Boys! I knew they was up to something because they'd look up at me and then nod among themselves and whisper: 'That's him, all right. Uh-huh, that's him.'

"All this time, y'understand, the ol' head was clear as a bell. I knew perfectly well what I was doing.

"So I jumped right at them—because that's the best way to get rid of the Brooklyn Boys, y'know. But they all got away, every single one, and I got back in bed again, thinkin' I was safe now for sure. Well, d'ye know what?"

"What?" asked somebody.

"Why, I hadn't but barely got back in bed when I looked down and there on the floor was *thirty-five thousand* Brooklyn Boys! And this time each one had a little musket over his shoulder. Well, the leader he lines them all up and waved his sword up toward me in the bed and yelled: 'That's him, boys! That's the guy, up there!'

"Then he yelled: 'Ready!' . . .

"Then he yelled: 'Aim!' . . .

"Well, now, as I said, all this time the ol' bean was workin' beautifully. I saw just what they was up to and before that Brooklyn Boy that had the sword could yell, 'Fire!' I'd jumped clean out of bed and through the window."

George paused, and wetted his throat with an appropriate liquid.

"Of course," he added, "my room is on the third floor an' I got sort o' banged up—as you fellas notice. But just think what might have happened if I'd been drunk and couldn't a' made that jump in time!"

§ 243   When O. Henry Met the Poet Scout

Bob Davis of *Munsey's Magazine,* who has a mania for bringing celebrities together just to see how they react on each other, was strolling along Broadway with O. Henry in the latter hours of the nineteenth century, when Captain Jack Crawford, the poet scout, his hair waving in the wind, came sailing across Madison Square. Davis introduced the pair and dragged them off to lunch.

Captain Jack, like most poets, having memorized all his own verse, never let a chance go by to hold the willing or unwilling listener spellbound. He opened up on the Bagdad Scribe before the oysters arrived. He spilled frontier poetry all over the premises, shook his hair out in a burst of blank verse, wedded the Pecos River to the Rocky Mountains, swept through the Yellowstone, tramped the plains, shot Indians, broke horses and piled the rhythmic dust of pioneer days all over O. Henry.

Captain Jack did all the talking and all the reciting that was done at that luncheon, which lasted two hours. About 3.30 P. M. the party broke up and O. Henry staggered out into the fresh air waving Davis and Crawford a mute farewell.

In the morrow's mail Bob received the following note:

"My dear Colonel Davis:

"How is your friend Captain Crack Jawford, the go it spout?

"O. Henry."

§ 244 Our Institutions Approved

A candidate for citizenship came to a naturalization bureau in New York to take out his first papers. The applicant was a Russian who spoke badly broken English. With him was a friend and sponsor from the East Side.

Under examination the candidate betrayed a tremendous lack of knowledge of national history and institutions and public men. Finally the examiner turned to the alien's companion:

"Here," he said testily, "this man's ignorance is appalling. Take him away and explain something to him about the Constitution and the government of the United States. Don't bring him back until he is better qualified."

The East Sider led his crestfallen fellow-countryman away. Within an hour they both returned.

"Here," said the Examiner, "what brings you here again?"

"Everything is all right," stated the East Sider. "I took my friend out and read to him out of the Constitution, and he says he likes it first-rate."

§ 245 The Annoyed Mr. Goldstein

A gentleman named Goldstein graduated out of the buttonhole-making line into practical politics. He gave his allegiance to the Republican party.

That year the Republicans carried New York state. They also carried Mr. Goldstein's election district which was an even more notable victory inasmuch as it was in a heavily Democratic section. At that time Chauncey Depew was U. S. Senator from New York;

also head of the New York Central Railroad and likewise Republican state chairman.

Bright and early on the morning after election day Mr. Goldstein was at the outer doors of Mr. Depew's offices in the old Grand Central terminal building. He sent word in that Mr. Goldstein, the politicianer, desired to see the head of the line.

Being admitted, he directed Mr. Depew's attention to the result of the voting in his neighborhood and claimed credit for the showing. Mr. Depew agreed with him that he had done well and that his labors in behalf of the party entitled him to recognition and reward. He desired to know how he personally or the G.O.P. might serve his friend.

At this Mr. Goldstein confessed to an ambition. He straightway desired, he said, to become a dispatcher for the railroad.

Depew directed his caller's attention to the fact that a dispatcher, among other essential qualifications, must have more or less knowledge of telegraphy. It then developed, that Mr. Goldstein thought a dispatcher was one of those functionaries in blue uniform who, through megaphones, called incoming and outgoing trains in the station.

Behold, then, Mr. Goldstein on a night, one week later, arrayed, in blue and brass, proudly pacing the main waiting-room, a megaphone under his arm and conscious dignity, conscious power and conscious pomp in his manner. Presently his chance comes. He lifts his voice and this statement comes from him:

"Say, efferbody, listen. It gifs me the outmost bleasure to announce that a lofely train, mit cushioned seats und a conductor und ef'rything pleasant—say, you'd like that train—is now aboud leafing on track Number Fife for Albany, Uticcer, Ro-chester, Syracuse, Buffaler und points on the Vest. Who would like to go in a nice train for some points on the Vest?"

Plainly pained at the failure of the populace to leap forward and avail itself of this opportunity he is about to repeat the announcement when he feels a tug at his coat tail. He turns impatiently to find a person of lowly aspect, who is burdened with hand baggage.

"Vell," he demands, "vot is idt?"

"When does the last train go to Cleveland?" inquires the stranger.

Into Mr. Goldstein's tones comes pity for such ignorance.

"Ven, on the Noo Yawk Central, does the last train go for Cleveland?" he repeats as though he scarcely can believe his ears. "Mine friendt, you should live so long!"

§ 246   Darkness Before the Dawn

A barn-storming troupe, specializing in Shakespearean repertoire, was fighting its difficult way through the middle west. For a month salaries had not been paid. One constable and two hotel-keepers were now traveling with the company, hoping to collect their claims. On Tuesday morning of a certain week the leading man approached the manager.

"Let me have half a dollar, will you?" he said.

The manager gave him a hurt look.

"Say, what's the matter with this gang, anyhow?" he demanded; "always wanting money. What do you think I am—a National bank, or something? It's only yesterday that the heavy man kept nagging after me for two dollars. Said he wanted to get his laundry out. What does he need with laundry? Am I bothering about my laundry? No. Here I am working like a tiger to dig up railroad fares for you people and square up hotel-keepers and keep this show moving across the country until we run into some good territory. And now you come yelling for dough. What do you want with a half dollar, anyhow?"

"I'll tell you what I need with it," said the leading man. "You announced 'Romeo and Juliet' for the bill tonight, didn't you?"

"Yes. What of it?"

"Well, you're expecting me to play Romeo, ain't you?"

"Sure I am."

"Well, how in thunder do you figure I'm going to play Romeo with a three days' beard? I've got to have a shave—so Romeo won't come on with a quarter of an inch of black whiskers on his face."

The manager considered the thick dark stubble on his star's chops and saw the force of the argument. Slowly, he rammed a reluctant hand into his pocket, then, as a smile of relief broke over his face, brought it out empty.

"Tell you what we'll do," he said briskly, "we'll change the bill to 'Othello'!"

§ 247   A Scandal in the Family

A young Irishman whose family was scattered pretty well over the English-speaking portions of the globe emigrated to America. Soon after his arrival in New York he paid a visit to the Bronx

Zoo. He halted in front of a cage containing one of the largest kangaroos in captivity. After watching the curious creature for some time in an awed silence, he hailed a keeper.

"What's that thing?" he asked.

"That," said the keeper in his best professional manner, "is a marsupial, a mammal that carries its young in a pouch on its breast, lives on roots and herbs, can jump twenty feet at one leap, is able to knock a human being down with a kick from either hind leg, and is a native of Australia."

"For the love of Hiven!" cried the Irishman, bursting into tears. "Me sisther's married to wan of thim!"

§ 248   Aiding the Sheriff's Vision

The late Charlie Case, for many years a headliner in vaudeville, was, I think, one of the funniest men and certainly one of the most original that the American stage has produced. He used to come sidling out of the wings in a diffident, apologetic sort of way and while twisting a string in and out of his fingers, tell side-splitting stories of what a mythical father of his had been saying and doing. The one I loved best had to do with Father's famous lapse from sobriety. As nearly as I recall Case's own rendition it ran as follows:

"Father came mighty near getting into some serious trouble her« the other day. A lot of folks wanted to have him arrested fo' obtaining money under false pretences; but he got out of it all right

"Here's the way the thing happened: A fellow up in the mountains made some moonshine whiskey and he gave Father a quart of it. So Father took three drinks of it and then, he went down town and rented a vacant store and began charging people ten cents apiece to come in and see the animals and the snakes. Right away they raised a row. Father could see the snakes and animals all right but they couldn't see anything but just an empty store.

"So some of them got mad and they went away and found the sheriff and swore out a warrant and told the sheriff that they wanted to have Father locked up in jail until he'd given them their money back. The sheriff put on his badge and came around to arrest Father.

"But Father gave the sheriff one drink out of the bottle and sold him a half-interest in the show for three hundred dollars."

§ 249 The Affair in Half Moon Street

Ever since I first heard it—and that must be fully ten years ago now—I have treasured the story of the gentleman, living at Number 5 Half Moon Street, who inserted the advertisement in the Agony Column of the London *Times*.

The advertisement stated, in effect, that a person of scientific attainments, living at Number 5 Half Moon Street, was preparing to go on a journey of exploration into Equatorial Africa, and desired, as a paid companion, a young man who was a good rifle-shot, experienced in the tropics and acquainted with the languages of the native tribes.

The same evening a youth-about-town was sitting in his club. He picked up a copy of that morning's *Times* and his eye fell upon this advertisement. He read it through and then he said to himself what an Englishman always says when confronted by anything which seems to him striking or interesting.

"Most 'straordinary! Most remarkably 'straordinary that any Johnnie living in Half Moon Street should wish to leave his diggings and go to Africa and take a strange Johnnie with him!"

The impression of what he had read lingered in his mind all through the evening. Pondering it over, he drank more perhaps than was good for him. At least, what he drank was not good for his speech—it made it thick and hiccuppy. Also it tangled his legs.

At 1 A. M. he arose and, leaving the club, set out for his lodgings. He rambled off his route and presently he found himself in Half Moon Street. By another coincidence he was directly in front of Number 5. Groggily, he stood for a space trying to couple these facts with some foggy recollections which lurked in the back of his brain. Then he remembered.

He made his fumbling way up the steps to the door and rang the bell and rang it again and again. At length footsteps sounded in the passage within and the door was opened by an individual who, despite his state of partial undress, plainly was a butler.

"Well, sir?" he asked.

"I desire (hic) to shee your master," said the inebriate. "Mush shee him at once."

"But the hour is very late, sir," remonstrated the servant. "The master has retired. He is in bed asleep. Can't I take the message, sir, and deliver it in the morning?"

"Not at all," said the clubman. "Thish is mosh pressing and

imperative. Businish is strictly between your master (hic) and myself."

So the butler went away, leaving him there, and eventually there appeared in the doorway, a middle-aged gentleman of an irritable aspect, in dressing-gown and slippers who plainly had just been aroused from slumber.

"Well, sir, well, sir," he snapped, "what is it you wish to say to me?"

"Are you the gen'l'm who inserted (hic) advertishment in *Times* stating you wished engage servishes of a young man 'company you to Africa?"

"I am. What of it?"

"Well, (hic) I jus' happened to be passing and I dropped in to tell you that, pershonally, I can't shee my way clear to going."

§ 250 Everything Coming Out Just Right

This is one of those post-war stories. However, it is said to have the advantage on its side of being true. It seems there was an English nobleman whose estate shrunk frightfully between 1914 and 1918. He decided, in order to replenish the family fortune, to go into business. But neither nature nor experience had qualified him for a commercial career and he made a frightful hash of the venture.

Eventually, a receiver took over his affairs. The receiver engaged an expert accountant who went over the books and struck a trial balance.

His Lordship scanned the document and exclaimed:

"What a remarkable coincidence! What an extraordinary coincidence! Why, the totals on both sides are identical!"

§ 251 Delivered Through a Middleman

In the year after the Great War started there was a German who ran a saloon in Bridgeport, Connecticut. Close by was a munition factory where explosives were being manufactured for the Allies. As one who had a sympathy for the cause of his Fatherland, the German nursed a deep grudge against the neighboring industry. He included the operatives in the plant among his enemies.

One day, as he sat behind his bar, a husky Irishman in overalls entered.

"Say," he began, "I'd like to open a small account with you. I'd like to come in here for me drinks and on Saturday night whin I get paid off I'll come over and settle. I'm a square guy and I always pay me debts. How about it?"

"Vell," said the German, "for my regular gustomers sometimes I put it on der slate; only, you are a stranger to me. Where you work?"

"Right across the street here," said the Irishman.

"In der munitions factory? Nutt'n doin'!"

"Well, they told me," said the Irishman, "that you was kinda sore on us fellers over there but I was thinkin' that if you knew we was makin' shells for the Germans now maybe you'd act different."

The Teuton's face broke into a broad smile.

"For the Chermans now you make 'em, eh? Say, dot's fine— dot's pully. Have someding on me. We drink togeder, huh?"

They drank together. Three times more, as rapidly as the Irishman emptied his beer-glass the German replenished it, each time stating that for this festive occasion, at least, there would be no charge for the refreshment. The hospitable rites having been concluded the new patron was moving toward the door when the German was moved to put a question. Until now, in his exuberance, he had forgotten to ask for details:

"Say," he said, "how you get dose shells over to der Chermans?"

"Well,' said the Irishman, edging a little nearer toward the door, "we don't exactly send 'em to the Germans direct, you understand."

"No? Then how you do it?"

"Oh, we sell em to the English and they shoot 'em over."

§ 252 Back to God's Country

Soon after the Civil War ended a former trooper of Morgan's cavalry moved from his home in the Bluegrass region to California. He was a gentleman of genial habits and a natural orator. It was almost inevitable, therefore, that sooner or later he should enter politics. He was announced as a candidate for the legislature on the Democratic ticket. He made a spirited campaign, but when the primary returns were in, of three candidates the ex-Confederate had finished third.

He called a meeting of his friends and made a speech. It was short but complete.

"Gentlemen," he said, "I'm going to quit this cussed country. I'm going back to Kentucky—the only fit place for a gentleman to live—where the niggers make your crop for you and the sheriff sells it."

§ 253 Hail and Farewell!

An amateur pugilist in a small town in Ohio accepted the invitation of a visiting professional who announced that he was ready to meet all comers.

The local prodigy mounted the stage, climbed through the ropes and gave his name to the announcer. As the announcer was introducing him the amateur tugged at his sleeve and whispered something in his ear.

"Kid Binks desires me to state," said the announcer, "that this is his first appearance in any ring."

He stepped back and the two men squared off. The professional ducked a wild swing, led with his right and knocked the amateur down with such violence that he fairly splashed when he hit the floor.

The master of ceremonies stood over the fallen one, counting him out. At eight the dazed youth got upon his knees. At nine he spoke in a husky whisper.

The announcer raised his hand for silence.

"Kid Binks also desires me to state," he said, "that this is his last appearance in any ring."

§ 254 Calculated to Work Improvements

Two sympathetic friends called at a house of mourning in the Bronx. Mrs. Levinsky, wife of a wealthy white-goods importer, had passed away, following upon her return from a Southern trip.

The callers were shown into the parlor where the bereft husband sat alongside the casket. They advanced and looked upon the face of the deceased.

"Don't she look wonderful?" said one of them.

The widower raised his head.

"Why shouldn't she look wonderful?" he asked. "Didn't she spend the whole winter at Palm Beach?"

§ 255 Improvements in the Language

The infusion of Russian and Polish stocks into New York has been responsible for some curious additions to the language of the Manhattan Cockney. Most of us are familiar with the story of the small East-Side boy who told his father that what he liked best about the arithmetic he studied at school was Gozinta.

"What do you mean, Gozinta?" asked his parent.

"Why, 2 gozinta 4, 4 gozinta 8, 8 gozinta 16."

Of somewhat more recent coinage is the one which recites how a teacher asked if any member of her class knew the meaning of the word "Stoic."

Up rose a small second-generation American from Rivington Street.

"Sure, teacher, I know what is a stoic," he said.

"Well then, Sidney, suppose you tell us what a stoic is."

"A stoic is the boid wot brings the babies."

But of all such yarns I believe I like best the tale of the transplanted Pole who had made a fortune by building cheap apartment-houses. He had just completed the erection of a flat-building near Riverside Drive, whereas theretofore all his operations had been confined to the more crowded down-town districts. A friend said to him:

"Meyer, that's a mighty nice-looking flat-bulding you've just put up. Have you got a name for it yet?"

"Soitinly," said the capitalist. "I've decided I should call it the Cloister Apartments."

"Strikes me as a rather curious name. Why call it that?"

"Because," said Meyer, "it's cloister the subway, it's cloister Central Park and its cloister the river."

§ 256 An Abiding Delusion, Too

A prominent citizen of an Oregon town was an ardent believer in the cult of mental-healing. Wherever possible this gentleman, with the zeal of a devotee, preached his doctrine. One day on the main street he hailed an impressionable youth from the country.

"Billy," he said, "how's your daddy?"

"Oh," said the youth, "paw's mighty bad off. He's been porely all spring. Now he's down flat in bed and ailin' stiddy. We're feared paw's powerful sick. He's feared, too."

"Nonsense," snorted the older man. "Your father isn't sick—he only thinks he's sick. Tell him I said so."

"Yessir, I will."

A fortnight later the same pair met again in the same place.

"Billy," said the citizen cheerily, "how's your father now?"

The youngster heaved a deep sigh:

"He thinks he's dead."

§ 257   Bordering on the Unreasonable

The hero of this story was one of those persons who accept whatever happens as a manifestation of the divine power. It was not for him to question the workings of a mysterious Providence.

Misfortune dogged his footsteps, yet never once did he complain. His wife ran away with the hired man. His daughter married a ne'er-do-well who deserted her; his son landed in the penitentiary; a cyclone destroyed his residence, a hailstorm spoiled his crop and the holder of the mortgage foreclosed on his farm. Yet at each fresh stroke he knelt and returned thanks to the Almighty for mercies vouchsafed.

Eventually, pauperized but still submissive to the decrees from on high, he landed at the county poorhouse. The overseer sent him out one day to plow a potato field. A thunderstorm came up but was passing by when without warning a bolt of lightning descended from the sky. It melted the ploughshare, stripped most of his garments from him, singed off his beard and mustache, branded him on the back with the initials of an utter stranger, and hurled him through a brushfence.

Slowly he got upon his knees, clasped his hands and raised his eyes toward heaven. Then, for the first time, the worm turned:

"Lord," he said, "this is gittin' to be plum' rediculous!"

§ 258   A Slight for the Kellys

Somebody was reminded the other day—and, by the same token reminded me—of one that I hadn't heard for at least ten years. The best authorities agree that a good story stands revival every five years.

As the tale runs, the parish priest called on a well-to-do parishioner named Kelly, for a substantial contribution to the fund for purchasing a bronze bell for the church. Mr. Kelly was in a generous mood. He gave a larger sum than any other member of the congregation gave.

The bell was purchased and installed. Meeting Mr. Kelly a few days later, the clergyman said:

"What do you think of the new bell?"

"I'm sorry I gave a cint," said Mr. Kelly, shortly. "If I'd known what was goin' to happen ye'd have had no money from me."

"You astonish me," said the Father. "What's wrong with it?"

"I'll tell ye what's wrong with it," said Mr. Kelly; "whin that bell rings do ye hear it speakin' me name? Ye do not. All ye hear it sayin' is: *'Doolan, Donlan, Donovan, Dugan!'*"

§ 259 The Luck of the Absentee

This was a favorite with Mark Twain. Whether he made it up or whether he had it from other sources and merely stood sponsor for it I have no way of knowing.

Twain said that a Nantucket sailor fell in love with a girl in his home town. She objected to his habits but promised if he took the pledge she would consider his suit favorably.

In his desire to win the young woman the suitor was willing to go farther even than that. He made application in the local Total Abstinence League, and on the same evening sailed on a whaling voyage. According to Clemons, he was gone nearly two years and during the entire time touched not a drop of strong drink. His mouth watered when the other members of the crew downed their grog allowances, but he, as befitting a good templar, stood fast.

The voyage ended. The reformed one hurried to his sweetheart's house to claim her hand. A shock awaited him. For eight months she had been the wife of a stay-at-home citizen.

"But," expostulated the poor sea-faring man, "you told me that if I would join that temperance lodge you'd be waiting for me when I got back."

"Oh," said the young matron, "you never heard the news, did you?"

"What news?"

"That very night, about two hours after you sailed, you were blackballed."

§ 260 Everything Happens for the Worst

This one is dedicated to pessimists and is included in this book especially for their consideration.

The setting is a country store. The proprietor is reading a newspaper which has just arrived from the city.

Uncle Henry, the official grouch of the neighborhood, bites off a chew of tobacco and masticates it with a morose intensity. This done, he is moved to ask a question:

"Ezra," he says, addressing the storekeeper, "I persoom that durned paper is jest as dull tonight as 'tis every other night in the week. No news wuth tellin', I reckin?"

"Well," says the proprietor, "there's one item on the front page that's sort of interestin'. It says here that a lot of those scientists all over the world are gettin' together in a scheme to change the calendar and have thirteen months to the year instead of twelve."

Uncle Henry gives a low despairing moan:

"It'll be jest my luck for it to be a winter month an' me plum' out o' fodder!"

§ 261 Spreading the Glad Tidings

A gentleman who evidently thought well of himself entered a restaurant and with commanding mien beckoned the head waiter to him. He ordered a seven course dinner, winding up with this instruction to the obsequious servitor:

"Now, don't forget to tell the cook that these things are for Colonel Brown—understand, Colonel Brown. Just mention my name to him and he'll understand."

A person of mild aspect had been a witness to this. As the headwaiter turned over Colonel Brown's order to an underling the mild man caught his eye.

"Just a minute, please," said the second patron. "I want to give an order, too. Got any fresh clams?"

"Yes, sir, some very fine clams to-day."

"Good. Here's my visiting card. Now go down to the cellar, open twenty-four clams, put 'em on some cracked ice, and while you're doing it, mention my name to every damn' one of 'em."

§ 262 Out of Business Hours

To realize what the antiquity of this one is you first must look up the date of General Tom Thumb's death and then hark still farther back to the yet more remote period when that little man was at the height of his fame.

Under the management of P. T. Barnum, the most famous of all our dwarfs was touring the country. Between engagements he stopped over Sunday at a country hotel in New England.

A lady of the neighborhood called and sent up her card with the request that she be permitted to meet the General. The message was received by a member of Barnum's staff, who happened at the moment to be in the General's room. This person, who was six feet tall and broad in proportion, and also something of a wit, asked that the lady be shown up.

Presently she knocked at the door and he answered it.

"I am looking," she said, "for General Tom Thumb."

"Madam," he said, "proceed to look."

"Surely you are not the celebrated midget?" she cried.

"Certainly I am," he answered. "But just as the present moment, Madam, I happen to be resting."

§ 263   In the Ascending Scale

A person who had been so incautious as to sample a bootlegger's wares was endeavoring to negotiate the opening into a hat store. Another man, who was perfectly sober and apparently had no sympathy with any persons who also were not perfectly sober, shoved the inebriated one aside and entered the establishment. The jostled person, straightening himself with difficulty, followed through the door.

Just inside a salesman bowed before the sober man.

"I want a hat," said the latter. "A derby hat. Size $6\frac{7}{8}$."

Having found a hat to his liking he departed. The clerk turned to the soused individual, who, while the sale was in progress, had been regarding the first purchaser with a baleful eye.

"And what can I do for you, sir?" inquired the clerk.

"I want a lid, too."

"Yes sir. What size?"

"Whasch size 'at other feller take?"

"$6\frac{7}{8}$."

"Alri'—then gimme 9-10-11!"

§ 264   A Family of Imitators

In the old days there was an ex-miner who opened a hotel in Reno, Nevada. Alongside the clerk's desk he installed a cigar-stand and stocked it.

One day a traveling man, who had sold him his original supply and who was in the habit of serving him, dropped in and inquired whether there was anything in his line that the proprietor desired to-day.

"Sure, pard," said the ex-miner. "You kin ship me another thousand of them Madero cigars. You needn't send me any more of them punks made by Colorado Madero. And say, who in thunder is this young Clara Madero who's busted into the cigar business and is tryin' to git away with it by tradin' on the family name?

"Me for old man Madero—to hell with his relatives!"

§ 265   Two Conundrums and a Tragedy

I do not know why it is that nearly all the stories having to do with frugality should be aimed at the Scot. Your average Scotchman does not particularly wish to hoard his money; he merely desires that when he spends it, he shall obtain a proper return.

You know of course the ancient conundrum which was printed years ago in London *Punch*. As I recall it, this conundrum ran as follows:

"How, at the conclusion of a railroad journey, can you definitely fix the nationality of an English passenger, an Irish passenger, and a Scotch passenger?"

The answer was:

"The Englishman hurries to the lunch-stand; the Irishman hastens to the bar; the Scotchman goes back through the train to see if anybody left anything."

Here recently, a friend fired this one at me:

"Why," he asked, "have the Scotch a sense of humor?"

"All right," I asked, "I'll bite; tell me, Mr. Bones, why have the Scotch a sense of humor?"

"Because," he said, "it's a gift."

A still later addition to the crop has just been received. It is stated that an Englishman, standing treat to a Scotchman at a pub recommended that his guest try some very fine brandy which the establishment had in stock at three shillings a drink. With glistening eyes the Scotchman agreed. He waited until the bar-maid had poured out the brandy and then with a sudden leap he pounced upon the glass, seizing it in both hands as in a vise.

"Why do you do that, old dear?" asked the astonished host.

"Because," said the Scotchman, "when I was a verra young man, back in Edinburgh in the year 1862, I saw one of them spilled."

§ 266 In the Very Lap of Comfort

An aged couple from the East Side were visiting their married daughter in Brooklyn. One afternoon on a sight-seeing stroll they drifted into a near-by cemetery.

Presently, a huge marble mausoleum caught their eye. They halted before it in admiration.

"Ain't that peautiful!" said the old man. "I pet you, Esther, that cost fully dwenty thousand dollars. Who is buried there, I wonder?"

His wife, whose eyesight was better than his, spelled out the name carved over the entrance to the tomb.

"It says: 'August Kohn.'"

"August Kohn, huh?—so! Then it must be the millionaire silk-goods importer vot's puried there." He wagged his beard in tribute. "Vell, them rich peoples certainly do live vell."

§ 267 Making It a Sweepstakes

This is one of my standbys. Every time I hear it—and I hear it on an average of at least four times a year—I like it better. I hope the reader may feel the same way about it.

The principal characters are an Irishman, with red whiskers, and a Hebrew with black whiskers. They fall into an argument over the relative glories of the two great races they severally represent. It is finally proposed by the Semitic debater that for every great Jew he names he shall be permitted to pluck one hair from his adversary's face. For every famous Irishman listed the other man may claim the tribute of a hair from the Jew's beard. The first to cry enough, or the first to be entirely denuded will be the loser.

A chosen referee gives the signal for the start. It is the Jew's turn.

"Moses," he cries, and yanks a hair from the Irishman's chin.
"Brian Boru," shouts his opponent.
"Abraham."
"St. Patrick."
"Baron Hirsch."
"Daniel O'Connell."
"Rothschild."
"Jawn L. Sullivan."
Inspiration seizes the Hebrew.

"The Twelve Apostles," he whoops exultingly, and snatches an even dozen of auburn hairs from where they grew.

With a triumphant whooroo the Irishman fixes both his hands in the Hebrew's beard:

"The A.O.H.!" he bellows, and brings away the entire crop.

§ 268   Filling a Long-Felt Want

An amateur investigator made a trip to a state lunatic asylum. While strolling about the grounds he happened upon an old man of a benign aspect sitting under a tree.

"Good evening," said the venerable gentleman. "A stranger here I assume?"

"Yes," said the caller. "I am. I take it that you, too, are a visitor."

"Unfortunately," said the old gentleman, "I am an inmate."

"But—pardon me—but you don't look like——" began the astonished stranger.

"I'm not, either," said the old gentleman. "My son, I am the victim of circumstances. Members of my family coveted my property. On trumped up charges they had me declared of unsound mind, and I was railroaded off from my home and brought to this place where I have ever since been in confinement. And yet, if only the truth were known, I am engaged in a great scientific literary work—an undertaking which has busied me for many years and which, if justice is ever done, will some day make my name famous throughout the English-speaking world."

"And what, may I ask, is this work?"

"I am engaged," said the old gentleman, "in compiling a complete index to The Unabridged Dictionary."

§ 269   Spoken from the Heart Out

In an effort to link practice with preaching, the Sunday-school teacher asked her class of small boys to recite appropriate quotations from the Scriptures as they added their free will offerings to the regular collection. The youngsters had a week in which to find and memorize suitable texts.

On the following Sunday the scholars advanced, one by one, each with a coin ready and his brow furrowed by the effort of trying to remember the quotation he meant to deliver.

First, as was fitting, came the brag pupil and, as he deposited a dime in the plate, he said:
"The Lord loveth a cheerful giver."
"Beautiful," said the teacher approvingly. "Now, Harry, what are you going to say?"
"The liberal soul shall be made fat."
"Willie?"
"Whoso giveth to the poor, lendeth to the Lord."
"Bobby?"
"Freely thou hast received, freely give."
"Very good, indeed. Tommy, it's your turn next."
Tommy's hand came slowly forth from his pocket, bringing a penny.
"A fool and his money are soon parted," said Tommy.

§ 270 Where Proper Relief Lay

Late in life, Messrs. Abrams and Jacobs took up golf. Both were retired cloak and suit merchants of the type made famous in Montague Glass's immortal stories.

On a glorious September afternoon they were going over the links of their country-club. They were playing for a stake of a dollar a hole, and the competition was spirited.

Mr. Abrams drove into a bunker. With his iron he made four ineffectual swipes, raising the sand in clouds. Then he stooped down, picked up the half buried ball and tossed it out on the fairway.

Mr. Jacobs stiffened with indignation.

"Look a' here!" he whooped. "You couldn't do that. It's against the rules."

"I already have done it," said Mr. Abrams, calmly.

"But again I tell you it's against the rules," declared Mr. Jacobs. "I have been playing this game longer as you have and I tell you it says in the book where you should not touch the ball with your hands at all. What am I going to do if by such tricks as that you should win the match?"

"Sue me," said Mr. Abrams.

§ 271 No Repetitions for Hubby

A few months ago an English illustrated paper published a joke which struck me as having merit. When I repeated it in company a gentleman who is supposed to know nearly all the jokes in the world told me that in slightly different guise the same wheeze was current on the Pacific Coast twenty years ago. He may or may not have been wrong. In any event, I like the British version.

A couple from the country have come up to London for a week's visit. They have seats in the first gallery for a performance of a society drama. To them the play proves exceedingly tiresome. In one of the intervals the husband, stifling a yawn, turns to his deeply bored wife:

"What comes next?" he asks.

She consults the program.

"It says 'ere, 'Act four, sime as Act one.'"

"Ow!" he exclaims, "let's 'op it. I couldn't sit through all that hawful mess again."

§ 272   There Was No Hurry about It

A brawny negro prize-fighter made application at an athletic club which was putting on a series of bouts, for an opportunity to meet some suitable opponent. He announced that he was a dark cloud, a whirlwind, a tempest, a tornado, a hurricane and a sirocco.

His language impressed the match-maker and for the preliminary go he was entered against a dependable colored scrapper. The stranger made a deplorable showing. For two rounds his opponent hammered him all over the ring. Early in the third round the beaten darky decided he had enough. He took an easy poke on the jaw and flattened out on the canvas to be counted out.

The referee was halfway through with his tally when disgust moved him to interpolate a speech:

"Say, nigger," he growled out of the corner of his mouth, "you ain't hurt. Get up from there! Ain't you goin' to fight any more?"

Without stirring from his comfortable recumbent position the whirlwind made answer:

"Oh, yassuh, I'm gwine fight some mo'—*but not to-night!*"

§ 273   An Attack on the Affiliated Talent

Two professional confidence-men made the acquaintance of a wealthy sportsman. He admired their sprightliness while privately deploring their vocation.

When the acquaintance had ripened into friendship he invited them to shoot in his private preserve. Before daylight they were paddled out in a skiff and put in a blind which, the night before, had been stocked with wooden decoys. There the guide left them, for the time being.

As the dawn began to break, one of the pair suddenly was aware of the wooden birds bobbing about in front of him. The light was poor and he was green at the duck-shooting game. He arose and fired both barrels of his gun into the flock.

His partner straightened up, took one look, and cried out in distress:

"My God! You're shootin' the boosters!"

§ 274 The Deceased Had Been Forehanded

A few months after the Eighteenth Amendment went into effect a Texan passed from this life.

While the funeral services were in progress at the late home of the deceased, two of the men mourners stood on the front porch of the house lamenting the passing of their friend and praising his virtues.

Said one of them:

"There wasn't no finer feller anywhere than what Bill was, but the main trouble with him was he wasn't forehanded. He had a wife and a whole passel of children and he should a-been more saving than what he was. He might a-knowed he couldn't live on forever. But no, he lived up to everything he made. And here now, right in the very prime of life, with a family on his hands, he gets sick and dies without leaving no estate as I knows of."

"The hell he didn't leave no estate!" exclaimed the other. "He left mighty nigh a gallon!"

§ 275 How the Reform Worked

When the Union troops under Grant, early in the Civil War, took possession of West Kentucky, some difficulty was encountered in controlling the populace, for that end of the state was a hot-bed of Southern sentiment. General Grant issued proclamations stating that no citizen would be molested unless he undertook to give aid and comfort to the enemy.

In one town in the invaded district, though, there was an elderly gentleman whose sympathies with the Southern cause were especially outspoken. Whenever word came of a victory for the Southern armies his jubilation was undisguised.

The Union provost-marshal, hearing complaints from his men of this man's actions and words, decided to make an example of him. He sent a squad to arrest the offender and presently, under guard, the old gentleman was brought before him.

"Look here," said the officer, "I'm getting tired of your behavior. Every few days I hear that you've been going about again spreading reports that our forces have been defeated. Now then, I've decided to reform you. Either you take the oath of allegiance to the Union right now or off you go to a military prison. Which shall it be?"

The prisoner decided to take the oath. After it had been administered the officer felt that a further admonition might be in order. "Now then," he said, "I hope you understand what this thing means? If ever again you utter a word of disparagement for the Union cause or a word of approval for the Confederates, and I hear of it, you'll suffer severely; because now you're a loyal Unionist. A single disloyal remark makes you guilty of treason."

The reclaimed one thanked him for the warning. On his way out he stopped at the door.

"Major," he said, "they ain't no law against thinkin', is they?"

"That depends," said the Major. "What's in your mind now?"

"Well," said the Kentuckian, "I was just thinkin' that them Rebels certainly did give us fellers hell day before yistiddy down below the state line."

§ 276 Where Higher Education Would Have Landed Him

Some fifteen years ago there landed in New York a friendless and almost penniless Russian immigrant who found lodgings on the East Side and at once, with racial perseverance and energy, set out to earn a living.

He was of a likeable disposition, and speedily made acquaintances who sought to aid him in his ambition. One of them sponsored him for the vacant post of janitor, or *shammos*, to use the common Hebraic word, of a little synagogue on a side street. But when the officers of the congregation found out the applicant was entirely illiterate they reluctantly denied him employment, inasmuch as a *shammos* must keep certain records. The greenhorn quickly rallied from his disappointment. He got a job somewhere. He prospered. Presently he became a dabbler in real-estate.

Within ten years he was one of the largest independent operators in East Side tenement-house property and popularly rated as a millionaire. An occasion arose when he needed a large amount of money to swing what promised to be a profitable deal. Finding himself for the moment short of cash, he went to the East Side branch of one of the large banks.

It was the first time in his entire business career that he had found it necessary to borrow extensively. He explained his position to the manager, who knew of his success, and asked for a loan of fifty thousand dollars.

"I'll be very glad to accommodate you, Mr. Rabin," said the banker. "Just sit down there at that desk and make out a note for the amount."

The caller smiled an embarrassed smile.

"If you please," he said, "you should be so good as to make out the note and then I should sign it."

"What's the idea?" inquired the bank manager, puzzled.

"Vell, you see," he confessed, "I haf to tell you somethings: Myself, I cannot read and write. My vife, she has taught me how to make my own name on paper, but otherwise, with me, reading and writing is nix."

In amazement the banker stared at him.

"Well, well, well!" he murmured admiringly. "And yet, handicapped as you've been, inside of a few years you have become a rich man! I wonder what you'd have been by now if only you had been able to read and write?"

"A *shammos*," said Mr. Rabin modestly.

§ 277   Scarcely a Lucrative Calling

A group of wealthy Southerners, Virginians and Carolinians mostly, were on a train returning from a meeting of the National Fox-Hunting Association. Naturally the talk dealt largely with the sport of which they were devotees. A lank Vermonter, who apparently had never done much traveling, was an interested auditor of the conversation.

Presently, when the company in the smoking-compartment had thinned out, he turned to one of the party who had stayed on. He wanted to know how many horses the Southerner kept for fox-hunting purposes and how large a pack of hounds he maintained and about how many foxes on an average he killed in the course of a season.

The Southerner told him. In silence for a minute or two the Vermonter mulled the disclosures over in his mind.

Then he said:

"Wall, with fodder fetchin' such high prices, and with dog-meat for hounds a-costin' what it must cost, and with fox pelts as cheap as they are in the open market, and takin' one thing with another, I don't see how you kin expect to clear much money out of this business in the course of a year."

§ 278 A Plea for Studied Action

Two ball teams, made up of inmates of San Quentin in California, played a game for the prison championship. One team was composed of negroes, the other of white men.

In the seventh inning, with the score a tie, the pitcher for the colored team, a long-term man, grew nervous under the strain. He wound up too quickly. In his haste he made wild pitches. He gave two opposing batters their bases on balls.

Over on the side lines a negro rooter raised his voice in steadying words to the champion of his race:

"Tek yo' time, black boy," he clarioned. "Tek yo' time! You ain't needin' to be in no hurry. You got a-plenty time to win dis game—you got nineteen yeahs!"

§ 279 The Current Rate on Suckers

The late Tom Williams dropped into a gambling house in Reno, Nevada, one night, and, playing roulette, speedily dropped his roll, but not before he had made up his mind that the game was crooked.

On his way downstairs in deep disgust he met the proprietor, Long Brown.

"What kind of a dump is this you're running?" demanded Williams. "I've just been skinned out of four hundred dollars."

"Who brought you in here?" said Brown.

"I brought myself in," said Williams.

"Oh, if that's the case," said Brown, "I owe you eighty dollars."

"How come?"

"Well, you see, I pay twenty per cent. apiece for all suckers that are steered in. You appear to have steered yourself in. Here's your eighty."

§ 280 Going and Coming

Two scholars, a Frenchman and an Italian, were having an argument. Each insisted his own country had produced the most distinguished literary figure that had ever lived.

"Dante," said the Italian, "was the greatest of all writers. Dante went to hell."

"Bah!" cried the Frenchman, "Baudelaire was a thousand times greater than Dante. Baudelaire came from hell."

§ 281 The Evils of Intemperance

A certain newspaper proprietor in New York who always was—and still is, even in these prohibition days—a total abstainer, dropped into the office just before press time, and found the assistant managing editor in charge.

"Where's Blank?" he asked, naming the managing editor.

"Off on one of those periodical tears of his," answered the assistant.

"Where's the city editor?"

"Pie-eyed—down in Perry's bar."

"I didn't see the make-up editor as I came through the composing-room. What's become of him?"

"He's in a Turkish bath over in Brooklyn, getting a bun boiled out of him."

The proprietor dropped into a chair, shaking his head sadly.

"Well," he said, "for a person who never touches a drop I seem to suffer more from the effects of drunkenness than any man in this town."

§ 282 Not a Family of Musicians

A self-made Western millionaire built the finest house in his home town. He imported decorators to furnish it, and managed to get it finished by the time his eldest son arrived from the East, where the youth had been completing his education.

The proud father escorted the young man through the shining new mansion, followed by the other members of the household. When the grand tour had been completed the millionaire inquired whether the son had any suggestions to make.

"Well," said the young man, "to me it seems complete in every possible detail except one."

"What's missin'?" demanded the parent.

"You ought to have a chandelier in the music-room," said the boy.

"All right," said the father. "I'll order one by telegraph to-night, but I'll bet a thousand dollars there ain't a damn one in the family can play it."

§ 283 The Reverend Had a Little Lamb

The pastor of a colored church in Louisiana was haled before the board of deacons on serious charges. It was alleged that, although married, he had been caught in the act of embracing a comely female member of the congregation, in the vestry room. The evidence against him appeared to be conclusive. Three presumably unbiased witnesses testified to the fact.

The accused was asked whether he had anything to say in his own defense. He answered at length and with eloquence. He led off by pointing out that the word "pastor" was a Latin word meaning "shepherd." Therefore, he properly was a shepherd. He also called the attention of the court to the fact that in pictures and paintings and more frequently in stained-glass memorial windows the Master Himself was shown as a shepherd, carrying a lamb.

Now then, he contended, it naturally followed that when he, as the shepherd, took a member of his flock in his arms, he merely was carrying out the Scriptural example.

In the minds of the deacons there seemed to be no way of controverting these arguments. Accordingly they went into executive session and drew up resolutions exonerating the preacher. But they added a proviso.

The concluding clause of the document, as read by the senior deacon before the congregation on the following Sunday night, ran as follows:

"And, be it finally resolved, ef in future our beloved pastor should feel de desire stealin' over him to tek one of de lambs of de flock in his arms, dat he shall tek a ram lamb!"

§ 284 God Save the King's English!

A London firm received from a merchant in Porto Rico a letter which, properly framed, now hangs on the walls of the home office—

proof in denial of the ancient libel that the English don't know a joke when they see it.

The letter read as follows:

"Why, for God's sake, you send me pump without handle? My customer hollar like hell for water.

"P. S.—Since writing I find the dam handle in the box."

§ 285   The Kink in Mr. Jones

Mr. Jones was one of those nervous persons, and inclined to hypochondria. His imagination, from time to time, afflicted him with maladies which never really materialized. Nevertheless, his devoted wife continued to share his apprehensions at each fresh alarm.

One afternoon, long before his usual hour for returning from business, he fell into the house. His face was white as chalk, and in his eyes was a stricken look. He was bent forward. He tottered to a chair, and, still curled into a half-moon shape, dropped into it.

"Maria," he gasped, "it's come at last! I'll never be a well man again!"

"Merciful Heavens!" she cried. "Henry, what has happened?"

"There was no warning," he said. "All of a sudden, a while ago, I found I couldn't straighten up. I can't lift my head. I feel all drawn."

"Is there any pain?" she asked, fluttering about in her distress.

"No," he said, "there's no pain—that's what makes me think it must be paralysis. Run for the doctor!"

She ran. Returning in a few minutes, she brought with her the family physician. She ushered him into the room where the sufferer was and waited at the door, wringing her hands and dreading the worst.

Almost immediately the physician emerged. He had his face in his hands and his shoulders heaved and shook as though under the stress of an uncontrollable emotion.

"Oh, doctor," cried the agonized Mrs. Jones, "is there any hope for him?"

"Well, madam," he said, "it'll help a good deal if he'll unhitch the third buttonhole of his vest from the top button of his trousers"

§ 286 Better than Believing in Santa Claus

Two typical wayfarers of the Bowery, penniless and tattered and with their feet half out of their wrecked shoes, were limping through the crooked streets of Chinatown. One of them found a small vial containing cocaine which, presumably, had been dropped by a dope fiend.

The tramps had heard many times of the stimulating and invigorating effects of this drug. Also, from association with habitués they knew the common method of taking it. They decided to experiment.

The finder uncorked the vial, poured a quantity of the white crystals into the palm of his hand and sniffed the stuff up his nostrils. His companion finished the bottle.

The effect was magical. They straightened their bent figures, drew their rags about them and stepped out briskly. Presently one of them spoke. There was a bloom in his cheeks and his eyes glistened:

"I've about decided," he said, "to make a few investments. I'm going to buy all the diamond mines in South Africa and after I've done that I'm going to buy all the gold mines in Australia."

His transformed partner made answer:

"Hold on," he said, "I don't know that I'm prepared to sell 'em!"

§ 287   The Curse of an Active Mind

My father, for the greater part of his life, was in the steamboat business. He was an official of a company operating packets on the lower Ohio River. The headquarters of the line was the gathering place of pilots, captains, mates, clerks and engineers—a collection of quaint types and homely philosophers. I was a small boy but I still remember it as though it were yesterday, when on a summer afternoon the talk drifted to the subject of mules. Somebody ventured the opinion that the mule was a stupid animal.

Instantly our champion romancer spoke up:

"Don't you believe it," he said. "The average mule has got more sense than the average horse has got. What's more, every mule has got something that no horse ever had—and that's imagination. Why, I know of an instance when a mule was killed by the power of his own imagination.

"It happened forty years ago when I was a young shaver, on my uncle's farm up the Tennessee River. My uncle owned an old gray mule. He had the mule on pasture in a ten-acre lot. In the middle of the lot was a log crib full of popcorn.

"Along about the middle of July came the most terrific hot spell that ever occurred in this country. The thermometer went to 118 in the shade and stayed right there day and night for three weeks. At the end of the third week, on the hottest day of all, the sun set fire to the roof of that corncrib and it burned to the ground. Naturally, the heat popped all the corn and it fell three inches deep, all over that ten-acre lot. The mule thought it was snow and laid down in its tracks and froze to death."

§ 288　A Way Out of the Difficulty

Whether we expect to go there or not, stories about Heaven almost always have an appeal for us. Here is one which has done service for a good many years:

An exceedingly rich man who had been noted all his life for taking a good and a loving care of his money, passed away. In due time he knocked at the Golden Gate and craved admission to the Celestial City. St. Peter received his application. The Angel Gabriel was called in, also, to pass on the petition.

"Your name," said the Saint, "is not entirely unfamiliar to us. We have heard of you while you were on the earth. I ask you now to search your mind and see whether you can recall any deed ever done by you in the flesh which, in your opinion, entitles you to enter Paradise and dwell among the blessed. Under a new ruling the record of a single noble act will secure admittance."

The millionaire gave himself over to intensive thought.

"Well, there was one thing," he finally said, "of which I was always very proud. One cold winter's night on the street I met a little crippled newsboy. He was crying. I stopped and spoke to him. He said he cried because he couldn't sell his papers; so I bought a paper from him. The price of it was only a penny, but I gave him three pennies for it."

"Excuse me for one moment," said St. Peter. "I must ask my confrère to consult the files and see whether your statement is correct."

The Angel Gabriel looked through the Doomsday book and, finding there a certain entry, nodded his head. St. Peter and Gabriel consulted together in low tones. It appeared that they could not go behind the returns. At length Gabriel slammed the covers of the great volume together and exclaimed:

"Oh, just give him back his three cents and tell him to go to hell!"

§ 289   Stylish Language, Indeed!

For years, a certain worthy and highly intelligent old colored woman did our family washing. One Saturday night after she had fetched the week's laundry she sat in the kitchen of our home before she started on her return trip to her own house a mile and a half away. My mother came to the kitchen door to chat with her a little while.

From remarks which the old woman let fall, my mother gathered that Aunt Milly, although very devout, did not seem to care deeply for the present pastor of her church.

"Mis' Manie," said Aunt Milly, "I'm goin' tell you how I put that there biggety preachin' man in his place. Yere yistiddy evenin' jest 'fo' suppertime, I wuz settin' on my front po'ch w'en the Rev'n Rogers come along by. He sees me settin' there an' he stops an' fumbles wid the gate latch an' he sez to me he sez, 'Sist' Carter, I would have speech with thee?'—jest lak that.

"Now, Mis' Manie, I ain't aimin' to let no nigger whatsoever, even ef he is a min'ster of the gospel, use mo' stylish language 'en whut I kin. So I sez right back to him, I sez, 'Rev'n, draw nigh an' ye shall be heard!'

"So he undo the gate an' come on up the walk to my do'step. But no sooner do he start in to speak 'en I know whut 'tis he's fixin' to say. He fixin' to ax my sympathy on 'count of that tore-down limb of a onmarried daughter of his'n havin' got herse'f mixed up in a scandalizin' an' bein' tawked about all over the neighborhood. So, jest soon ez I sees whut he's drivin' at, I th'ows up my right hand like this, an' I sez to him, I sez,

" 'Rev'n,' I sez, 'hold! Yere last fall,' I sez, 'w'en my husband, Isaiah Carter, at the age of seventy-fo' w'en he should a'knowed better, wuz mekin' hisse'f kind of promisc'us by hangin' 'round two of the lady members of the congregation, an' I went to you,' I sez, 'an' axed you, az the pastor, to 'monstrate wid him, whut did you do? Jest because he'd done give you five dollars fur the new organ fund, you tole me to shet up my black mouth an' go on home an' 'tend to my own bizness.

" 'Rev'n,' I sez, ' "ez ye sows, so shall ye reap!" Rev'n, pass on!' "

§ 290   The Original Package

Marjorie, aged four, marched into the grocer's to tell the news.
"We've got a new baby brother up at our house," she said.
"You don't tell me!" said the grocer. "Is he going to stay with you?"
"I guess so," said Marjorie; "he's got his things off."

§ 291   The Voice of a Husband

An Eastern college professor, on his first visit to Yellowstone Park, attempted to study at close range the grizzly bears that came down to the garbage heaps back of the Fountain Hotel for their provender. An irritable she-bear, with a cub in tow, resented his scientific curiosity. She hauled off and slapped him about fifteen feet and was preparing to claw him when Mrs. Professor came running up, armed with an umbrella, and by opening and closing it repeatedly, so frightened the bear that she departed without doing any serious injury to the startled investigator.

On the following day, two cowboys who, in the season, served as park guides, were discussing the affair. Said the first one:

"I claim that was a powerful brave woman, takin' her own life in her hands to save that fool husband of hers."

"I don't see nothin' so brave about it," said his friend. "Anybody would do that."

"Like hell they would! Spose'n some bear had your wife down and was fixin' to claw her to death—what would you do?"

"Me? I'd give three loud ringin' cheers."

§ 292   The Passive Rôle

It is set forth that during the Civil War a young officer in the Union Army was taking a stroll along a road in Virginia when he met an old negro man and engaged him in conversation. The ancient darky returned such quaint answers to the Northerner's questions that the latter was moved to quiz him humorously.

"Uncle," he said, "you know, don't you, that this war between us and the Rebs is largely on your account?"

"Yas, sah, dat's whut I done heared 'em say."

"Well, you crave to have your freedom, don't you?"

"I 'spects I does."
"Then why aren't you in the army yourself?"
The negro scratched his head reflectively.
"Boss," he said, at length, "did you ever see two dawgs fightin' over a bone?"
"Yes, many a time."
"Well, wuz de bone fightin'?"

293 The Suggestion of a Scandal

In a high state of excitement little Evelyn runs into the house.
"Oh, mother!" she cries out. "Our pussy-cat has got some kittens and I didn't even know she was married!"

§ 294 A Warning Word to a Friend

Two Irishmen, newly landed, got jobs as laborers in a small machine shop on the second story of a loft-building, so-called, on the lower West Side of New York. Under the fire regulations, smoking by the operatives was not permitted while they were on duty. During their first morning in the new place one of the green hands, whose name was Donlan, craved a few comforting whiffs from his pipe. He voiced his desire and a friendly fellow-employee confided to him that in such cases it was customary to ask leave of the foreman to go to the washroom and there to steal a clandestine smoke.

Thus advised, Donlan approached his boss and inquired the whereabouts of the washroom.

"Go down the hall," said the foreman, "and take the first turn to the right, and the second door you come to after that is the door to the lavatory."

Donlan undertook to follow instructions but he made a mistake. In the darkness he took the turn to the left instead of the right-hand turn, and, opening the second door, stepped into the elevator shaft and struck with a bump on the ground floor below.

Presently he came back upstairs. He was sweeping up rubbish when O'Day, his buddy, asked him where was the washroom.

Donlan gave him the direction as he remembered it, and, as O'Day turned to go, he called out to him:

"But say, Larry, look out for the top step—it's a son-of-a-gun!"

§ 295 Obstructing the Highway

There is a corner in a Southern state, down near the Mississippi River, where formerly lynchings occurred more frequently than they do these times. In the days before the rural-free-delivery system was adopted, Uncle Gip Thomas held the contract for delivering the mail in this neighborhood. So regular was he that the residents almost could set their clocks by him.

But one day he was nearly two hours late in reaching the end of the line, where there was a tiny cross-roads hamlet. Just as the citizens were forming a posse to set out in search of him, in fear that some mishap had befallen him, Uncle Gip ambled into view.

"What delayed you, Uncle Gip?" asked the postmaster. "Did you happen to an accident or did an accident happen to you?"

"Nary one, nor both," stated Uncle Gip. "But about ten o'clock this mornin', jest before I crossed the creek, I come to where some of the boys had done left a nigger hangin' right thar in the public road. Well, suh, my mare she got skeered and shied back, and I jest natchelly couldn't make her go past him noways; so finally I had to tear down a panel of rail fence and lead her through the gap and lay the fence back up again and go through the woods down into the hollow and ford the creek and then tear another gap in the fence before I could get back again on the turnpike—and that was what kept me so late." Uncle Gip paused a moment and then went on again in an aggrieved tone:

"Honest, boys, it does look to me like there oughter be a law against leavin' a nigger hangin' in the public road."

§ 296 In Part Settlement

The men who earn their living on the waters and in the marshes of the Great South Bay of Long Island are a race unto themselves. They are a sturdy, independent lot, and, almost without exception, are endowed with a quaint native wit.

One winter's day a party of baymen sat around a red-hot stove in a little oyster shanty on one of the farther bars. The talk veered this way and that until finally there arose the ancient question:

"What would you do if you had a million dollars?"

One of the company allowed he'd buy himself an ocean-going yacht and tour the world. Another rather thought he'd adopt orphans and educate them. And so forth and so on.

All this time, Old Man Banks, locally celebrated as the most shiftless man in the county, had sat in silence, rolling his quid and staring reflectively into the hot coals.

"Say, Banks," quoth one of the group, "you been keepin' pretty quiet; what would you do if somebody was to hand you a million in cash?"

The ancient deftly spat in through the open stove door before he answered:

"Well," he said, "I don't know exactly, but I reckon I'd pay it on my debts ez fur ez it went."

§ 297   The Apostolic Switch

An Irishman walked up Fifth Avenue one Wednesday night, dropped into a place of worship and immediately went to sleep. After the prayer-meeting services were over the sexton came and shook him by the arm.

"We are about to close up," said that functionary, "and I'll have to ask you to go now."

"What talk have you?" said the Irishman. "The cathedral never closes."

"This is not the cathedral," said the sexton. "The cathedral is several blocks above here. This is a Presbyterian church."

The Irishman sat up with a jerk and looked about him. On the walls between the windows were handsome paintings of the Apostles.

"Ain't that Saint Luke over yonder?" he demanded.

"It is," said the sexton.

"And 'tis Saint Mark just beyant him, if I'm not mistook?"

"Yes."

"And still farther along Saint Timothy?"

"Yes."

"Young man," demanded the Irishman, "since whin did all thim turn Protestant?"

§ 298   In One of His Tamer Moments

Fred Kelly, the writer, was standing on a street corner in Cleveland waiting for a car. A small man, densely grown up in whiskers and with a mild manner and a diffident way of speaking, sidled up to him.

"Excuse me," he said, "are you acquainted with this town?"

"More or less," said Kelly.

"Well," said the stranger, "maybe you can tell me, then, where the street fair is going on."

It so chanced that Kelly knew the location where a carnival company was holding forth for the week, and he gave the directions for reaching the spot. Then, as the little meek-looking man started off, Kelly was moved to put a question on his own account:

"Are you running one of the concessions over there?" he asked.

"No," said the little fellow, "but I'm working in one of them."

"What do you do?"

"I work in a side-show that they've got over there. I'm the wild man."

§ 299   That Thick Hotel Crockery

A Northern man was stopping at a small hotel in Alabama. One night after he had retired there came a knocking at his door.

"Who is it?" he asked, sitting up in bed.

"Hit's me, boss," came the somewhat cryptic answer.

"Who's 'me'?"

"One of de bell-boys."

"What do you want at this time of night?"

"Got a telegram fur you, boss."

"Oh, that's it? Well, it's not very important, I guess. I'll read it when I get up in the morning. Just shove it under the door."

There was a pause. Then, in a voice made sharp by the fear of losing a tip, the darky spoke:

"I can't—hit's on a plate!"

§ 300   A Reduction for Cash

Any Scot will tell you that, while as a race the Scotch are thrifty, it is in Aberdeen that thrift becomes an exact science.

And it was in Aberdeen, so the story runs, that an especially frugal citizen entered an apothecary's shop or, as we would say in America, a drug store. He told the proprietor that he wished to purchase threepence worth of morphine.

The chemist pondered over a request so unusual. Customarily he sold the drug only on a physician's prescription; but this customer was known to him as reputable and responsible. Nevertheless, he must make sure the purpose was proper.

"Thr-pence worth of morphine, eh?" he said. "What would ye be wantin' it for?"

The native thought a moment.

"Tuppence," he said.

§ 301   Extending Down to the Very Bottom

Let us not forget the story of the young woman who had a tooth which must come out. She agreed with the practitioner that it should be drawn, but each time he brought the forceps into view she clenched her jaws tightly together and refused to open them until he put down the shining instrument to argue with her.

Finally he had an inspiration. He bade his woman assistant get a long hatpin from her hat and station herself just behind where the obdurate patient sat.

"Now, then," he counseled her, "when I get the forceps right close to her lips I'll give you the signal and you jab the hatpin clear up through the seat of the chair. Naturally, she'll open her mouth to say 'Ouch!' and then I'll get that tooth. It's very loose—it'll come out in a jiffy."

The artifice worked. As the dentist held up the ousted tooth he said soothingly:

"Now, then, that wasn't so bad after all, was it?"

"No," said the relieved sufferer; "only one sharp, darting pain. But oh, doctor, I had no idea that the roots of a tooth went down so deep!"

§ 302 Belated but Sincere

The funeral was over. The elderly widower, having returned from the cemetery, sat on the front porch of his small New Hampshire cottage whistling to himself. A neighbor passed, and saw the solitary figure in the shadow of the porch, and halted his team.

"Well, Uncle Gil," he said, striving to put sympathy into his tones, "how air you bearin' up?"

"Fust-rate, Eph," said the supposedly bereaved one, cheerfully. "Dun't know ez I ever felt better."

"I thought mebbe you'd be missin' her," said the neighbor. "She was a good wife—tuck keer of your home and raised your children and always done mighty well by you durin' all the thutty years you lived together."

"Yas; I know that," stated the widower. "She done all them things and I lived with her thutty years, jest ez you was sayin'. But, gol-dern her, I never did like her!"

§ 303 An Expert Opinion

When I hear of medical experts disagreeing in a consultation I think of a diagnosis which was made once by a colored person from down South who came North to drive a car for a friend of mine. This was in the days when automobiles were more prone to functional disorders than at present. The darky was a fair-enough chauffeur and he professed to be a good mechanic, but as subsequent events proved, no reasonably prudent person would entrust him with a nutpick.

One bright Sunday he took his master for a spin over on Long Island. Suddenly, on a lonely road, the car developed a racking cough and a hectic flush and after panting along for a few rods came to a dead stop.

The chauffeur descended from his seat, selected an armload of wrenches and other utensils from the tool-box and wriggled his way under the balking auto. There he hammered and tinkered for twenty minutes. Eventually he crawled out, covered with dust and streaked with grease, and delivered his opinion to his employer.

"Mr. Miner," he said, "I reckon you'll have to find yore way back to town the bes' way you kin. They's fo' sep'rit things de matter wid dis yere cyar—an' I dunno whut nary one of 'em is."

§ 304   A Well-Merited Rebuke

"Vaiter, vaiter, here vaiter—gif me some addension, uf you bleaze!"

The gentleman rapped with impatient knuckles on the table top. At his call, a servitor came hurrying to his side.

The scene was a Yiddish restaurant in Grand Street on New York's East Side. The hour was the luncheon hour. The speaker was a heavily bearded person who had just made his entrance. All about him conveyed the idea that here was a business man in a rush.

"Vaiter," he said, "you should right avay bring me a knife und a fork und a napkin und a blate; ulso ein glass water. Und make it snappy!"

The waiter, somewhat puzzled, produced the articles called for, then stood by awaiting the order. To his surprise the patron waved him back and then before his astounded eyes drew from one coat-pocket a knuckle of rye bread and from the other a pickled herring and proceeded to make a light but satisfying meal.

Ablaze with indignation the waiter spun on his heel and dashed away to find the proprietor.

"See that guy yonder?" he said, pointing toward the bewhiskered one. "Well, of all the scalded nerve ever I seen in my life—say, you know what that guy done, boss? He come in here a minute ago and made me fetch him a set of feedin' tools and then, be gee, he hauled out his own chow and started eatin'. Ain't you goin' to give him a call-down?"

"I certainly am," stated the owner. He ranged up alongside the offender.

"Say," he demanded with terrific sarcasm, "wot kind of a place do you think I'm runnin' here, anyway?"

The stranger looked up from his repast:

"Vell," he said calmly, "since you ask me, I got to dell you—der service here iss rotten! Ulso, for why ain't der orchestra playing?"

§ 305 For Business, Not Pleasure

The newly organized Ku Klux Klan, having had its first parade, was now in session behind locked doors for the purpose of conferring the secret work upon a batch of new members. A stranger tried to shove his way into the hall. The keeper of the outer portals shooed him away. Presently the persistent intruder returned.

"Say, look here," said the warden, "you don't belong in here." He took a closer look at the stranger. "I'm sure of it. Ain't you Jewish?"

"Shure, I'm Jewish," answered the other, with an ingratiating smile.

"Well, don't you know the Ku Klux Klan don't let no Jews join it?"

"I don't vant to join."

"Well, what do you want then?"

"I vant to see the feller vot buys the bed-sheetings."

§ 306 Let There Be Light!

A young negress visited a dentist of her own race late one afternoon to have an aching molar removed.

"Does you want gas?" inquired the dentist.

"Suttinly I wants gas," she answered. "Does you think I crave to have a strange man foolin' 'round me in de dark?"

§ 307 A Little Bed Time Tale

If you have for a friend a clergyman who is slightly deaf, it is proper to tell this story on him, adding that you were present when it happened. As a matter of fact, it has been attributed to every distinguished churchman in this country who is hard of hearing. However, it goes better, I think, when you make the central character a bishop—by preference a very dignified bishop—who is attending a dinner-party.

Seated next to him, on his deafer side, is a young lady who, being naturally diffident, is now deeply awed by her proximity to so famous a man. She hesitates to address him, preferring to wait for what she regards as a favorable opportunity; yet she craves conversation with him.

Toward the end of the meal, fruit is passed about. The nervous guest seizes on this for her cue. Gently she joggles her great neighbor's elbow.

"I beg your pardon, sir," she says, "but are you fond of bananas?"

His Reverence inclines a stately head in her direction, at the same time cupping his hand behind his ear.

"What did you say?" he asks.

Blushing, the young woman raises her voice:

"It's really of no consequence," she says; "I merely asked you whether you liked bananas."

By now, all the others at the table are listening. The bishop considers for a moment and then replies:

"Well, my dear, if you wish my honest opinion, I have always preferred the old-fashioned night-shirt."

§ 308   A Growing Suspicion

For years Mrs. Grauman, wife of the wealthy retired shirt-waist manufacturer, had been ailing. Or anyhow, she thought she was ailing. She tried one specialist after another, patronized a succession of sanitariums, took the cure here, there and elsewhere. Yet nothing seemed to help her. She remained a chronic complainer.

The husband's patience sorely was tested. Also there was a constant drain upon his checkbook. Mr. Grauman didn't so much mind the latter. Always he had been a generous provider for his family. What secretly irked him was a conviction that the lady's trouble was more or less imaginary; an unspoken but none-the-less sincere belief that his money was being spent to gratify a neurotic whim. Had Mr. Grauman known the words "malingerer" and "hypochondriac" these undoubtedly were the words he would have applied in his own private diagnosis of the case.

Nevertheless, the invalid, after long months of treatment, succumbed to her mysterious malady. She became no more.

On the night before the funeral the mourning widower sat alone by the bier. For long hours he communed with himself. Finally he reached forth a caressing hand and softly patted the casket.

"Vell," he said, "maybe Mommer *vas* sick!"

§ 309 Caught in the Jam

There is an actor in New York who is distinguished among other qualities for his frugality. There have been other frugal actors from time to time, but probably none quite so much so as this gentleman is. His passion for personal economy has come to be proverbial. Let us for convenience call him Jones, which isn't his name at all.

One day in the early part of December of last year a gentleman of a waggish turn of mind came, with a look of concern on his face, into the Lambs Club. He approached a card table where four brother members were playing bridge.

"Did you hear about the accident to Jones?" he asked.

"No," they chorused. "What was it?"

"Well, it just happened over on the East Side. While Jones was doing his Christmas shopping he got crushed between two push-carts."

§ 310 And Getting Worse All the Time

The transcontinental flier had pulled out from Chicago for the long run to the Coast and the conductor had made his rounds, when the passengers in one of the coaches became aware of signs of concern on the part of a fellow traveler. This was an elderly bearded man in old-fashioned garb and of fatherly aspect. He sat with his head in his hands muttering to himself in Yiddish and at intervals uttering low moaning sounds.

They sympathized with his grief and among themselves wondered what ailed him. The common theory was that the poor old fellow must be on his way across country, hoping to reach the bedside of some dear one who was in sore affliction. Or, possibly, he was going west to attend a funeral.

Next morning, as the train entered Kansas, his grief seemed greater even than it had been the night before. He groaned almost continuously, beating himself gently on the breast and at intervals exclaiming:

"Oi! Oi!"

This continued all through that day and the day following. The patriarch seemed so alone in his sorrow; so completely desolated. Kindly eyes regarded him and all on the train wished they might do something to soothe him and comfort him. But he was a stranger and, after all, there wasn't anything really they could do; besides, they felt it was not proper that they, who never before had seen him, should intrude upon his distress.

Finally, though, on the next afternoon when they were crossing Southern California and were within a few score miles of Los Angeles, one big-hearted man could contain himself no longer. He approached the seat where the old man sat in a huddle of misery and extending a cordial hand, he said:

"Sir, I do not know you. I do not wish you to think that I am inquisitive, but I have been sorely moved by your grief and perhaps now that we are approaching our destination I can be of some small assistance to you. Is there anything I can do?"

Tears gushed from the old man's eyes as mutely he shook his head.

"I'm so sorry. Pardon me for asking, but have you suffered a personal bereavement?"

The ancient shook his head in the negative.

"Is it worse than that even?"

A nod.

"Well, then, what is the matter?"

"Listen, Meester: T'ree days already I am on der wrong train!"

§ 311   A Temptation to His Majesty

The steamer was calling at the principal port of one of those remote South Sea islands regarding which so much romance has been written these last few years by gifted fictionists and imaginative travelers. In canoes the natives paddled out to welcome the strangers from other climes. At the head of the volunteer reception committee came the ruling monarch, King Some-thing-or-Other, a huge brown man with an air of heavy dignity and a battered high hat upon his head. He was accompanied by the Imperial staff and also by his household retinue, the party including all of his wives, many of his children and his prime minister. The latter was a Cockney beach-comber who had been stranded here years before and who, having been adopted into the tribe had risen to a place of high favor in the eyes of the copper-colored potentate.

The king, his premier, and his body-guard were welcomed aboard ship. The subjects remained alongside, in broken English begging the passengers to throw pennies down to them. Whenever a coin struck the water, half a dozen islanders at once dived for it.

One of the visitors was generously inclined. When he had emptied his pockets of coppers he began flinging out small bits of silver and correspondingly, the excitement among the amphibious natives increased. In the hope of moving them to an even more spirited exhibition of their powers, the white benefactor fished about until he found a silver dollar. He was in the act of hurling it over the side when the prime minister caught his arm.

"Please, sir," begged the Cockney, "don't do that, sir. Hi ask you to restrain yourself, sir. You'll be 'aving 'Is Royal 'Ighness overboard next!"

§ 312   Giving the Lady the Air

A country girl went to Charleston, South Carolina, to have some work done on her teeth. The operator was cleansing a cavity with a small blow-pipe. The patient flinched.

"Do you feel that air?" asked the dentist.

"That air whut?" said the young lady.

§ 313   Complete in Every Detail

The gentleman who entered the popular-price restaurant must have had a great night the night before. Because he felt so miserable this morning. And looked it! He was disheveled; his eyes were wan and bloodshot; his hand trembled. In short, it was plain to any eye that he suffered from what, technically, is known as a hang-over.

He fell into a chair at the table, took one look at the breakfast menu and gagged. To him, all affability, came a colored waiter.

"Well, boss," began the servitor genially, "whut's it goin' to be this mawnin'?"

"Oh, I don't know," said the sufferer. He sniffed the close air of the little place and turned slightly paler. "I feel like the devil. About all I want, I guess, is two fried eggs and a few kind words."

"Lemme see ef I got that right?" said the waiter. "You is feelin' kind of puny so all w'ich you craves frum me is two fried aigs an' a few kind words."

"That's it."

The colored man hurried to the kitchen. Presently he returned balancing a small platter. On the cloth before the nervous patron he placed a dish containing two eggs.

"Boss, here's part of yore awder." He sank his voice to a discreet whisper. "An' yere's the rest of it:

"Don't eat 'em!"

§ 314   A Bare Statement

The eminent Dr. Blank, specialist in bone and muscular diseases, was a busy man. The routine in his offices was devised with a view to facilitating the handling of cases. He had a full staff of nurses, clerks and attendants.

On a certain morning a neatly dressed and diffident-appearing youth entered the outer room and told the nurse in charge that he wished to see Dr. Blank.

"Have you an appointment?" she asked.

"No, ma'am," he said.

"Then this must be your first visit?"

"Yes, ma'am."

"Very well, then. Go to that dressing-room down the hall, second door on the left, and remove all your clothing, including your shoes. Presently a bell will ring and you may then enter the adjoining room where Dr. Blank will be waiting to see you."

Blushingly, the young man started to say that he didn't think all this was necessary. With an authoritative gesture the nurse checked him.

"If you really desire to see Dr. Blank you must do exactly as I tell you," she stated. "This is the invariable rule for all who call upon him for the first time."

Still protesting, the stranger repaired to the disrobing chamber. Sure enough, within a few minutes a bell tinkled, and, wearing nothing at all except his embarrassment, the youth stepped timorously across a threshold into an inner room where the distinguished specialist sat at a desk.

"Well sir," snapped the expert with professional brusqueness, "what seems to be the matter with you?"

"There ain't nothin' the matter with me," said the newcomer.

"Well, then, what do you want? What did you come here for?"

"I came," said the youth, "to see if you didn't want to renew your subscription to the *Ladies Home Journal*."

§ 315 One Right Behind Another

Some years ago the editor of a popular publication had an inspiration. He made up a list of men and women distinguished in art, religion, literature, commerce, politics, and other lines, and to each he sent a telegram containing this question: "If you had but forty-eight hours more to live, how would you spend them?" his purpose being to embody the replies in a symposium in a subsequent issue of his periodical.

Among those who received copies of the inquiry was a humorous writer. He thought the proposition over for a spell, and then by wire, collect, sent back this answer:

"One at a time."

§ 316 How Time Flies, to Be Sure!

A negro in Sunflower County, Mississippi, was tried and convicted of murder and sentenced for a certain date. After he had been returned to his cell to await the time of execution it would appear that he practically was forgotten. The lawyer, who had been appointed by the court to defend him, lost interest in the case. He neither moved for a new trial nor did he take an appeal from the verdict.

Time slipped by until, finally, it dawned upon the condemned darky that, unless he took steps in his own behalf, something of a highly unpleasant nature shortly would be happening. So he sat down and himself wrote a letter to the governor of the state, reading as follows:

"Dere Guvnor:

"The w'ite folks is got me in the jail here at this place and I is in the middle of a right bad fix. So I teks my pen in hand to ax you please, Mister Guvner, to do something fur me right away?

"Because dey is fixin' to hang me on Friday. And here 'tis Wednesday already!"

§ 317 Honor Where Honor Was Due

A certain distinguished English actor whom we will call Walker-Smith plays a persistent but terrible game of golf. During a visit to this country he visited the links of a country club in Westchester County, New York State.

After an especially miserable showing one morning, he flung down his niblick in disgust.

"Caddy," he said, addressing the youth who stood alongside, "that was awful, wasn't it?"

"Purty bad, sir."

"I'll have to confess that I am the worst golfer in the world," continued the actor.

"Oh, I wouldn't say that, sir," purred the caddy, soothingly.

"Did you ever see a worse player than I am?"

"No, sir, I never did," confessed the boy truthfully; "but some of the other boys was tellin' me yistiddy about a gentleman that must be a worse player than what you are. They said his name was Walker-Smith."

§ 318 On Her Own Motive Power

I am reliably informed that this one really happened down in Winston-Salem, which is the only town in North Carolina that parts its name with a hyphen. A lady who lives there was my informant. She heard it from her pantry window one summer afternoon.

Her cook, Aunt Cilly, was sitting in the kitchen door. The organizer of a new lodge was entreating Aunt Cilly to become a charter member. At length and with eloquence he painted the advantages of belonging to the society. He pointed out its manifold advantages. To begin with, it had a beautiful name made up of noble long words. Its ritual was impressive, its uniform dazzling. Practically every member would hold office, and so forth and so on.

In silence Aunt Cilly harkened until the solicitor ran dry. Then she spoke:

"Tell me dis, Br'er Sawyer, befo' you goes any fu'ther—do dis yere lodge of your'n fune'lize de daid?"

"To tell you de truth, Sista', we ain't quite got 'round to dat part yit," confessed the orator. "Dey's been so much else to do. But in due time we aims to 'range 'bout de sick benefits an' de buryin' fund an' all dat."

"Br'er Sawyer, bresh by," commanded the sagacious Aunt Cilly. "Yo' new lodge done lose its taste fur me already. I 'members whut happen' to dat shiftless flight-haided Fanny Meriwether whut lived jest a little piece up dis same street. Yere two years ago she took an' up an' j'ined one of dese yere new-fangled lodges w'ich a strange nigger got up in dis town, same ez whut you's aimin' to do now. An' dat lodge didn't specify 'bout no buryin' money, neither. Well, Fanny Meriwether hauled off one day an' died widout ary cent of money laid by fur to fune'lize her. An' whut wuz de upshot? W'y, she laid 'round de house daid fur goin' on three days an' den dat pore gal had to git to de cemetery de best way she could."

§ 319 Who's Who in Newark

Back in those old sinful wet days, two gentlemen, both far overtaken in alcoholic stimulant, were seen under a lamp-post on a street corner in Newark, clinging to each other for support.

As a spectator passed them he overheard the following dialogue carried on in somewhat fuzzy accents:

Said Souse Number One:

"Do you know Bill Talbot?"

Said Souse Number Two after a moment of reflection:

"No; whuzziz name?"

Said Souse Number One:

"Who?"

§ 320   Hives, Perhaps, But No Honey

On their bridal tour the young couple went, as many young couples do on their bridal tours, to Washington. They stopped at one of the larger hotels. For two days they did the usual sight-seeing stunts. They visited the Capitol and the White House and they crossed over to Arlington and they ascended the Monument.

Early on the morning of the third day the husband remained in the room to write some letters. The bride ran out to do a little shopping. Half an hour later she returned. She had left the elevator at her floor and was passing through the long hallway when she discovered that she had forgotten her own room number. She was sure, though, she knew which was the right door, but, when she turned the knob and tried to enter, she found it locked.

She rapped on the panel.

"Let me in, honey," she said. "I'm back."

There was no reply.

She rapped again.

"Honey, oh, honey!" she called, "I want to get in."

From the other side of the door came the voice of a strange man— a dignified and an austere voice:

"Madam, this is not a beehive; it is a bathroom."

§ 321   A Mystery Revealed

This yarn, which is of English origin, requires quite a bit of stage-setting. We are expected to imagine a village green in the morning. The official village drunkard is revealed in the foreground. It is evident that he has had a hard night. He leans against the village pump, pressing his throbbing temples to the cool iron work. Ambling up to him with a smile of gratification on his chubby cheeks, comes the curate of the parish.

"Good morning, Walker," says the curate briskly.

"Mornin'," says Walker, opening one eye wanly but not shifting his position.

"Walker," continues the curate, "I want to tell you that I was most pleased—although, I must confess, a bit surprised as well—to see you among those present at vesper services last evening."

"Ow," says Walker; "so that's where I was, was I?"

§ 322 It Very Often Proves Fatal

A literal and simple-minded man, by birth a German, sent his wife to the hospital for an operation. The operation was performed in the forenoon. In the afternoon, when he quit work, the husband called to inquire how the patient had stood the ordeal. The nurse told him that she seemed to be improving.

Early the next morning he was on hand asking for the latest tidings from the sick-room, and again he was informed that his wife still appeared to be improving. Twice daily all through the week he received similar reports.

But one morning when he called he was met with the distressing news that she had passed away. In a daze the widower started down the street to find an undertaking establishment. On the way he met an acquaintance and the latter said:

"Well, how's your wife to-day?"

"She iss dead," answered the bereft one.

"Ach!" said his friend. "That's too bad. I thought she was getting along first rate. What did she die of?"

"Improvements."

§ 323 Proving That Figures Don't Lie

Three patricians of the coal yards fared forth on mercy bent, each in his great black chariot. Their overlord, the yard superintendent, had bade them deliver to seven families a total of twenty-eight tons of coal equally divided.

Well out of the yards, each with his first load, Kelly and Burke and Shea paused to discuss the problem of equal distribution—how much coal should each family get?

"'Tis this way," argued Burke. "'Tis but a bit of mathematics. If there are 7 families an' 28 tons o' coal ye divide 28 by 7, which is done as follows: Seven into 8 is 1, 7 into 21 is 3, which makes 13."

He triumphantly exhibited his figures made with a stubby pencil on a bit of grimy paper:

7/28/13
7
—
21
21
—
00

The figures were impressive but Shea was not wholly convinced. "There's a easy way o' provin' that," he declared. "Ye add 13 seven times," and he made his column of figures according to his own formula. Then, starting from the bottom of the 3 column, he reached the top with a total of 21 and climbed down the column of 1's, thus: "3,6,9,12,15,18,21,22,23,24,25,26,27,28." "Burke is right," he announced with finality.

This was Shea's exhibit:

13
13
13
13
13
13
13
—
28

"There is still some doubt in me mind," said Kelly. "Let me demonstrate in me own way. If ye multiply the 13 by 7 and get 28, then 13 is right." He produced a bit of stubby pencil and a sheet of paper. "'Tis done in this way," he said. "Seven times 3 is 21; 7 times 1 is 7, which makes 28. 'Tis thus shown that 13 is the right figure and ye're both right. Would ye see the figures?"

Kelly's feat in mathematics was displayed as follows:

13
7
—
21
7
—
28

"There is no more argyment," the three agreed, so they delivered thirteen tons of coal to each family.

§ 324   The Exact Locality

Little Willie came running into the house stuttering in his excitement.
"Mommer," he panted, "do you know Archie Sloan's neck?"
"Do I know what?" asked his mother.
"Do you know Archie Sloan's neck?"
"I know Archie Sloan," answered the puzzled parent; "so I suppose I know his neck. Why?"
"Well," said Willie, "he just now fell into the back-water up to it."

§ 325   A Two Part Serial

This story naturally resolves itself into two parts. Thus:

Part 1

Two midgets, members of a traveling troupe, are waiting at the Atlanta station for a train to New Orleans. The train is due at midnight but it is late. The dwarfs go into the lunch room for a bite. One of them drinks two large cups of black coffee, then immediately begins to lament his indiscretion.
"I had no business doing that," he pipes to his companion. "Now I know I won't sleep a wink till broad daylight."
The train arrives and the little men get on. The coffee-drinker has a sleeper ticket calling for Upper Eleven. The other little man holds a reservation for Upper Twelve.
The porter boosts the diminutive passengers into their respective berths and the train moves on.

Part 2

On the following morning two traveling-men meet in the washroom of the Pullman.
"Hello, old chap," says the first, "I didn't know you were aboard. What space did you have last night?"
"I was in Lower Eleven," said the second man.
"How did you rest?" asks number one.
"Rotten! I guess it must have been a fancy, but I had the feeling that all night long somebody was walking up and down just over my head."

§ 326   A Tribute to the Father

Over the alley fence the colored grass widow was calling her small black offspring.

"Morphy!" she shouted. "Oh, you Morphy! Come yere to me."

The passing white man was moved by curiosity to halt and ask questions:

" 'Morphy'?—isn't that rather a curious name for a boy, Aunty?"

"Dat ain't his full name," she explaimed. "Dat's jest whut I calls 'im fur short. Dat chile's full name is Morphine."

"Well, then, why Morphine?"

"Ain't you never heered de word 'Morphine'?"

"Certainly; but never in this connection. Would you mind telling me why you chose it when you were christening this child?"

"I chose it 'cause it wuz de mos' suitable one dey wuz. 'Bout de time he wuz bawn, I heerd one of de w'ite folks readin' out of a book dat Morphine wuz de product of a wild poppy.

"An', Mista, ef evah a chile had a wild poppy, dis is de chile!"

§ 327 The Personal Touch Was Lacking

Among gamblers there is a saying, and a true one, that no matter how wise a guy may be in his own line he's always a sucker at some other fellow's game. The expert confidence man goes against the crooked roulette wheel. The promoter of fixed footraces blows his loot on faro.

It has remained for a sporting person whose specialty is poker to explain why, in his own case, he fails to garner any profits when he invades a kindred field of endeavor. He went to Belmont track one day to play the races. When he returned home in the evening he was penniless. The hand book-makers had stripped him of his last dollar.

His wife took him to task.

"You certainly are a boob," she said. "Every time you go to the track you come home cleaned out. Why is it you always lose there when you always can win at cards?"

"Well," he said, "I've been thinking about that very thing myself, and I guess the answer is that I don't shuffle the horses."

§ 328 Straight from the Scriptures

Several versions of this story are current but the one I like best of all goes like this:

There was a colored preacher who served a term in state's prison in West Virginia for horse-stealing. After his release he changed his name and moved to Alabama. There he became the pastor of a prosperous flock. He figured that his past life was entirely buried. None of the congregation had the slightest suspicion that he was an ex-convict, and he hoped to go on until the end of his days enjoying the confidence of the community.

But one Sunday as he entered the pulpit, he suffered a distressing shock. Sitting in a front pew was a black man he instantly recognized as a former cell-mate in the penitentiary. That wasn't the worst of it. He could tell by the expression on the other's face that the latter also had recognized him. He had a feeling either that he must submit to blackmail or suffer exposure and lose his present charge. The distracted parson did some quick thinking. Then he opened the Good Book, fixed his eyes meaningly upon the countenance of the interloper, cleared his throat and began as follows:

"Brethren an' Sistren. I had figgered to disco'se to you-all dis Sabbath mawnin' 'pun de subjec' of de parable of de Prodigal Son; but sence steppin' into dis holy place I has changed my mind an' I shall preach frum de fo'teenth Chapter of Ezekiel, nineteenth Verse, w'ich sez: 'Ef thou seest me an' thinkest thou knowest me, don't say nothin', fur verily I say unto you, I'll see you later.'"

§ 329   The Real Fromage, in Fact

Two of Broadway's typical products were invited to spend an evening at the Fifth Avenue home of a wealthy patron. The guests knew a great deal about musical shows and about picking winners at the tracks and, when it came to rolling a sucker for his money, they acknowledged no superiors. But in certain other departments of knowledge both of them were just a trifle shy.

Observing that they seemed somewhat self-conscious, their host undertook to make them feel more at home. He made the mistake, though, of picking on literature as a topic. Across the dinner-table he said to one of them:

"How do you like Omar Khayyam?"

"Oh, pretty good," said the person addressed; "but a bottle of this here red Chianti suits me better."

On the way home the second Broadwayite took his friend to task for his ignorance.

"Bo," he said, "when you don't understand a thing why don't you keep your mouth shut? Why, you big stiff, this here Omar Khayyam ain't no wine. It's a cheese."

§ 330   Practically No Reason for It

There once was a clerk of the hotel in a small Maine town who had a unique way of keeping a diary. Each evening he wrote on the bottom lines of the page of the register for the current date a brief account of the principal daily doings in the community, usually coupled with a summary of his own personal reactions to them. Sometimes his phraseology was unusual but always it was amply descriptive.

A friend of mine was stopping at the hotel, having gone up to Maine on a fishing trip. He fell into the habit of glancing through the back pages of the register, more for the enjoyment he got from the quaint language of the entries than because he was interested in bygone neighborhood history.

On succeeding pages of the book for a week of the early spring of the year previous, he found these progressive records of a local tragedy:

Tuesday: "While fishing through the ice yesterday, Henry Whippet fell in the Saco River up to his neck. He was drawed out and took home."

Wednesday: "Henry Whippet is in bed with a powerful bad cold His folks are thinking some about calling in a doctor."

Thursday: "Henry Whippet is rapidly continuing to get no better. It now looks like he is fixing to break out with the pneumonia."

Friday: "Henry Whippet is sinking rapidly."

Saturday: "At nine o'clock this morning our esteemed fellow-citizen, Henry J. Whippet, Esq., went to his Maker entirely uncalled for."

§ 331   He Couldn't Stick to Any One Thing

Carried away by a spirit of patriotism, a New York song-writer, of indolent habits, signed up for a citizens' training-camp. On his arrival he was assigned to an awkward squad under charge of a sergeant of the regular army.

Bearing a dummy musket, our hero lined up with the rest of the green hands. Facing them, the drill-master proceeded to rattle off the manual.

"Attention!" he shouted. "Carry arms—present arms—shoulder arms—parade arms!"

The song-writer flung his wooden rifle down.

"I quit!" he declared. "I'm through, right now."

"What's the matter?" demanded the astonished sergeant.
"The trouble with you is you change your mind too darned often!"

§ 332 Reserve Ammunition

Either the mule which drew the decrepit wagon along the sandy road through the pine-barrens, was balky or else perhaps he merely was conservative by nature. Despite prayers, pleas, curses and commands from the lanky Georgian who drove him, each being accompanied by a terrific blow with a long heavy club, the obstinate animal merely blinked its eyes and continued to amble at the slowest of all possible gaits. The city man, who came along just now in his automobile, drew up to watch the spectacle. Ordinarily the passer-by was a humane man and believed in treating the dumb brutes with all possible kindliness. But the sight of this long-eared malingerer made him forget his sentiments.

"My friend," he said, "I marvel at your patience. Is that beast, by any chance, sick?"

The Cracker shook his head:

"Naw, suh," he answered, "there ain't nothin' ailin' him. This is jest the way he acts all the time. Even down here on this flat land I have to keep beatin' him all the time this a-way to make him move a-tall."

"Why don't you climb down out of that wagon and kick him in the stomach?"

"Naw, I reckin not. You see, I'm savin' that up fur the hill yonder."

§ 333 Dust to Dust

In the Pinenut mining region of Nevada during the early nineties, rich gold-bearing veins were discovered in the foothills. Coincident with this discovery came the development of placer claims in the beds of the valley streams. There was a tremendous rush of prospectors from neighboring mining towns, and Pinenut became the center of much activity. Unfortunately, it proved to be a superficial bonanza and petered out in a short time. A few fanatics still lingered on, hoping that a sharp pick in hopeful hands would open a new Golconda at an unexpected moment.

As Robert H. Davis tells the story, one of the hangers-on had the bad taste to die. It was the custom in new mining camps for the District Recorder to perform the services of the church and to lay to rest those who expired with or without their boots on. The ceremony was the same for both. This particular funeral took place in the dry bed of the creek. A hole six by two by three had been scooped from the gravel. The deceased reposed in a rude coffin.

The Recorder, from the Book of Common Prayer, read the service in a solemn voice:

"Ye brought nothing into this world and ye shall take nothing out."

The coffin was lowered by horny hands.

"The Lord giveth and the Lord taketh away. Blessed be the name of the Lord. Dust to dust!"

Reaching down he gathered a handful of dirt and gravel which sifted through his fingers and fell with a rattaplan upon the wooden box.

"Ashes to ashes!" But instead of either dust or ashes the gleam of a nugget flashed back from the coffin lid. There it lay, resurrected from eternity while the lamented was being returned to the mould.

Without a moment's hesitation the Recorder dropped his prayer-book, jumped into the grave, heaved the deceased out of the property and exclaiming in a loud voice:

"I claim everything seven hundred and fifty feet North and South and six hundred feet East and West. Everybody get off the premises."

He pulled out two six-shooters, cleaned his estate of spectators and put up his location notices without delay.

The interment took place the following day in a vegetable garden.

§ 334 No Trouble to Show Goods

Holbrook Blinn, the actor, was playing an engagement in London several years ago. One afternoon he went out to Epsom Downs for the racing. In the crush at the paddock he was addressed by a Cockney of a slinky appearance:

"Sye, Guv'ner," said the stranger, "wouldn't you like to buy a diamond scarf-pin hat a bargain?"

Blinn shook his head and started to move off, but the importuning stranger detained him:

"Wyte a bit please, Guv'ner," he pleaded, in an eager half-whisper; "don't go yet, you'll never get another chance like this. Hy pledge you me word of 'onor you won't regret it if you buys this 'ere pin. Pure w'ite stone and a nobby settin'. Worth twenty quid, if hit's worth a penny. And yours for four pound cash."

A LAUGH A DAY KEEPS THE DOCTOR AWAY

Interested in spite of himself by the insistent one's eloquence, Blinn said:

"Well, let me have a look at it."

"Hi ain't got it wiv me—yet. But I can give you a look hat it."

"How can you give me a look at it if you aren't carrying it with you?" asked the puzzled American.

"Turn your 'ead slow, Guv'ner," said the Cockney, dropping his voice. "See that fat bloke yonder wiv the gray coat on?" He pointed a cautious finger and sank his voice still lower. "Hit's in 'is necktie."

§ 335 Fun for Little Isadore

Mr. Pincus, the delicatessen dealer, was visiting Mr. Rabinowitz, the retailer in second-hand garments at the latter's flat in Allen Street. To the host came his little son, Isadore, aged six.

"Popper," he asked, "vould you gif me a quarter?"

"Shure," said the parent. He hauled a coin from his pocket, dropped it with a generous gesture into the outstretched hand of his offspring and, as the child trotted away, made as if to resume his interrupted conversation with the caller. But Mr. Pincus, who had been observing the byplay with distended eyes was the first to speak:

"Rabinowitz, have you gone crazy or something? Your boy asks you for a whole quarter und right avay you give it to him. What an extravagance!"

"That's right," said Mr. Rabinowitz, with a proud smile. "Every night comes my little Isadore und asks me for a quarter, und alvays I gif it to him."

"But ain't it teachin' him bad habits, having all that money to spend on himself?" insisted Mr. Pincus.

"Pincus," said his friend, "I tell you a secret: he ain't spendin' it on himself; alvays he goes und puts it in his savings bank, only, it ain't a savings bank—that's what he thinks it is. It's the gas meter."

§ 336 An Awful Blow for Mr. Barnum

The late Alf T. Ringling, of Ringling Brothers, loved the lore of the circus. In his library he had shelves of books and pictures and documents and ancient posters pretaining to life under the big tops. Also he knew hundreds of anecdotes, humorous and otherwise, modern and ancient, which related to some aspect or another of the business he all his active life had followed. A year or two before his death he told me this one, which he vouched for as having been an actual occurrence:

It was back in the days before the Ringling Show had attained large proportions, when Barnum and Bailey's circus was, as its billing proclaimed, The Greatest Show on Earth.

The aggregation, with its menagerie, its three rings and its elevated stages and hippodrome track, and all, was touring the South. A day or two earlier, an acrobat who just had closed a season with a traveling burlesque troupe—by special request of its manager—applied for a job with the circus and was given it. His act did not give full satisfaction to the director of performances, who so reported to Mr. Barnum, and the latter sent for the new performer, and told him that his work fell short of the desired standard.

"You recommended yourself pretty highly when you came around the other day," said Mr. Barnum. "In fact, as I recall, you told me you were the best man in your line anywhere. Now I hear that you haven't made good."

Being an artiste, the young man naturally had his share of temperament.

"Is that so?" he answered with heavy sarcasm. "Well, lemme tell you somethin'—there ain't nobody can reflect on my abilities without answerin' to me. If I hear any more of this sort of talk I'll quit!"

"All right, then, quit," said the famous showman.

"You said it," answered the indignant trouper. "I've quit. I've resigned. Do you know what that means, Mr. Barnum?"

"I think so," said the older man. "It means you've quit."

"Think again. Do you happen to know what town this is?"

"Certainly I do—Pine Bluff."

"That's it. Now you've got it. Here right in the middle of the season I'm leavin' Barnum and Bailey's circus flat on its back in Pine Bluff, Arkansas."

§ 337   An Over Sensitive Deer

An Englishman was visiting on a big ranch in the southern part of Texas. The country abounded in game and the visitor, who had done very little shooting in his life, became filled with an ambition to kill a deer.

His host fitted him out with a rifle and sent him on a still hunt under the guidance of a negro hand who had considerable experience at stalking. The darky led the greenhorn to a likely place on the edge of a thicket. Before the pair had traveled very far the keen eyes of the negro spied out a handsome buck feeding in the thickets and by slow degrees moving in their direction. He drew the Englishman down into a handy clump of chaparral; but when the buck almost was within easy gunshot of them he suddenly quit feeding, raised his head, sniffed, snorted, and instantly was gone. The disappointed amateur turned to his guide:

"Surely the brute didn't see us? I did not move, I know," he said.

"Naw suh, he ain't see you—dat I'm sho'," said the negro, "but I think, boss, he must a' smell' you."

"But that couldn't be," said the still puzzled Englishman. "Why, I had a barth only this morning!"

§ 338 The Proper Rate of Exchange

The late Charles E. Van Loan, a splendid story-teller in his own right and equally adept as a story-writer, used to love to tell this one:

An ambitious promoter undertook to stage a prize-fight between two heavy-weights at a little town just over the international boundary between Mexico and California. The fight was advertised to go for twenty rounds.

From both sides of the line a great crowd gathered, the majority of those present being Mexicans.

A somewhat inexperienced but quick-witted Texan acted as referee. It subsequently developed that, contrary to the ethics, the referee had a private bet on one of the scrappers. Midway of the fight, it appeared highly probable that his favorite would shortly be knocked out and so, to save his money, the referee, at the end of the tenth round, declared the bout a draw, and ended it right there.

Enraged and disappointed, the audience rose up, shouting threats. The native contingent was especially vociferous. A first-class riot was threatened.

But the imperiled referee had a smart notion in reserve. By waving his arms and shouting that he had a statement to make, he secured comparative silence. Then he made his announcement and it proved eminently satisfactory. The Americans present saw the point of the joke; the Mexicans were appeased because the explanation seemed to them perfectly sound.

"Gentlemen," the referee said, "this was advertised as a twenty-round fight and that's exactly what it is—twenty rounds Mex. or ten rounds American."

§ 339 Classifying the Delinquent

Years ago, when I was a reporter for a New York evening paper, and covered trials at the Criminal Courts Building, there was an elderly and very devout Irishman who had a job in Part Two of General Sessions. It was his duty to keep order and to act as doorkeeper, on occasion, and sometimes as a sort of usher. But he particularly shone on those occasions when he was called upon to aid in taking the so-called pedigree of a newly convicted defendant.

In this matter a certain routine invariably was followed. The prisoner would be arraigned at the bar. The old Irishman would range alongside him and in an undertone ask of him certain questions, then call out the answers to the clerk sitting fifteen feet away, who duly recorded them on the back of the indictment. This ceremony was more or less automatic, since from long experience the old man knew exactly what facts regarding the prisoner's past life he must ascertain. As the convicted man usually made his responses in an undertone, only the functionary's voice would be heard as he chanted his own version of the disclosures just made to him.

One day a youth of a most forbidding appearance, who had been found guilty of attempted highway robbery, was brought up. The old Irishman edged up to him and in a friendly confidential half-whisper asked him for his right name.

"Henry Smith," returned the youth, in a surly grumble out of one corner of his mouth.

"He says Henry Smith, Mr. Penney," called out the Irishman. Then he turned again to the malefactor:

"Born in the United States?"

"Sure—Brooklyn."

"Native-born, Mr. Penney."

"Any religious instruction in your youth, young man?"

"No," shortly.

"PROTESTANT, Mr. Penney."

§ 340 A Touch of the Swedish

Personally I do not know a great many persons of Swedish birth. But those Swedes I have met struck me nearly always as being keen-witted. Nevertheless, it is customary among after-dinner speakers, at least, when telling a yarn purporting to deal with slow thinking, to make the central character of it a Swede, and preferably a Swede farmer.

For instance, there is the classic of the Wisconsin politician who, in the presidential campaign of 1912, toured the back districts of his native state to electioneer for his party. In a remote neighborhood he came upon a tall Scandinavian sitting on a log in a clearing. The stranger hauled up his team and greeted the resident, who replied with a nod.

The politician explained that he was sounding out the sentiment in the district.

"What do you think about Wilson?" he asked.

"Aye don't know," drawled the other.

"Well, how about Roosevelt?"

"Aye don't know."

"Maybe you like Taft?"

The alien shook his tawny head dumbly.

"Well, now, look here then, you must have some opinion," said the visitor. "You and your neighbors must have talked the thing over among yourselves. Who do you think has the best show?"

The simple Swede gave this question lengthy consideration. Then, with a faint change of expression, he said·

"Aye tank Ringling Brothers got the best show."

Then there is the time-honored yarn of the Swede farm-hand in Minnesota who, on the witness stand, was called upon by the attorney for the railroad to furnish details touching on the tragic death of a companion.

"Aye tell you," he answered. "Me and Ole we bane walkin' on railroad track. Train come by and Aye yump off track. By and by, when train is gone, Aye don't see Ole any more, so Aye walk on and pretty soon Aye see one of Ole's arms on one side of track and one of Ole's legs on other side of track, and then pretty soon Aye see Ole's head, but Ole's body is not there, so Aye stop and Aye say to myself, 'By Yupiter, something must a' happened to Ole!'"

§ 341 Calling for Night Work, Too

A well-known public lecturer occasionally tells this story on the platform as illustrative of the enterprise and instinctive commercial sagacity of the young American. He vouches for it as an actual personal experience. His version of it runs somewhat as follows:

"Two summers ago I was motoring up in New England. Taking a short cut over a dirt road I ran into a miry place and the car bogged down and stuck fast. Providentially, as it would seem, a farmer boy immediately hove into sight, driving a team of big horses.

I entered into negotiations with him and the upshot was that for two dollars he agreed to undertake the job of rescuing me from my predicament. The price seemed reasonable and we closed the bargain.

"He hooked his horses to the axle of the stalled automobile and soon had the car upon high ground. I was struck by the brightness of the lad and the skill he had shown in extricating the heavy car from the mire. After I had paid him I led him into conversation, taking occasion to compliment him upon his smartness.

" 'Well,' he said, 'I've had considerable practice, Mister. This makes the third car that I've pulled out of this mudhole to-day.'

" 'Did each one of them pay you two dollars?' I asked.

" 'Yep,' he said. 'That's my regular price for this job.'

" 'Then you've earned six dollars to-day?'

" 'Yep, that's right,' he said.

" 'Pretty fair wages for a boy of your age, I should say,' I commented.

"Before answering me, the youngster withdrew from my immediate vicinity and mounted one of his horses.

" 'Well,' he said, 'this has been a 'specially good day. I don't always earn this much, and anyhow, 'tain't as easy as you might think for me to earn this money. All day I've got to be hangin' 'round waitin' for one of you city fellers to get bogged down and start callin' for help and that ain't the worst of it neither; except when it rains, I've got to be around here a good part of every night.'

" 'What do you do here at night?' I asked.

"He drew his team off the road and started away through the woods. Then, over his shoulder, as he vanished, he replied:

" 'Oh, night-times I have to draw water and fill up this here mudhole so as it'll be ready for business the next day.' "

§ 342 Returning in the Regular Manner

This one was a favorite with the late Joseph H. Choate. I heard him use it more than once when he was making after-dinner speeches.

"I had a friend once, named Smith," said Mr. Choate, "whose son, although of comparatively tender years, was addicted to the reprehensible habit of indulging in alcoholic beverages. The father packed him off to Harvard in the hope that the youth might become interested in educational matters and lose his craving for hard liquor.

"It appeared that the father's hopes were to be gratified, because the young man, in writing home to ask that his allowance be increased, told his sire that he had mended his ways and now was devoting himself exclusively to the undertaking of acquiring learning. The senior was most highly gratified. He decided to run up to Cambridge and personally congratulate his offspring upon the reformation which had been effected. To make the meeting more pleasant he would take the youngster by surprise. So, without announcing his intention, he started.

"But the train was delayed and Mr. Smith did not reach Cambridge until after midnight. He got in a cab and rode to the boy's boarding-house. The building was dark.

"He felt his way up the walk, rang the doorbell and pounded on the door. Eventually an upstairs window was opened and an elderly lady, the proprietor of the establishment, showed her head.

"'Well,' she called out, 'what is wanted?'

"'Does Henry Smith, Jr., live here?' asked the father.

"'Yes,' said the old lady, wearily. 'Carry him in.'"

§ 343 Or in Other Words, Slightly Confused

I have always been interested in the character of Daniel Boone. It seemed to me that of all our early pioneers he, perhaps, was the most gallant and the most picturesque, and certainly the most typical

A few months ago a collector of early Kentucky lore told me a story of the great pathfinder. I leaped upon it with loud cries of joy. I said to myself that if it were not true it deserved to be true. So far as my informant knew, it had never been printed but instead had been handed down by word of mouth from one generation to another. So I just was making ready to plunge into the arena with a brand new contribution to pioneer Americana when I sustained a severe shock.

This shock was the discovery that the same anecdote, in substantially the same form in which I heard it told by my Kentucky friend, already had appeared in print. It was published a trifling matter of one hundred and two years ago. Even so, I offer it here again for the reason I believe it has merit in it entitling it to perpetuation.

It appears that in 1819 Chester Harding, an artist, being prompted by a patriotic impulse made the long journey from his home on the eastern seaboard to Missouri, which then was in the far West, for the purpose of meeting the aged Boone and painting his portrait. At the time of Harding's arrival Boone had left his log-cabin home and had gone on one of his periodical outings into the wilderness. The visitor followed along an obscure trail until he came to a tumbledown shanty. To quote Harding's words, "I found him engaged in cooking his dinner. He was lying in his bunk, near the fire, and had a long strip of venison wound around his ramrod, and was busy turning it before a brisk blaze, and using pepper and salt to season his meat.

"I at once told him the object of my visit. I could tell that he did not exactly know what I meant. I explained the matter to him, and he agreed to sit. He was nearly ninety years old, and rather infirm; his memory of passing events was much impaired, yet he would amuse me every day by his anecdotes of his earlier life. I asked him one day, just after his description of one of his long hunts, if he never got lost, having no compass. 'No', said he, 'I can't say as ever I was lost, but I was *bewildered* once for three days.'"

§ 344 A Squirrel without a Peer

In the wicked days when drinking still was going on, Riley Wilson, the official humorist of West Virginia, met on the streets of Huntington a friend of his from up in the mountains. Extending the customary hospitalities, Wilson invited the hillsman to have something. The visitor was agreeably inclined. They crossed the street and entered the swinging doors of a life-saving station.

At one end of the bar an electric fan was buzzing. The gaze of the mountaineer froze on this novel object. So absorbed and interested was he that he almost forgot to help himself from the bottle which the barkeeper set out for him. He put down his emptied glass and, walking close up to the fan, continued to watch it in a fascinated silence.

"Well, old man," said Wilson, "are you ready to move along?"

"Riley," answered the mountaineer without turning his head, "ef you don't mind, I'm goin' to stay here a spell longer. I don't know how long I may be here, 'cause I aim to wait until this here critter stops spinnin' this wheel around so I can git a good look at it. I've seen some peart squirrels caged up, in my time, but this shore must be the peartest one that ever was ketched."

§ 345 The Triumph of the Novice

By way of a beginning, it is incumbent to me to explain that the negroes of the Coast country of South Carolina and Georgia have a distinctive *patois* which differs radically from the speech of members of their own race up country. "Gullah talk," as it is called, has but one gender—the masculine. Everything—a man, a woman, a bull, a cow—is "he."

With this bit of explanation we may proceed. An Englishman, desirous of killing some big game during his visit to America, accepted the invitation to visit a plantation-owner on one of the sea islands lying below Charleston. In honor of the visitor a deer drive was arranged.

The Britisher, chaperoned by an old negro man, was assigned to a "stand" on one of the best "runs." Beforehand he had been told to shoot only at bucks, as the does enjoyed protection.

Presently, to the ears of the nervous Englishman where he crouched with his black companion in a thicket, came the sound of the hounds' baying. The dogs had found a fresh trail. They were drawing nearer and nearer.

Suddenly, fifty yards away across an open glade, a darting patch of tawny brown showed in the undergrowth. The Englishman fired, and a convulsive thumping in the brush told him that he had not missed.

The old negro left his covert and ran forward to see what it was that had been shot.

"Did I kill him?" called the excited amateur.

"Yeah, boss. You kill 'im," answered the darky, as he bent over the stricken creature. Then, as he straightened, seeing that the fallen animal had no horns, he added: "'E a doe do'."

At this moment the host hurried up, having heard the shot from his place of ambush a short distance away.

"Any luck?" he called out as he approached.

"Oh, yes," answered the Britisher exultantly. "I thought I saw a deer and dropped it, but your black fellow yonder has just told me that it is a dodo—a creature which I thought was entirely extinct. Luck, eh, what?"

§ 346   The Gift of Tongues

To arrive at an estimate of the approximate age of this one, try to recall how many years ago it was that Robert Ingersol died and then take it into further consideration that the incident here to be narrated is supposed to have occurred quite a long time before that date.

The great infidel was sitting one day in his library. A genius out of a job came to him seeking advice.

"Mr. Ingersol," said the caller, "I speak seven languages fluently but somehow or other I don't seem to be able to make a living. I can't get work anywhere. At this moment I owe a month's rent. What can you suggest?"

"My friend," said Ingersol, "I don't think I could suggest anything for a person who can express himself in seven languages and can't pay his rent in any one of them."

§ 347   Inquiry Regarding the Stranger

This little incident dates back to the time when a certain well-known publisher of New York was somewhat younger than he is at present. His only daughter, now a charming young matron with a baby of her own, had just passed her fourth birthday. Let us call her Clara, which is not her real name. Since before his marriage the gentleman in question had worn a beard. The little girl had never seen her father excepting with mustache and whiskered chops.

One Saturday night, moved by a whim, he told the barber to give him a clean shave. Then he went home and went to bed. Next morning early little Clara came from the nursery to visit her parents. The mother was awake; her daddy still snoozed.

The child was in the act of kissing her mother, when her gaze fell upon the smooth face on the pillow in the adjacent bed. Her eyes widened in astonishment.

Leaving her mother's side, the little thing tip-toed across the room and subjected the countenance of her father to a puzzled stare. Then she crept back again to where the wife was.

"Mother dear," she said in an awed whisper, "who is the gentleman?"

§ 348   When Appearances Were Deceitful

The native was making a slow headway with a hoe against the weeds and sassafras sprouts which covered the slope with their scrubby growth. Behind him rose the knobby field with deep furrows in it where the rains had washed out gulleys in the thin soil. Further on a rotting rail fence ran in crazy zigzags across the brow of the eminence and on all sides the clearing was enveloped by a bleak and poverty-stricken landscape.

The Northern tourist, who was making a detour through the foothills, halted his car and hailed the industrious worker.

"My friend," he said, "you look like a live chap and a hustler."

"Well," said the native, "I aim to keep busy." He laid down his hoe and advanced to the edge of the road.

"That's what I said to myself as soon as I saw you. I'm wondering why you're content to slave your life out in this God-forsaken country. I never saw such poor-looking soil in my life. Why don't you pull up stakes and move up into Ohio where I live?"

The resident hillsman shook his head.

"You see, stranger," he answered, "I've always lived 'round here and I guess I'll stay awhile longer."

"Well," said the tourist, "every man to his own fancy, and I guess a fellow might get attached even to such a spot as this. But what can you expect by staying on? You are bound to get poorer and poorer all the time."

"Mister," said the hillsman, "I'm a blamed sight better off than what you seem to think. Why, I don't own nary acre of this here land."

§ 349 The Curious Ways of Sheep

They tell this story on Charlie Russell, Montana's famous cowboy painter, who by a very great many is regarded as Frederic Remington's successor as the greatest delineator of Western life. Probably it isn't true, because Russell, as an old cow hand, naturally would have the utmost contempt for all phases of the sheep-growing industry; but as the story goes, he once fell upon hard times and in this emergency accepted a position as herder for a sheep man.

Now, Russell knew about all there was to know about beef cattle and about horses but his education regarding the ways and habits of sheep had been neglected. All the same, he went out on the range with a flock of woolly baa-baas. Ten days passed, and he returned to headquarters to replenish his supply of provisions. The boss met him at the ranch-house.

"Well, Charlie," he asked, "how goes it?"

"Oh, all right," said Russell.

"Satisfied with your new job, eh?" pressed the employer.

"I guess so," said Russell. "But if you want me to keep on working for you there's one thing you'll have to do."

"What's that?"

"You'll have to get another lot of sheep. That first bunch has done lit out on you."

§ 350 Where They Take Things as They Come

Down in the old malarial belt below Mason and Dixon's Line, the indolence of the dwellers in the Low Grounds is proverbial. In illustration of this attribute a story used to be told by the late Polk Miller, of Virginia.

Miller said that in a remote district a prominent resident was being buried. The funeral procession, on its way from the church to the graveyard passed a cabin where an ancient couple resided.

The pair in question were engaged that afternoon in the pursuit of their favorite occupation of doing nothing whatsoever. The old man was stretched on the earth with his back against the wall of the house, and facing the road. His wife, in a rickety arm-chair, was facing in the other direction, massaging her front teeth with a snuff stick. Presently she spoke:

"Whut's that I hear passin'?"

"It's Jim Coombs' fune'l jest goin' by."

"Much of a turn-out?"

"Biggest I ever seen in these parts," he answered. "More'n twenty hacks and waggins, looks like, and a whole passel of mo'ners on foot."

The old woman fetched a little resigned sigh:

"Well," she said, "I certainly do wish I was settin' turned 'round the other way—I'd like mightily to see that there fun'el."

§ 351 A Mystery Unraveled

There was a member, now deceased, of a New York club much frequented by members of the theatrical profession, who suffered in the latter years of his life from a curious internal disorder. Always involuntarily and often at inopportune moments, he gave off weird rumbling and wheezing sounds.

One evening with three fellow members he was playing bridge. He was suffering at the moment from an especially violent attack. A certain comedian, who had been imbibing heavily, approached.

Immediately the newcomer's attention was focussed upon the strange, ghostly noises which at intervals occurred. Just as he had traced these mysterious manifestations to their source the afflicted gentleman, after an especially violent outburst, spoke:

"I beg your pardon, gentlemen, for causing this disturbance. I assure you I cannot help it—the thing is entirely beyond my control. I really don't know what is the matter with me."

"I know what's the matter with you," cried out the inebriated one, "you're haunted!"

§ 352 Already Showing Signs of Use

"Well," said the friendly grocer, "I hear you've got a little baby brother up at your house. What do you think of him?"

"I don't like him," said Mildred frankly. "He's got a funny red face and he cries all the time."

"Well," asked the grocer, "why don't you send him back where he came from?"

"Oh, I'm afraid we couldn't do that," she said. "We've used him two days already."

§ 353 A Hint to the Wise Is Ample

Here of late as all readers of the daily press know, the Ku Klux Klan has been rather active in parts of the state of Arkansas. In a small town north of Little Rock, the colored population has been much exercised over the midnight marches and the occasional visitations of the masked brotherhood.

In this town two negroes met. One of them said:

"Look yere, Henery, whut would you do ef you wuz to git a notice from them ole Ku Kluxes?"

"Me?" said Henry. "I'd *finish* readin' it on de train!"

§ 354 Just Before the Shooting Started

Just before hostilities ended in 1918, a young lieutenant of my acquaintance was detailed to duty as a drill officer at a camp of colored draft troops in Mississippi.

He said that late one night he was returning from a near-by town to his quarters. As he neared the sentry lines, out of the darkness came a voice calling: "Halt!"

He halted, gave the countersign and started on. Immediately, in the gloom, there was a rattle as of a rifle being shifted in the sentry's hands and again the same voice cried: "Halt!"

"You've halted me once already," he said sharply, rightly figuring that the unseen one must be a green trooper, "and I've given you the password. What more do you want?"

"But, boss," said the sentry, drawing nearer, "I don't know you."

"Very probable," said the captain. "What has that got to do with it?"

"It's got a whole heap to do wid it. W'en the sergeant put me yere to-night he p'intedly sez to me dat ef somebody comes by w'ich is a stranger to me I is to cry 'Halt!' th'ee times an' den shoot 'im."

§ 355   The Limit of Helplessness

Only too often does the average after-dinner speaker reach a point where he has nothing to say and yet feels that he must say it. Usually he does, too,—at great length. I know, because in my time, before I reformed, I was addicted to the vice of after-dinner speaking myself.

To those offenders who still persist in their wicked ways of trying to be humorous to order across the dinner table, without having the proper materials in stock, I respectfully would recommend the following highly illustrative little anecdote:

A New England husbandman was driving up a steep hill with a load of provender and gardening implements in his motor truck. In a rough place on the grade the tail-gate slipped from its catches and, item by item, the cargo spilled out. The farmer steered along oblivious of his losses. He reached the crest of the hill, coasted down into the valley, and there, in a miry place, he stuck fast. He climbed down from his seat, and then, for the first time realizing the full depth of his misfortune he exclaimed to himself:

"Stuck, gol darn it! Stuck in the mud—and nothin' to unload!"

§ 356   The Most Unkindest Cut of All

On the stage of a music hall in the East End of London a memory wizard with a pronounced Cockney accent was offering an exhibition of his skill. In response to questions from the audience he gave, off-hand, and promptly, the dates of historic events, the distance from the earth to the moon, and other facts and figures without limit.

It was quite evident from the language of some of his statements that the performer was a most patriotic Briton. Invariably, when mentioning a great Englishman or a great English achievement, his voice rose exultantly.

Sitting well down in front were two Americans. They figured that the wizard must have accomplices in the house to ask him questions prepared beforehand. To find out whether or not the performer did have the powers of memory he boasted and with a view also to arousing his patriotic fervor to a still higher pitch if possible, one of the Yankees called out:

"Professor, please tell me what memorable event occurred on July the Fourth, 1776?"

Without a moment's hesitation the professor shot back his reply:

"A h'infernal h'outrage, sir!" he shouted.

§ 357 The Position of a Young Man

A minor-league baseball manager received a letter from a young player who gave an unabridged and highly flattering account of the author's ability to make good in any company. Also he declared he could hit 'em harder and higher and farther than Babe Ruth ever did. It so happened that the manager was very much in need of a utility player but the young man had neglected to say whether he was a pitcher, catcher, infielder or outfielder.

He answered the letter, inquiring what position the prospective phenomenon played.

A reply came back accompanied by a snapshot of a youth in uniform, crouched and apparently awaiting the arrival of a grounder.

"You can see by the inclosed photograph," wrote the young man, "that I play in a stooping position, with one hand on each knee."

§ 358 No Detail to Be Overlooked

It was the last night of the revival meeting. The evangelist was going strong. His subject was eternal damnation. With all the eloquence at his command, he urged the congregation to flee from the wrath to come.

"Ah, my friends," he exclaimed, "on that last dread day there will be weeping, and wailing, and gnashing of teeth!"

In a rear pew stood up an elderly woman.

"Elder," she said tremulously, "I ain't got no teeth."

"Madam!" he shouted back, "teeth will be provided!"

§ 359 At the Extreme Rear

Up toward Chateau Thierry in the big shove of 1918, a brigade commander of the A. E. F., temporarily separated from his staff, was making a sort of private reconnaissance toward the front. It was night-time. Directly ahead of him, he knew, was a negro infantry regiment, now under fire for the first time.

All at once he encountered a straggler. Perhaps it would be unfair to refer to this person as a straggler, for he was giving a spirited imitation of a foot-racer.

"Halt, there!" shouted the outraged brigadier.

The fleeing private slowed up.

"What do you mean by running away in this disgraceful manner?"

"Boss," quavered the black man, "I ain't been aimin' to run away, but these yere feets of mine jest natchelly carried me out of dat mess up yonder."

"Well, you face about and rejoin your company immediately."

Reluctantly the unhappy soldier reversed himself and started to obey. Then he hesitated and over his shoulder he put a question:

"Who is you, to be givin' me dese yere awders? You ain't no cap'n, is you?"

"I am the general commanding this brigade—that's who."

"Lawsy me!" quoth the darky, half to himself. "I sho' must a' run a long ways to git clear back to where the gene'ls stay!"

§ 360   He Knew Where to Find Paw

The gentleman from the city had rented a country-place in the White Mountains for the summer. Returning from a walk he noted, as he neared his front gate, signs that a mishap had occurred on the road. A load of hay had been overturned while in transit. It was piled in a great shock at the edge of the highway where its weight had caused it to slide from the wagon upon which it was being moved. The team were nibbling grass in the ditch. A fourteen year old boy, dripping with perspiration, and plainly very tired from his exertion, was forking the hay back on the wagon with tremendous energy.

"What happened?" asked the gentleman—a somewhat unnecessary question in view of the evidence.

"The wheels went down in a rut," said the boy, "and this here jag of hay turned bottom-side up."

"Well, you look all tired out," said the sympathetic city man. "This seems to be a pretty big job for one of your years, too. Suppose you quit for awhile and go on up to my house yonder with me and have a bite to eat and a drink of cold lemonade or buttermilk."

"I wouldn't dast to do that," said the boy. "Paw wouldn't like it ef I didn't get this here hay put back right away."

"Oh, that'll be all right. Nothing is going to happen to your hay while you're gone or to your team, either. Come along with me; I'm sure your father won't mind."

Half reluctantly, as though swayed by conflicting emotions the youngster laid down his fork and accompanied the hospitable stranger. Twice, during the course of the meal which was provided for him, he paused from eating to voice his fears that "Paw" would be seriously annoyed for his failure to complete the job of replacing that hay. Each time his host reassured him, meanwhile pressing fresh helpings of this and that upon his young guest.

Finally, at the end of half an hour or so, the boy pushed his chair back from the table and rose up.

"I guess I'll be goin' now," he said. "Paw'll want I should get that hay forked up. I expect he'll be mighty pestered with me."

"Why need your father know anything at all about it?" said the gentleman.

"Why, Paw must know about it already," explained the youngster.

"Where is your father?" asked the city-man. "I didn't see him as I came along."

"He's under the hay," stated the youngster simply.

§ 361 Consolation for the Imperilled One

In a California town is an old family physician with rather a caustic wit. He was in attendance at the confinement of a lady whom we will call Mrs. A—a wife of a year. There were no complications; the affair was progressing as well as might reasonably be expected.

But the husband was in a distressful state. While sympathetic friends endeavored vainly to calm him he walked the floor of the room adjoining the sick room. At frequent intervals he beat upon the connecting door and from those within pleaded for assurance that all was going well. Yet the answers, while consoling, did not avail to soothe his agitation. What the midwife told him only seemed to harass him the more. Messages of cheer from the trained nurse were received by him with choked groaning sounds.

Finally he called through the keyhole that he must have a word personally with the officiating practitioner. The old gentleman came forth.

"Doctor," exclaimed the suffering young man, "I've been waiting for hours now. I can't stand this terrible suspense any longer. Doctor, for my own sake, please tell me what the prospects are?"

"Well, son," said the doctor. "I can only say this to you: I've been bringing babies into the world for forty-odd years now—and I never lost a father yet."

§ 362   Examples of the Higher Criticism

Whenever actors get together it is almost inevitable that sooner or later the subject of dramatic criticism will come up and that someone present will quote a notice favorable or unfavorable—but generally favorable—touching on his own work.

No symposium of this sort is complete without reference to the instance of tact displayed in print by a local reporter on a certain historic occasion in a small middle-Western city when ambitious non-professionals gave an incredibly awful performance of a classic drama. The newspaper man who had been detailed to cover the performance was wishful to avoid giving offence to the members of the cast yet, in honesty, he could say nothing complimentary. So he merely wrote this:

"For the benefit of the new hospital fund, our leading amateurs presented 'Lady Audley's Secret' at the theatre last night before a large audience of our best townspeople. The orchestra rendered several pleasing selections and the acoustics of the hall were never better."

Then there is the famous criticism done by an editor in Rising Sun, Indiana, when a certain native-born prodigy essayed the rôle of the melancholy Dane. The criticism ran something like this:

"Among scholars there has long been a dispute as to whether the works attributed to Shakespeare were written by Shakespeare or by Bacon. The editor of this paper has hit upon a satisfactory way of settling for all time this ancient question. Let the tombs of both be opened. The one who turned over in his grave last night was the author of Hamlet!"

I am reminded also of what Kin Hubbard, better known as "Abe Martin," had to say years ago of a certain theatrical entertainment. For brevity and yet for completeness I think it would be hard to beat this:

"Al Jeffreys' 'Uncle Tom's Cabin Company' played at the opera-house last night. The Siberian blood hound was badly supported."

Hap Ward, the comedian, furnishes one from his own experience:

"We were playing a one-night stand in Oregon," said Hap. "On the morning following the performance I found a notice of our show on the front page of the town paper. The opening sentence was promising—I smiled to myself as I saw it. For it read as follows:

"'Ward and Vokes' show, as given here last night, was not half bad.'

"Then I read the second sentence and quit smiling.

"'On the contrary, it was all bad!'"

§ 363   The Prize Smell of the Circus

Harry Dickson, the writer, probably knows as much about the Southern negro as any white man can ever expect to know. But even so, in his search for local color and quaint lines with which to illuminate his stories, he constantly is striking a new angle of thought or a new angle of observation on the part of some one or another of his dusky neighbors down in Mississippi.

Once upon a time Dickson was on a hunting trip in a remote county. While there, he met an old negro guide, a bear-hunter of superior attainments and a person of a quaint and an original philosophy. All his life the old man had been buried at the back edge of the canebrakes. Only once or twice had he been to a large town. The dream of his life, it developed, was to see a circus. He had heard of circuses, he had talked with persons who had seen circuses and he treasured a tattered program of a circus performance which a white man had given him. But the marvels of the red wagon and the white top never had revealed themselves to him.

Learning of the old man's ambition, Dickson had an inspiration. It was an inspiration born partly of philanthropy and partly of selfish and mercenary motives; for he scented a chance to get some prime material for one of his stories. He promised Uncle Jim that when next the circus visited Vicksburg, he, Uncle Jim, should see it.

In the middle of the following summer Ringling Brothers came along with their show. Dickson sent Uncle Jim money for his railroad fare and bade him be in Vicksburg at daylight of a certain morning. He met Uncle Jim at the train.

That day was probably the most crowded day and the most eventful in Uncle Jim's entire life. His patron took him up into the yards to see the circus unload from the cars, and took him thence to the show lot to watch the raising of the tents. Under escort of Dickson the old negro viewed the street parade, the afternoon performance and the side-show and heard the concert. He saw it all—menagerie, hippodrome, freaks and the rest of it. His widely popped eyes and the look on his face testified to his enthrallment at beholding these wonders, but not a word either of commendation or admiration fell from his lips. Harris was rather disappointed. He had expected a constant flow of "copy."

Still maintaining his silence, Uncle Jim trailed Dickson to his home when the day was ended. He had dinner in the kitchen with the servants and a little later was to be taken to the train which would carry him back to his home in Sunflower County. Toward dark Dickson went to the back of the house to bid his guest farewell.

Uncle Jim, with his shoes off, sat on the lowermost step of the porch easing his tired feet.

"Uncle Jim," said Dickson, "I'm afraid you haven't enjoyed your trip very much."

"W'y, Mist' Dickson," said Uncle Jim, "whut meks you think dat? I ain't never gwine furgit whut I seen to-day ez long ez I lives, an' I's always gwine be grateful to you, suh."

"But you haven't said anything about the circus. What made you so dumb?"

"Well, suh, my eyes beheld so much dat it seem lak my tongue forgot to wag."

"Oh, that was it? Well, of all the things you've seen to-day what impressed you most?"

"All of it 'pressed me—frum de start to de finish."

"Yes, I know, but there must have been some one thing that stands out in your mind above all the others—something that seemed to you more amazing than anything else. Think the whole day over, now, and see if you can tell me what that thing is."

"Well, suh, Mist' Dickson," said Uncle Jim, after a period of reflection, "ef it comes down to jes' one thing, I'd say de thing w'ich hit me de hardest was dat air beast w'ich dey calls de camel. Uh,—dat camel!"

"Why the camel particularly?" asked Dickson.

"Mist' Dickson," said Jim, "he's got such a noble smell!"

§ 364   A Tribute—with One Reservation

A distinguished member of the Little Rock bar was notable for two things: his capacity for chambering good, red liquor and his ability to speak eloquently at short notice upon any conceivable subject. Oratorically, he was even as the rock which Moses smote—one cue, one suggestion, one invitation and from him there would pour a glittering, noble stream of language. One night at a banquet in his home city the toastmaster conspired with certain of the guests to play a trick upon this talented gentleman; in fact, I believe a wager was laid. The plot was launched early in the evening when he was informed that, contrary to the local custom, he would not be called upon for any remarks. Then privily, a waiter was instructed to station himself behind the chair of Colonel Doolove—that being the orator's name—with orders to see to it that the

Colonel's toddy glass was replenished as often as he might empty it. So well did the waiter obey his orders that by the time the hour for the speech-making rolled around the Colonel appeared to be almost in a state of coma. The toastmaster felt that the moment had come for springing his surprise. Perhaps I should have stated earlier that the bet was to the effect that there was at least one toast to which the Colonel, drunk or sober, could never respond with fitting words.

With a confident wink at some of his co-conspirators the toastmaster arose, and said:

"In view of the fact that one of the guests of honor has disappointed us to-night, and in order that this feast of reason and flow of soul may properly be rounded out I am going to take the liberty of calling upon one whose name does not appear on the postprandial program. I shall ask our distinguished friend, Colonel Doolove, to favor us with a few remarks in his inimitable style. I ask him now to speak to the toast—water."

Groggily the Colonel rose in his place. With difficulty he fixed his wavering vision upon the company and then without further hesitation delivered himself of the following:

"Mr. Toastmaster and Gentlemen, I speak to-night of water. What visions does that word conjure up! What delectable thoughts does it bring to the contemplative mind. Water, I maintain, is the most beneficent, the most benign and the most beautiful of all the elements with which a generous Creator has endowed this mundane sphere.

"Is water beneficent? I ask of the rolling tides which, in obedience to the command of the Almighty, ebb and flow at their ordained times, now retreating, now advancing, upon the wave-kissed beach. I ask of the oceans which bring to us the freighted argosies of other climes. I ask of the rivers which bear upon their currents the commerce of nations, making possible communication and intercourse between peoples. Yea, verily, water is beneficent.

"Is water benign? Consider the dews which freshen the flowers of the field and make glad and glorious the summer morn. Consider the rains which descend upon the parched and arid desert, causing fragrant blossom to burgeon where before there was but sand and waste. Consider the harnessed power of dashing streams which turns the wheels and gives impetus to applied industry. Consider these things and then dare to say water is not benign!

"Is water beautiful? The answer is found in impetuous Niagara. It is found in the roaring cataract, in the purling brook, in the racing mountain torrent, and upon the bosom of the sheltered lake illumined with the glorious colors of the sinking sun, and reflecting,

244 A LAUGH A DAY KEEPS THE DOCTOR AWAY

as a mirror, every shifting play of radiance from the skies, every dancing frond of the lofty evergreens caressed by the breezes of the evening. It is found in the teardrop of the mother as she bids her son go forth to fight for his imperiled country.

"Never, while man has speech, is it to be gainsaid that water is beneficent, that it is benign, that it is beautiful. But, gentlemen, as a beverage it is a dadburned failure!"

§ 365   Staving Off the Fatal Blow

"Rabin," said Mr. Moscovitz to his friend, "I think I have lost a pocketbook with two hundred dollars in it."

"Have you looked for it good?" asked Mr. Rabin.

"Sure I have looked," said the desolated one. "I have looked in all my coat pockets, in all my vest pockets, in my front pants pockets and in one of my hip pockets—and nowheres it ain't there."

"Why don't you look in the other hip pocket?" asked Mr. Rabin.

"Because," said the stricken Mr. Moscovitz, "that's the last pocket I got."

"Vell, vot of it?"

"Because, Rabin, if I should look in that pocket and still it ain't there, then I drop dead."

§ 366   SPECIAL EXTRA—To Be Read Only in Leap Year

It must be all of thirty-five years now since the thing happened. But the memory of it still abides in my mind, as the finest exhibition of spontaneous humor that ever came within my own experience.

I was a small boy in a Kentucky town. John Robinson's circus paid us its annual visit. For the afternoon performance, my father took me and my younger brother and half a dozen little girls and boys, the children of neighbors, along with him. At the last moment two old ladies joined the party. One of them lived across the street from us and the other just around the corner. Mrs. Slawson, the senior of the pair, was exceedingly deaf. She used one of those old-fashioned, flexible rubber ear-trumpets with a tip at one end and a bell-like aperture at the other. Her crony, Mrs. Ream, had a high-pitched, far-carrying voice.

On a blue-painted bench, with the old ladies at one end, my father at the other and the row of youngsters in between, we watched the show. The time came for the crowning feature of a circus of those times. Perhaps the reader is of sufficient age to recall what this was. Elephants and camels and horses would be close-ranked at the foot of a springboard. Along a steep runway, which slanted down to this springboard, would flash in order, one behind another, the full strength of the troupe. The acrobats would tumble over the backs of the animals to alight gracefully upon a thick padded mattress. The clowns would sprawl on the backs of the living obstacles. Always there was one clown who, dashing down the runway, would suddenly halt and fling his peaked cap across. There was another, dressed as a country woman, who, as he somersaulted, lost a pair of bifurcated white garments, while the audience whooped its delight.

This season, though, a culminating treat had been provided by the management: The lesser gymnasts had done their stunts. Now, to the head of the runway mounted the premier tumbler. He stood there grandly erect in his rose-colored fleshings, his arms folded across his swelling breast and his head almost touching the sagging canvas of the tentroof. The band, for the moment, stopped playing. The ringmaster mounted the ring-back and proclaimed that Johnnie O'Brien, foremost athlete of the world, would now perform his death-defying and unparalleled feat of turning a triple somersault over two elephants, three camels and four horses! For many this announcement had a special interest; they knew Johnnie O'Brien was a native-born son of our town.

So an expectant hush fell upon the assemblage. Mrs. Slawson turned to Mrs. Ream, and in the silence her voice rose as she asked:

"What did he say?"

Mrs. Ream brought the blunderbus end of Mrs. Slawson's ear-trumpet to her lips and, through its sinuous black length, in a voice so shrill that instantly every head there was turned toward the pair of them, she answered:

"He says that that pretty man up yonder with the pink clothes on is goin' to jump over all those animals without hurtin' himself!"

On the sawdust, in his baggy white clothes, squatted one of the clowns. On the instant he leaped to his feet, ran to the head of the larger elephant, and in both hands seized that creature's long black dangling trunk which now, as everyone saw, looked so amazingly like Mrs. Slawson's ear-trumpet, and raising its tip to his mouth he shrieked out in a magnificent imitation of Mrs. Ream's falsetto notes:

"He says that that there pretty man up yonder with the pink clothes——"

If he finished the sentence, none there heard him. From every side of the arena there arose a tremendous gasp of joyous appreciation and, overtopping and engulfing this, a universal roar of laughter which billowed the tent. Strong men dropped through the seats like ripened plums from the bough and lay upon the earth choking with laughter. The performers rolled about in the ring.

And through it all Mrs. Slawson and Mrs. Ream sat there wondering why the band did not play and why the pretty man in the pink clothes up at the top of the runway seemed to be having a convulsion.

[THE END]